# THE PHILOSOPHY OF MARTIN SCORSESE

# The Philosophy of Popular Culture

The books published in the Philosophy of Popular Culture series will illuminate and explore philosophical themes and ideas that occur in popular culture. The goal of this series is to demonstrate how philosophical inquiry has been reinvigorated by increased scholarly interest in the intersection of popular culture and philosophy, as well as to explore through philosophical analysis beloved modes of entertainment, such as movies, TV shows, and music. Philosophical concepts will be made accessible to the general reader through examples in popular culture. This series seeks to publish both established and emerging scholars who will engage a major area of popular culture for philosophical interpretation and examine the philosophical underpinnings of its themes. Eschewing ephemeral trends of philosophical and cultural theory, authors will establish and elaborate on connections between traditional philosophical ideas from important thinkers and the ever-expanding world of popular culture.

SERIES EDITOR

Mark T. Conard, Marymount Manhattan College, NY

BOOKS IN THE SERIES

*The Philosophy of Stanley Kubrick,* edited by Jerold J. Abrams
*The Philosophy of Martin Scorsese,* edited by Mark T. Conard
*The Philosophy of Neo-Noir,* edited by Mark T. Conard
*Basketball and Philosophy,* edited by Jerry L. Walls and Gregory Bassham

# THE PHILOSOPHY OF
# MARTIN
# SCORSESE

## I.C.C. LIBRARY

Edited by Mark T. Conard

THE UNIVERSITY PRESS OF KENTUCKY

Publication of this volume was made possible in part by
a grant from the National Endowment for the Humanities.

*Editorial and Sales Offices:* The University Press of Kentucky
663 South Limestone Street, Lexington, Kentucky 40508-4008
www.kentuckypress.com

11  10  09  08  07          5  4  3  2  1

Library of Congress Cataloging-in-Publication Data

The philosophy of Martin Scorsese / edited by Mark T. Conard.
    p.  cm. — (The philosophy of popular culture)
  Includes bibliographical references and index.
  ISBN 978-0-8131-2444-5 (hardcover : alk. paper)
  1. Scorsese, Martin—Criticism and interpretation. I. Conard, Mark T., 1965-
  PN1998.3.S39P55 2007
  791.4302'33092—dc22

                    2007003156

# Contents

## Part 3. Vision, Salvation, and the Transcendental

# Introduction

In the introduction to *The Philosophy of Neo-Noir* (University Press of Kentucky, 2007), I noted the conspicuous absence in that volume of the films of Martin Scorsese, who might rightly be regarded as a master neo-noir filmmaker. Indeed, Scorsese is best known for his works centering on the noirish elements of gangsters and/or violence, such as *Mean Streets* (1973), *Taxi Driver* (1976), *Goodfellas* (1990), and *Casino* (1995), to the point where he's identified with these types of films in the way that Billy Wilder is often thought of as primarily a maker of screwball comedies (*The Seven Year Itch* [1955], *Some Like It Hot* [1959]) or Woody Allen is often seen as the maker of existentialist comedy/dramas (*Annie Hall* [1977], *Manhattan* [1979]). But we should remember that Billy Wilder also directed *Double Indemnity* (1944) and *Sunset Boulevard* (1950) and that Woody Allen's oeuvre includes *Interiors* (1978), *Another Woman* (1988), and *Match Point* (2005). The stereotyping of Scorsese is equally unjustified since, over his career of some thirty-four years and counting, his films have covered a wide range of topics and themes, from the Dalai Lama in *Kundun* (1997) and Jesus in *The Last Temptation of Christ* (1988) to Howard Hughes in *The Aviator* (2004), social roles and mores in nineteenth-century New York in *The Age of Innocence* (1993), pool hustling in *The Color of Money* (1986), and the boxer Jake La Motta in *Raging Bull* (1980). Indeed, Scorsese's work hasn't been limited to narrative feature films, also including documentaries (*The Last Waltz* [1978], *No Direction Home: Bob Dylan* [2005]) and music videos (Michael Jackson's *Bad* [1987]).

As I also noted in the neo-noir introduction, I omitted Scorsese from *The Philosophy of Neo-Noir* because I planned to devote an entire volume in the Philosophy of Popular Culture series to his films, and the present work is the fulfillment of that promise. *The Philosophy of Martin Scorsese* investigates the philosophical themes and underpinnings of the films of this master auteur as well as using the movies as a vehicle for exploring and explicating traditional philosophical ideas. It comprises thirteen essays from scholars in both philosophy and film and media studies. The essays are written in nontechnical language and require no knowledge of philosophy to appreciate or understand.

Part 1, "Authenticity, Flourishing, and the Good Life," begins with "No Safe Haven: *Casino,* Friendship, and Egoism," in which Steven M. Sanders uses Scorsese's film to explore the uneasy relation between egoist ethics, which claims that the only duty one has is to oneself, and friendship, which seems at times to require self-sacrifice. Next, in "God's Lonely Man: *Taxi Driver* and the Ethics of Vigilantism," Aeon J. Skoble investigates the story of the assassin/savior Travis Bickle, wondering when and under what conditions vigilantism is ever justified. In "*Goodfellas,* Gyges, and the Good Life," Dean A. Kowalski uses the case of the mobster Henry Hill to examine and evaluate Plato's claim in the *Republic* that the immoral, unjust person is necessarily unhappy. Last, in "*Mean Streets:* Beatitude, Flourishing, and Unhappiness," I use Scorsese's first masterpiece to examine different philosophical conceptions of unhappiness, raising the issue of whether unhappiness is the natural state and condition of human beings.

Part 2, "Rationality, Criminality, and the Emotions," begins with "The Cinema of Madness: Friedrich Nietzsche and the Films of Martin Scorsese," in which Jerold J. Abrams discusses a prevalent theme in Scorsese's films: the relation between madness, creativity, and criminality. Next, in "*The Age of Innocence:* Social Semiotics, Desire, and Constraint," Deborah Knight explores Scorsese's adaptation of Edith Wharton's 1920 novel, in which the characters' actions are scrutinized by a surrounding social group whose values are dominant and whose decisions will inexorably win out, much as with Scorsese's gangster characters. In "*After Hours:* Scorsese on Absurdity," Jennifer L. McMahon uses Scorsese's comedy to discuss the existentialist notion of absurdity. Last, in "The Pupkin Gambit: Rationality and Irrationality in *The King of Comedy,*" Richard Greene wonders whether it's rational to act as Rupert Pupkin does in Scorsese's film, risking short-term harm to himself and others for possible long-term benefits.

Part 3, "Vision, Salvation, and the Transcendental," opens with "*The Last Temptation of Christ* and *Bringing Out the Dead*: Scorsese's Reluctant Saviors," in which Karen D. Hoffman discusses the similar experiences of self-sacrifice and temptation of the protagonists of the two films. Next, in "Flying Solo: *The Aviator* and Libertarian Philosophy," Paul A. Cantor argues that Scorsese's Howard Hughes is the kind of visionary entrepreneur extolled by libertarian thinkers. In "Art, Sex, and Time in Scorsese's *After Hours,*" Richard Gilmore argues that Scorsese's film contains important lessons about our experience of time, our interpersonal relationships, and the power and meaning of art. In "The Ethical Underpinnings of *Kundun,*" Judith

Barad uses Scorsese's film about the young Dalai Lama to explore Buddhist ethics—particularly its commitment to nonviolence. Last, in "Scorsese and the Transcendental," R. Barton Palmer examines Scorsese's obsession with the spiritual, which pervades not only his European-style art films, such as *Kundun* and *The Last Temptation of Christ,* but also his genre projects, like *Taxi Driver* and *Goodfellas.*

At the heart of this volume lies our deep admiration for Scorsese's work. We sincerely hope and believe that our analyses of his films will not only enrich and deepen your understanding of them but also introduce you in a richly rewarding fashion to certain philosophical issues and ideas that are well worth considering.

**Part 1**

# AUTHENTICITY, FLOURISHING, AND THE GOOD LIFE

# No Safe Haven
## *Casino,* Friendship, and Egoism
*Steven M. Sanders*

With *Casino* (1995), Martin Scorsese leads us back into the noir landscape of damaged selves that he created to such stunning effect in the critically acclaimed *Goodfellas* (1990). In the words of the film historian David Thomson, ever since *Taxi Driver* (1976) Scorsese's work has reflected "a man happy with the fervent claustrophobia of film noir."[1] *Casino* is a significant addition to Scorsese's body of work in this vein, for the film does nothing less than restage the familiar noir themes of criminal violence, betrayal, loss, and the corruption of the American dream against the backdrop of 1970s Las Vegas.

*Casino*'s thematic elements are pursued with all Scorsese's relentless logic. The narrative opens with a pretitle sequence as Sam "Ace" Rothstein (Robert De Niro) lights a cigarette and gets into his car while in voice-over narration he utters the film's ominous opening lines: "When you love someone, you've got to trust them, there's no other way. You've got to give them the key to everything that's yours. Otherwise, what's the point?" Moments later, a car bomb explosion tosses him into midair. With this sequence, Scorsese lays the film's philosophical foundation stone: *There is no safe haven without its own trapdoor.* The safe havens—Ace's love for his wife, Ginger McKenna (Sharon Stone), his $2 million stash in a safe-deposit box in Los Angeles, the only key to which he has entrusted to Ginger—are no more important to Scorsese than the trapdoor, the way Nicky Santoro (Joe Pesci) exploits his friendship with Ace to manipulate the complex set of activities surrounding casino management for his own enrichment, even to the extent of placing Ace's well-being in jeopardy.

In a sense, *Casino* is less a crime drama than a set of essayistic excursions into the underside of the casino operation, with dramatic scenes added to the fact-based reportage provided by Scorsese's coscenarist Nicholas Pileggi, on whose book *Casino* the film is based.[2] Of course, *Casino* is much more than a sequence of excursions. Scorsese does not seem to care very much about gambling. His film neither explains nor seems very interested in the mechanics of poker, dice, or roulette, for example, or the psychology of the gambler. So he must be using the rituals of casino operation for an expedition into its heart of darkness. With its sense of the present prefigured in the past, its motifs of paranoid suspicion and ultimate betrayal, *Casino* is an exemplary film in the noir tradition, with the themes and stylization of those films noirs like *The Asphalt Jungle* (John Huston, 1950) and *The Killing* (Stanley Kubrick, 1956) that deliver on their promise to expose the human dimension of the criminal enterprise.[3]

## Las Vegas Noir

In *Casino,* Scorsese uses the backdrop of Las Vegas, a "new" noir city—unlike New York and San Francisco, the cities of classic film noir, shadowed in chiaroscuro—to create a galaxy of meanings, associations, and signifiers. Shot compositions, camera movements, decor, and design combine in relations of near orchestral partnership and balance. Dozens, perhaps hundreds, of gorgeous, intoxicatingly rich images bring 1970s-era Vegas to life, with the vernacular architecture and neon signage effectively camouflaging the Strip's sordid realities and the sound track music pushing the din and dissonance to extremes. The details steadily accumulate and anchor *Casino* in its time and place.

The Las Vegas setting provides the context for the social and psychological realism that fills *Casino* and propels the plot, whose moral center lies in a predetermined ending, another element found in film noir. Scorsese gives us acid-etched sketches of Ace's micromanagement of and manipulations at the Tangiers, the casino he runs for the mob, Nicky's increasingly self-destructive behavior, and Ginger's two-timing and squalid end. Scorsese likely excised, expanded, and otherwise altered the factual incidents in Pileggi's book to suit his own purposes. And, while we are not given enough backstory to fully understand what formed any of the protagonists, the coscenarists expose the characters of Ace, Nicky, and Ginger, who, in their incarnations as actual persons, would no doubt have not wanted to be so exposed.

Scorsese goes beyond the classic noir convention of the voice-over narration by presenting both Ace's and Nicky's points of view in their own voice-overs. Ace, the antihero and predominant narrator, is sufficiently savvy to know his success at running a licensed casino depends on maintaining the appearance of a clean operation, even as he functions as a cash cow and conduit to the Midwest mob bosses who await their monthly skim in

Kansas City, which, Nicky tells us, is as close as they could get to Las Vegas without getting arrested. Ace is a quick study, and succinctly explains the mood of paranoia surrounding the casino operation, where everybody watches everybody else: "Since the players are looking to beat the casino, the dealers are watching the players, the box men are watching the dealers, the floor men are watching the box men, the pit bosses are watching the floor men, the shift bosses are watching the pit bosses, the casino manager is watching the shift bosses, I'm watching the casino manager, and the eye in the sky is watching us all."

Nicky, who has been sent to Vegas by the mob bosses to make sure nobody interferes with Ace and the casino scam, sees Vegas as a place ripe for exploitation. "I saw it as untouched," he tells us, with bookies, pimps, and drug dealers to shake down and no one to run to for protection. "So I started getting everybody in line. Best of all, for the first time in my life, I figured out a way not to lose." As Ace tells us, Nicky "had tipsters all over town, bellmen, valet parkers, pit bosses, secretaries, and they all got a piece of the score." Nicky begins to accumulate a substantial stash of his own, without the Midwest mob's knowledge, of course, because they think that he is there to keep an eye on Ace. In Nicky's moral universe: "You gotta know that a guy who helps you steal, even if you take care of him real well, I mean, he's gonna steal a little extra for himself. Makes sense, don't it?"

Not least of all, there is Ginger, a fixer and user with her own ambition and greed. Ace unlocks her trunk of hustler's tricks for us even as he finds himself falling in love with her. "Who wouldn't want Ginger?" he asks rhetorically, going on to observe, apparently without irony: "She was one of the best-known, best-liked, and most respected hustlers in town." Ginger "knew how to take care of people, and that's what Vegas is all about. It's kickback city." She paid off the valet parkers "because they took care of the security guards who took care of the metro cops who let her operate."

## *Casino* and Egoism

The ethical dimension of *Casino* is ambiguous because of the prominence within the noir tradition of alternative strands of thought—particularly its nihilism, amoralism, and egoism. From *The Maltese Falcon* (John Huston, 1941) and *Double Indemnity* (Billy Wilder, 1944) to *Kiss Me Deadly* (Robert Aldrich, 1955) and *Basic Instinct* (Paul Verhoeven, 1992), all three positions have been dramatized by a preoccupation with the conflict, not to mention the repudiation, of moral values. Because nihilism, amoralism, and egoism are associated with the displacement of conventional morality, they may appear to be similar in outlook. But there are differences between them, and these differences matter. For example, nihilists insist that there are no objective values to ground moral judgments about what we ought to do or how we ought to live, and amoralists express indifference about such judgments. But egoists are moral realists: the justificational supremacy of self-interest reflects an objective moral reality. It may turn out that egoism is not the one true moral theory, but at least egoists believe that there *is* moral truth, whereas nihilists dismiss the idea of moral truth altogether, and amoralists deny that it is important.

By *egoism,* I mean the view that self-interest is the criterion of one's overriding value. But what counts as self-interest? Philosophers typically use *self-interest* in a generic sense to refer to happiness, well-being, flourishing, or, as I shall say, what makes one's life go best for one. On one view, what would be best for one and make one's life go as well as possible is what would give one the most pleasure; on another view, what would be best for one is what would best fulfill one's desires over the course of one's life; and, on a third view, what would be best for one might include such objective goods as knowledge, the development of one's abilities, liberty, and so on. We will not know very much about what egoism is in the absence of a fuller account of this notion of making one's own life go best.[4] However, I will not try to provide a detailed account of this notion. Instead, I want to show how certain problems with friendship arise in *Casino* and how they might be dealt with if egoism is assumed to have such a basis.

Many philosophers have argued that egoism has implications that appear to be in sharp conflict with some of our most firmly held beliefs about friendship, and a large part of the controversy between egoism and its critics concerns the most appropriate response to these implications. Some philosophers have argued that egoism itself incorporates constraints on self-interested actions harmful to others. In this way, they hope to remove the objection that egoism is unable to make sense of our moral thought about the value of friends and our responsibilities to them.[5] As I have argued elsewhere, these attempts fail because, in my view, they badly distort egoism in a misguided attempt to accommodate our nonegoist beliefs about our moral obligations and our responsibilities to our friends.[6] By way of contrast, a philosopher such as Jesse Kalin does not make this type of concession. Kalin is willing to say that each person should "pursue his own self-interest even to the harming of others when necessary" and concludes that this does not weaken egoism's appeal as a normative guide to action.[7] Construed in this way, egoism requires us to be disposed to take advantage of anyone, even a friend, if doing so is in our own self-interest. If this is the case, then, far from being a sound moral outlook, egoism is antagonistic to morality.

The relationship between Ace and Nicky takes on moral significance as an illustration of a type of egoist friendship. Nicky uses Ace for his entrée into Las Vegas social life and, more important to Nicky, for access to the network of activities surrounding the operation of the Tangiers. He is determined to make his own life go as well as possible, and Ace is an instrumentality to be used toward that end—and pretty clearly *only* an instrumentality. As the film opens, Nicky is heard to lament: "It should have been perfect. I mean, he had *me*, Nicky Santoro, his best friend, watching his ass." This will serve as our leitmotif, for *Casino* gives us a graphic illustration of some of the behavior and motivational forces surrounding a typical form of egoist friendship (if that is not an oxymoron).

Perhaps because friendship is so central to a happy life, every moral theory must include some account of its value. Yet egoism is often thought to be deficient in this respect. The principal objection is that egoism is unable to make sense of the moral value of friendship because it conceives of friends as being only instrumentally valuable—that is, valuable as a means to one's own ends—and not valuable as ends in themselves, that is, as persons whose ends have no less value than one's own. Consequently, egoist thought and practice are widely believed to be inimical to friendship. Taking *Casino's* depiction of egoist friendship as a point of departure, I argue that the pathologies displayed to such dramatic effect in the film follow from a common type of egoism that I shall call *maximizing* egoism. I shall suggest some egoist alternatives to maximizing egoism that support relationships we would recognize as friendships, though perhaps of an attenuated type. Clarifying the central contentions of egoism and following out egoism's normative implications for friendships of various types will lead to a better understanding of *Casino* and a more fulfilling experience when we watch it.

## Egoists and Their Friends

In order to develop our understanding of egoist friendship in *Casino*, let us ask whether Nicky (or any egoist) can have grounds for *exempting* his or her friends from interest-maximizing calculations. (By *friends* I mean those to whom the egoist stands in special relations we may call *friendships* without begging the question. I discuss below whether and in what sense these relations *are* friendships.) If Nicky can make exceptions of Ace and his other friends (his crew, e.g.) when he is calculating how to use others to his own advantage, the case for the possibility of egoist friendship will be greatly strengthened, even if, in the end, the way Nicky would be disposed to use those who are *not* his friends would remain unchanged.

The egoist's rationale for exempting friends from egoist interest-maximizing calculations is similar to the one that utilitarians, for example, use to extend the utilitarian justification further than one might have expected so that it embraces special cases, for example, loyalty to friends, partiality to spouses, parents, and children, and so forth.[8] Utilitarians try to show how they can exempt spouses, parents, and children from calculations that might compromise their special status if they were treated impartially. They give arguments for exempting parents, spouses, and children from the application of the utilitarian principle that people should be considered on a par, morally speaking, with each other. Utilitarians might argue that, because our parents, spouses, children, and friends have expectations of special treatment from us, such special treatment has greater utility than treating each as simply one among many, that the institutions of marriage and the family are socially beneficial and actions directed toward their maintenance are desirable, and that any steps toward the formation of cooperation, reliance, and trust between the parties to such relationships would be good. In these ways, utilitarians would argue that it is justifiable to exempt those who stand in special relations to us from treatment that we might initially expect, given utilitarianism.

Similarly, egoists might argue that they are justified in exempting those standing in special relations to *them* from treatment that, at first blush, we might expect from them. Rather than interfering, egoists would cooperate with their friends; instead of confronting, they would compromise; in place of duplicity and manipulation, they would offer candor and sympathetic understanding—as long as the price was not unjustifiably high. This qualification is, of course, central. The question, What's in it for *me?* would come easily to Nicky's lips, and, indeed, for him it is decisive. Once his friendship with Ace begins to create burdens that outweigh the (perceived) benefits to him, Nicky starts to alter things so that the relationship does not have this result. We see this, for example, in the way in which Nicky starts to skirt the edges of respectability once Ace has helped him establish his bona fides.

There may be other ways in which egoists can justify the exemption of their friends from interest-maximizing calculations, but I mention this one because I believe that it establishes the initial plausibility of the idea that egoists do not need to be disposed to take advantage of their friends, without having to modify egoism so drastically that the resulting view could not plausibly be said to count as an egoist view at all. From this, we might conclude that egoists are fully capable of friendships in which they show a genuine concern for others. And, if this is the case, it might be argued that the satisfactions derivable from friendships are no less available to someone like Nicky than they are to nonegoists. Still, I have done no more than try to establish the initial plausibility of this idea. I next explore an obstacle that stands in the way of giving the idea more than merely initial plausibility.

## Levels of Friendship

A distinction between kinds or levels of friendship is often used to support the claim that an egoist like Nicky cannot have the *relevant* kind of friendship. This type of criticism may be the most plausible one against someone like Nicky, who, it seems clear, has a severely limited grasp of, or commitment to, Ace. Consider, for example, how Nicky uses Ace and exploits him even to the extent of having sex with his wife.

Lawrence A. Blum argues: "There are many different levels of friendship, levels which are understood in moral terms of how fully one cares for the other." Blum concedes that "even a selfish person can wish another well" and "can be very attached to another person, e.g., a spouse or friend," though Blum also says that "such a friendship could not be a friendship of the most morally excellent kind." According to Blum: "Caring in the full sense . . . is incompatible with selfishness." But, leaving aside this questionable equation of self-interest with selfishness, does invoking kinds or levels of friendship amount to anything more than a contestable *claim* that some relationships, states, or experiences are more valuable than others? In order to succeed as an objection to egoism, such a claim would have to be *justified,* and Blum's altruistic account clearly begs the question against someone like Nicky, who might well ask why he should seek that deeper kind of friendship, which, according to Blum, "involves a high level of development and expression of the altruistic emotions of sympathy, concern, and care—a deep caring for and identification with the good of another from whom one knows oneself clearly to be other."[9]

Nicky would not believe that he *ought* to seek the kind of friendship in which Ace's good has the highest normative priority. Given his view that self-interest is the criterion of his overriding value, Nicky's highest priority is making his *own* life go best. This means, of course, that his friendship with Ace cannot be a friendship of the most morally excellent kind. But why should this matter to Nicky? It would not faze him unless this type of friendship mattered most *to him,* and it is clear that it does not. After all, Nicky will argue that the absence of morally excellent friendships is not a loss to him since he does not miss them. The argument Blum offers would not work against Nicky unless it could be established that the absence of morally excellent friendships in Nicky's life actually harms Nicky—that is, makes him worse off, whatever Nicky may think—and Blum has not shown the absence of such friendships to be harmful.

The level of caring that Nicky *can* have for Ace does not amount to true friendship, as *friendship* is defined by Blum. But this incapacity for true friendship does not have the significance Blum thinks it does. For it is relatively certain that, whatever demands friendship may make of us, there are limits. Friendship rarely demands commitment to another's welfare regardless of personal cost. In fact, it is unlikely that our friends would even ask us to make such significant self-sacrifices for their sake, so any alleged general incompatibility between friendship and self-interest is untenable. Now, if it is unlikely that we will often be in situations where friendship requires us to make significant self-sacrifices, it will be in our overall self-interest to have friends—even if doing so increases the likelihood that we will, thereby, be disposed to bear some burdens that we would not have if we had no friends. The relatively certain benefits of friendship will simply outweigh its unlikely burdens.

The fact that Nicky seems unwilling to comply with even this quite modest constraint on his behavior says more about the conditions of his acceptance of egoism than it does about egoism itself. What it shows is that, in evaluating egoism as a moral theory, we should distinguish between the *truth* conditions of the theory and the conditions of its *application* by specific persons.[10] The fact that Nicky might claim that egoism is the one true theory yet not act as though he accepts the theory is not a refutation of egoism as an account of morally justificatory reasons.

## Egoism and Psychological Dispositions

It seems implausible to maintain that no one could *ever* advance his genuine self-interest at the expense of a friend. Could there *never* be cases where what is best for oneself would be worse for one's friend? When your friend with the kidney condition needs one of your healthy kidneys, is it obvious that what is better for you (to keep both your healthy kidneys) is *not* worse for your friend? Or consider the situation of Elliot, Lee, and Hannah in Woody Allen's 1986 film *Hannah and Her Sisters*.[11] Hannah (Mia Farrow) is married to Elliot (Michael Caine), who believes that he has discovered the woman of his dreams in his sister-in-law Lee (Barbara Hershey). Their affair involves the deception and betrayal of Hannah, someone they both love and are disposed to act favorably toward. As Ian Jarvie notes, this is a "love that works partly with the help of lies and concealment."[12] Is it so obvious that what is worse for Hannah (not to be deceived and betrayed by her friends) is not better for Elliot and Lee (to take a chance at a far greater happiness than they might otherwise experience)? Are we even convinced that there can *never* be cases of short-term, guilt-free enjoyment that involve the temporary departure from the virtues of veracity and fidelity? I do not believe that we can rule out these possibilities if by *possibility* we mean what is consistently imaginable. Given the contingencies of human belief, desire, and preference ranking, such outcomes must be counted as genuine possibilities, and a theory that denied this could do so only at the cost of arbitrariness. In *Casino,* such cases are shown to arise when Nicky exploits opportunities to extort people with whom his friendship with Ace puts him in contact, such as employees at the Tangiers to whom Nicky lends money at exorbitant interest rates. If this is correct, then a situation *could* arise in which an egoist could make things go best for himself at the expense of his friend, and he would be disposed to act accordingly. For I take it that, if self-interest is the criterion of his overriding value, he would be disposed to act at his friend's expense.

But is this a psychological possibility? Is not Aristotle correct in observing that to live a life of virtue is to act in accordance with the right rule on all occasions?[13] The virtues are acquired by exercising them: if a person acts habitually in accordance with the dictates of the right rule, then he will do so also on occasions when his actions involve the possibility of self-sacrifice. Surely, Nicky could not possess the virtue of friendship and at the same time be disposed to take advantage of his best friend, Ace, when that would be in his self-interest. Following this Aristotelian line, Laurence Thomas has argued: "A person who shifts from being favorably disposed towards a person to being disposed to exploit that person every time he realizes that he can get away with it, cannot be one with a healthy personality." If this is true, then: "A person with a healthy personality cannot move from one to the other just like that."[14]

But this claim rests on a misunderstanding of the grounds of the *exceptions* that Nicky can make in exercising his dispositions. On the basis of this misunderstanding, Thomas and other philosophers have drawn dubious conclusions about what is and is not possible for a person with a healthy personality to be disposed to do. Egoism requires the exercise of dispositions that have as their principled rationale making one's own life go as well as possible. But the successful practice of egoism permits one to *restrict the exercise* of one's dispositions. Even if one were to concede that egoists would be disposed to deceive and betray people, this does not entail that such practices would be carried over into their every relationship. For example, organized crime figures can be disposed to use violence as an intimidation strategy yet be doting parents, as we have been shown from *The Godfather* to *The Sopranos*. In several scenes, in fact, Nicky is shown doting over his son, Nicholas Jr., as young Nicky is a source of great pride to him. The mobster as doting parent may have been overdone, but we have not been given reason to think it is impossible for an egoist to restrict the exercise of his dispositions so that his life may go as well as possible. As Nicky recognizes, cooperation, loyalty, and friendship can be pressed into the service of self-interest, even if he is prepared to deceive the very friend who has enabled him to set up his criminal enterprise. Of course, Nicky will not be disposed to make the shift from being disposed to be loyal to Ace to being disposed to take advantage of him just like that or "at the drop of a hat."[15] A commitment to a partner, whether in commerce or crime, will often be closely linked to other projects and possibilities, and a wise egoist will not jeopardize these at the drop of a hat. Egoists will not constantly be assessing their commitments and friendships in terms of egoistic utilities that arise on the fly or terminating them every time it appears that some other set of arrangements might maximize their personal expected utility.

## The Pervasiveness of Egoism

Perhaps the problem all along has been one that *Casino* illustrates with tremendous force and vivacity: Nicky's egoism implies the all-consuming aim of making his own life go as well as possible, which, as we have seen, undermines his commitment to Ace. The problem with the egoist's overriding commitment to himself, writes William H. Wilcox, "is that the practical effects of this particular commitment are so pervasive that little room is left for a concern for another's well-being to have much practical effect."[16]

This criticism assumes that egoists' commitments to, or concern for, their friends depend for their practical significance entirely on their weight in a calculation of purely personal interest-maximizing considerations. Against this, I have argued that, given the circumstances in which egoists are most likely to find themselves, caring and concern for, rather than taking advantage of, friends would be more conducive to life's going well for them. It would be unusual if it were not almost always the case that the interests of our friends were either among or compatible with our most important interests. And, since egoism does not require any particular way to go about realizing our aims, egoists might find their concerns for and commitments to their friends arising quite independently of their place in a calculation of personal interest-maximizing considerations. Such egoists would do many things for their friends that are not incompatible with living an egoist way of life. They could consistently care about their friends without compromising their overriding commitment to themselves.

However, the egoist who argues this way, writes Wilcox,

> overlooks a further distinction between being *committed* to something for its own sake and *merely caring about* something for its own sake (as an end). I care about the welfare of (probably) any stranger for its own sake. . . . But I am not *committed* to the well-being of any stranger; there are quickly reached limits to the effort I would be willing to make to save the life of a distant stranger. An undeceived egoist's attitude toward his "friends" would have to be much like my attitude to any stranger. But this attitude falls far short of any that has a place in friendship.[17]

Thus, Wilcox concludes that the egoist's overriding commitment to his own self-interest would be incompatible with friendship. But Wilcox implies a false alternative, as though strangers and friends were the only possibilities. He overlooks the fact that personal relations can be realized and combined with great complexity and variety in a person's life. This complex pattern of discriminations in personal relations can range from *acquaintance* to *friend* to *good friend* to *best friend* and might explain Nicky's greater emotional distance from a mere acquaintance (to say nothing of a stranger) than from Ace, a man he calls his dear friend.

## Maximizing and Satisficing Egoism

But, rather than leave the controversy here, let us ask why Wilcox believes that the easily reached limits to the efforts one would be willing to make for the sake of a stranger would apply to the egoist's friends. My suspicion is that the disposition to instrumental behavior that Wilcox identifies with the egoist's attitude toward his friend—and that we are shown so graphically in connection with both Nicky and Ginger—is an expression of what he takes to be a more fundamental egoist imperative to *maximize* his overall good. It is common to link egoism with the view that one must do all and only those acts that maximize personal expected utility. According to this view, it is the egoist's overriding commitment to promote his or her own good *to any extent* at the expense of another *to any extent*.[18] This is, of course, incompatible with friendship and many of the commitments we normally think people have toward each other.

This way of thinking about egoism conflates the *justificatory role of self-interest* with a *maximizing strategy*. Once the connection between these two notions is broken, one is free to think about egoism in a way more consonant with the commitments that friends are normally thought to have toward each other. Such an account provides a framework for understanding how friendship can be valuable for its own sake even if it is not the sole over-riding value. The satisfactions constituted by the feeling and involvement associated with deep friendship can, then, be seen as a manifestation of the commitment to making one's life go well, or at least well enough.

We can unlink the overriding commitment to our own self-interest from the requirement to maximize by rethinking egoism in terms of a strategy of *satisficing,* one that works well even if it is not the single *best* strategy. We would then, in the egoist view, have the needed flexibility. After all, in actual life one can rarely, if ever, identify the best outcome or course of action, and the attempt to do so often smothers spontaneity, whereas satisficing gives it scope, adding zest and freshness to living.[19] The egoist asks how he or she can make life go well for himself or herself, and this may involve *not* maximizing. For he or she may know that life will go better (or at least well enough) when he or she does not engage in calculations of personal utility in every situation, spending less time *calculating* about how to make things go as well as possible for himself or herself *in order that* things may go well. And, as seems clear from the case of friendship, we can avoid many of the unwanted practical implications of egoism if we reject maximizing in favor of satisficing.

To some, this proposal may sound heretical. The very notion of a sat-isficing egoist—one who aims at making his or her life *good enough,* even if it falls short of the *best possible* life—will strike some as absurd. After all, is it not the very point of the egoist to make life go *as well as possible* for himself or herself? If so, then satisficing egoism cannot be a genuine form of egoism at all, and the case is closed. But this brisk dismissal of satisficing egoism conflates the legitimate point that no position could be egoist that denied that chains of normative justificatory reasoning must terminate in self-interest, with the dubious claim that egoists cannot consistently aim at any outcome *except* making life go *as well as possible* (and not merely good enough) for themselves. While egoists rightly insist that self-interest is the criterion of overriding value, there is no reason why this requires maximiz-ing. To say that it does is simply to beg the question of the legitimacy of satisficing egoism.[20]

## Nicky and His Friends

*Casino* illustrates how egoism adds an individualistic emphasis to both moral theory and moral phenomena, including friendship, and one of the great merits of the film is to so powerfully illustrate the spectacle of unconstrained egoist excess. Much of the egoist emphasis in ethics can be traced to Nietzsche, who, with other philosophers, endorsed an ethics of individuality, will, authenticity, and dominance. But there is a danger of overdoing this emphasis, as, arguably, various critics of Enlightenment conceptions of moral rationality and agency, from the existentialists to the postmodernists, have done. While Nicky devotes his time in Las Vegas to activities that are designed to make him feared and wealthy, it is clear that he pays the price for this endeavor in an ignoble life and a horrific death. Of course, we should not interpret this end as nothing more than the price one must pay for doing business as a maximizing egoist. The fact that Nicky is portrayed as a psychopath makes it easier to equate his flouting of moral norms and his extremely violent behavior with egoism.[21] Nicky indulges his pervasive vices (gambling, drug taking, adultery, violence) while his self-deceptions pile up. His impulses toward self-assertion result, instead, in self-destruction.

Nevertheless, one can see how this outcome is an implication of Nicky's maximizing egoism. Nicky's disposition to take advantage of his friend Ace is exercised in a highly competitive subculture where access to the tangible rewards of life is limited and treachery and backstabbing are widespread. Recognizing in himself the capacity not only for equivocation and keeping things close to the vest but also for some of the more spectacular forms of treachery, Nicky will have no trouble imagining that his friends have similar dispositions. In this respect, the situation is far worse than the one that faces the satisficing egoist, for he at least could come to understand that his instrumental attitude toward his friends was interfering with securing the benefits of true friendship. He could, therefore, take steps to view his friendships in a less instrumental way, in the hope that this would make his life go better. But this adjustment in Nicky's *own* outlook and behavior would not help unless it led to an alteration in *others* of the disposition to treat *him* instrumentally, and he can hardly be certain of that. Insofar as having a healthy personality involves the absence of protracted anxiety, inner conflict, or chronic depression, is it not obvious that these conditions would be present in Nicky, who is disposed to act favorably toward the very same friends whom he must be disposed to regard as potentially dangerous adversaries to be watched or preempted? And, as *Casino* shows most graphically, it remains only for the mob bosses, eager to tie up loose ends and cover their tracks, to order the means of Nicky's death.

Given the widespread criticisms of egoism as a moral theory, it may appear to be foolish to argue that it best accounts for the kind of friendship dramatized in *Casino*. In one respect, of course, I accept this since I agree that egoism—even satisficing egoism—is not entirely congruent with all our beliefs about the value of friendship. It is important to remember, however, that what I have tried to do is elucidate a type of egoism that Nicky's friendship in *Casino* presupposes, not establish that everything in that presupposition is itself defensible.

## Notes

I am grateful to Mark T. Conard for his very helpful comments on earlier drafts of this essay and to Michael Almeida, Christeen Clemens, Edward James, and Aeon J. Skoble for valuable discussions of the topics with which it deals.

1. David Thomson, *The New Biographical Dictionary of Film*, expanded and updated ed. (New York: Knopf, 2004), 810.

2. Nicholas Pileggi, *Casino: Love and Honor in Las Vegas* (New York: Simon & Schuster, 1995).

3. I discuss Kubrick's film in "The Big Score: Fate, Morality, and Meaningful Life in *The Killing*," in *The Philosophy of Stanley Kubrick*, ed. Jerold J. Abrams (Lexington: University Press of Kentucky, 2007).

4. For the three views, see Derek Parfit, *Reasons and Persons* (New York: Oxford University Press, 1984), 3–4.

5. This type of approach to egoism is found in Edward W. Regis Jr., "Ethical Egoism and Moral Responsibility," *American Philosophical Quarterly* 16 (1979): 50–62.

6. I defend this account at length in "Is Egoism Morally Defensible?" *Philosophia* 18, nos. 2–3 (1988): 191–209.

7. Jesse Kalin, "In Defense of Egoism," in *Morality and Rational Self-Interest*, ed. David P. Gauthier (Englewood Cliffs, NJ: Prentice-Hall, 1970), 75.

8. I am indebted here to the discussion of utilitarianism in Bernard Williams, *Ethics and the Limits of Philosophy* (Cambridge, MA: Harvard University Press, 1985), 106–12.

9. Lawrence A. Blum, *Friendship, Altruism, and Morality* (London: Routledge & Kegan Paul, 1980), 73, 72, 73, 70.

10. See Peter Railton, "Alienation, Consequentialism, and the Demands of Morality," in *Consequentialism and Its Critics*, ed. Samuel Scheffler (New York: Oxford University Press, 1988), 115. Railton's concern is with act consequentialism, and his valuable, far-ranging discussion has influenced me throughout this essay.

11. I am grateful to Christeen Clemens for suggesting this example.

12. Ian Jarvie, "Arguing Interpretations: The Pragmatic Optimism of Woody Al-

len," in *Woody Allen and Philosophy*, ed. Mark T. Conard and Aeon J. Skoble (Chicago: Open Court, 2004), 55.

13. Aristotle discusses this idea in bks. 8–9 of *The Nicomachean Ethics*.

14. Laurence Thomas, "Ethical Egoism and Psychological Dispositions," *American Philosophical Quarterly* 17 (1980): 77.

15. Thomas writes that the egoist's disposition to take advantage of anyone when he has good reason to believe this would be in his self-interest and the disposition to act favorably toward his friends are "polar dispositions" and that "a person can no more shift between these two dispositions at the drop of a hat than can a person exhibit those traits that are fully characteristic of both the virtue of honesty and the vice of mendacity upon demand" (ibid.).

16. William H. Wilcox, "Egoists, Consequentialists, and Their Friends," *Philosophy and Public Affairs* 16 (1987): 79. Wilcox's essay is a reply to Railton's "Alienation, Consequentialism, and the Demands of Morality."

17. Wilcox, "Egoists, Consequentialists, and Their Friends," 79.

18. Ibid.

19. For a summary of a number of objections to maximizing strategies, see James Griffin, *Well-Being: Its Meaning, Measurement, and Moral Importance* (Oxford: Oxford University Press, 1986), 356 n. 33. Griffin himself by no means favors satisficing over maximizing.

20. Mark T. Conard registers an important source of dissatisfaction with my account of satisficing egoism. He argues that, by having friends and giving up some of what is in one's best interest (whatever that might be), one is, thereby, implicitly affirming that having friends is *better* than having those other things, that it leads to one's having a better life or, perhaps, even the best life possible. Thus, one is not actually settling for a life that is good enough but, rather, maximizing. I believe that a satisficing egoist would say that the *best* possible life would be to have all the benefits of friendship without having to make any of the sacrifices. Since that is not feasible (though it is not logically impossible), satisficing is a distinct and preferable policy.

21. I explore the topic of morality and psychopaths in "Why Be Moral? Amorality and Psychopathy in *Strangers on a Train*," in *Hitchcock and Philosophy*, ed. David Baggett and William Drumin (Chicago: Open Court, 2007).

# God's Lonely Man

*Taxi Driver* and the Ethics of Vigilantism

*Aeon J. Skoble*

Martin Scorsese's 1976 film *Taxi Driver* takes us through a brief but eventful period in the life of one Travis Bickle (Robert De Niro). We don't know much about Travis's background, except that he is an honorably discharged former marine and that he has trouble sleeping. He takes a job driving a New York City taxi because he's up all night cruising the streets anyway and figures he might as well get paid for it. But we come to find out some of what is on his mind, thanks to the sporadic voice-over segments. We learn early on, for instance, that although Travis is willing to work in parts of New York others are afraid of, he is disgusted by what he sees: "All the animals come out at night. . . . Sick, venal." He thinks that something should be done about the rampant depravity he witnesses nightly. He isn't sure what, but he is confident that it will happen eventually: after noting with satisfaction a cleansing rain, he muses: "One of these days a real rain will come and wash all this scum off the street."

*Taxi Driver* shows us the thoughts and actions of a protagonist who seems slightly deranged, but in many instances it is the rest of the world that seems crazy. Every night, Travis sees prostitution, violence, and drug use. One passenger (a cameo appearance by Scorsese) describes to Travis in detail his wife's infidelity and how he intends to kill her. Iris Steensma (Jodie Foster) thinks Travis is "square" because he disapproves of her life as a teen prostitute. ("You call that bein' hip?" he says. "What world are you from?") Travis, of course, is not entirely competent to distinguish which is which: initially he sees Betsy (Cybill Shepherd) as an angel in an otherwise hellish environment. ("Out of this filthy mess, she is alone.") But when he becomes disillusioned about her, the disillusionment morphs into a plan to assassinate Senator Charles Palantine (Leonard Harris), for whom Betsy is working. Though unrealized, the plan seems entirely the product of an unhinged mind. There is no logical reason it should follow from Travis's disappointment with Betsy.[1] On the other hand, his attempt to rescue Iris from her world of drugs and teen prostitution, though bloody in its achievement, isn't at all crazy and is, arguably, noble. By allowing us to get inside Travis's mind, Scorsese's film presents an opportunity for undertaking an exploration into the ethics of vigilantism. In this essay, I hope to use the film to explore the questions of when, if ever, vigilantism is justified, in what ways vigilantism is epistemologically or ethically problematic, and how we are to differentiate justice from revenge and madness.

By definition, vigilantes are those who, as the cliché has it, take the law into their own hands. We might distinguish between *self-defensive vigilantism,* as when Bernhard Goetz shot his would-be assailants on a New York City subway or, fictionally, when Travis defends a bodega owner against armed robbery, and *adventuresome vigilantism,* which is how we might characterize Travis's later actions and most of what comic book superheroes spend their time doing.[2] The former is, I suspect, largely unproblematic, although subject to constraints of proportionality. It is the latter that is more complicated.

The very existence of that clichéd formulation *taking the law into their own hands* implies that, according to most people, this is morally problematic. For example, John Locke argued that part of the defining conditions of civil society was that each individual gives up his or her right to private vengeance, delegating it to the consensually formed government for the purposes of objectivity.[3] If everyone were a judge in his or her own case, mistakes and overreactions would be legion, so, to be more secure in our rights, we form governments and delegate to them the authority to make and enforce laws. It makes us all more secure, on this theory, to have the pursuit and punishment of wrongdoers be the delegated task of some agency of the state. On this view, it's wrong for *me* to try to apprehend or punish robbers, as this is the assigned function of the state's police force and court system. Even on this standard account, however, there are exceptions. For example, I may defend myself against an attacker, and I may come to the aid of a third party suffering an attack, especially where authorized law enforcement agents are absent or powerless. Travis judges that Iris is a virtual prisoner of Sport (Harvey Keitel) and the Mafia underboss (Bob Maroff) he works for and, hence, needs rescuing. This is potentially debatable: at their breakfast date, Iris talks as if she is involved of her own volition and describes her plan to save enough money to move to Vermont. But it's pretty clear, not just to Travis, but to most viewers of the film, that Iris is indeed "trapped" in a situation not entirely within her control (and indeed is a minor, a child, not entirely capable of full legal autonomy). We see evidence of this later (although Travis does not) in the scene where Iris complains to Sport that she doesn't like what she's doing. Sport gets her to stay not with direct coercion (of the sort he used the night she tried to get in Travis's cab) but with lies: "If you ever liked what you were doing, you wouldn't be my woman." He keeps her in prostitution partly by lying about his love for her, which he senses is the most effective tactic with this very young girl: "I only wish that every man could know what it's like to be loved by you. That every woman everywhere had a man who loves her like I love you." While Travis isn't privy to this disturbing scene, he has seen the way she is guarded in her apartment. When he queries Iris about her plan to leave, he knows Sport won't be amenable:

> TRAVIS: So what are you going to do about Sport and that old bastard?
> IRIS: When?
> TRAVIS: When you leave.
> IRIS: I don't know, just leave 'em, I guess.
> TRAVIS: Yeah, you're just gonna leave?
> IRIS: Yeah, they've got plenty of other girls.
> TRAVIS: Yeah, but you just can't do that, what are you gonna do?
> IRIS: What should I do? Call the cops?
> TRAVIS: No, the cops don't do nothin', you know that.

If she cannot expect the police to help her, and she cannot help herself, then it becomes morally legitimate for Travis to help her. While it remains problematic what level of violence is justified in the course of his action, it seems plain that *taking* the action is permissible.

As a possible objection to this analysis, one might note that there are rules that bound this sort of "private justice," and among them, typically, is a rule that says: I may not go out of my way to look for trouble and then defend against it. In Michael Winner's 1974 movie *Death Wish*, it's true that the architect Paul Kersey (Charles Bronson) is defending himself (or others) against attackers, but the ostensible objection to his behavior is that he is going out at night *looking for attackers to defend himself against*. This is what causes the police to label him a vigilante. In *Taxi Driver*, however, it's less obvious that Travis is looking for trouble: Iris gets into his taxi trying to get away from Sport. It is a chance encounter that becomes part of Travis's growing determination to "do something." Another chance encounter occurs when Travis foils a robbery of a bodega, shooting the criminal. This is not a Kersey-like case of looking for trouble—Travis reacts fairly reasonably to circumstances that appear before him unbidden. His ability to do justice in this case, in contrast with his inability to help Iris that first time (and his general sense of inability to cleanse the city), is also a critical catalyst in his transformation from passive-if-disgruntled observer to vigilante.

## "I Got Some Bad Ideas in My Head"

In his voice-over at the beginning of the film, Travis simply yearns for a solution to the city's problems ("a real rain will come"). Later, he personalizes it, but abstractly ("Somebody's got to do something"). He tries to give the responsibility to Senator Palantine: "You should clean up this city here, because this city here is like an open sewer, you know, it's full of filth and scum. Sometimes I can hardly take it." When he becomes disillusioned with Palantine, Travis assumes responsibility himself: "Listen, you fuckers, you screwheads. Here is a man who would not take it anymore. A man who stood up against the scum, the cunts, the dogs, the filth, the shit. Here is a man who stood up." Travis comes to think (rightly or wrongly) that Palantine will not do anything about the crime in the city. He takes responsibility for doing justice partly because he increasingly feels that no one else will do so. Travis is "God's lonely man." He stands up against the evil because someone has to, and no one is. Spider-Man, while much more sane, offers a similar rationale for his becoming a vigilante: "With great power comes great responsibility."[4] His own failure to intervene earlier resulted in the murder of his uncle. Many superhero origin stories—from Zorro to Batman to Rorschach—involve the theme of "someone has got to *do* something" that Travis here appeals to.

The problem is that Travis is not entirely sure what it is he needs to stand up against.[5] There's a critical distinction between fighting evil and fighting perceived evil. How to tell the difference? It's relatively uncontroversial that Iris needs to be rescued from the Mafia, but it is far from obvious that Senator Palantine should be killed. Other than as an unwarranted inference from Betsy's rejection, there's no evidence in the film whatsoever to suggest that Palantine is an evildoer. So, when Travis is finally energized to "stand up," his initial object is actually unconnected to his disgust. Regardless of what he thought he might accomplish by assassinating Palantine, when he realizes that that won't work, he sets his sights more microcosmically: rescuing Iris.

This, then, is one of the key problems facing any discussion of the ethics of vigilantism: epistemology. One has to know that the target "has it coming." Since Paul Kersey waits until the muggers confront him, each of his targets is correctly chosen: someone intent on violently assaulting Kersey. This is a common trait among fictional vigilantes: they are, at least, correct about identifying deserving targets of their private justice. Historical vigilantes, for instance, lynch mobs, are frequently *incorrect* about who is deserving of their justice, even if, within their own false worldview, they have a framework for distinguishing good from bad. (For example, the Ku Klux Klan might offer its antipathy toward race mixing as a rationale for its vigilante tactics. My point is that, even if Klan members claim to have a good reason, and even sincerely believe they have a reason, that doesn't imply that they *actually* have a good reason.)

Comic book superheroes are, technically, vigilantes, and what makes them at least nominal allies with the police is that they correctly identify and harm only criminals.[6] From Bob Kane's staid Batman to Alan Moore's more unhinged Rorschach, the costumed vigilantes know who the evildoers are, so even though it's private justice, the bad guys "had it coming to them" every bit as much as when they're pursued by Dick Tracy or Eliot Ness. Comic book superheroes, then, are taking the law into their own hands *correctly.* One reason Travis Bickle is disturbing, more disturbing than Paul Kersey or Batman, is that he is sufficiently confused as to *lack* solid epistemological grounds for his vigilantism. While he's right to want to rescue Iris, he's wrong to want to kill Palantine.[7] More specifically: rescuing Iris is justice; assassinating Palantine is madness. If Travis is mentally unstable, that might tend to undercut the justifiability of his vigilantism, even it's true that Iris deserves to be rescued—it might be a case of Travis doing the right thing for the wrong reason. But it's not clear just how unstable he is. When he talks to her at breakfast about leaving, his reasoning is entirely correct: she needs to get out, and Sport won't be too keen to let her go. One needn't be insane to conclude that she needs rescuing, and indeed Travis's recognition of her legitimate distress is evidence that he isn't entirely deranged.

## "One of These Days I Gotta Get Myself Organizied"

That is not to say that Travis's *method* of rescuing Iris is entirely sane: he could have spirited her away in his taxi as easily as he met her for breakfast and driven her to the commune in Vermont. Instead, he elects to kill those participating in Iris's subjection. He really does get himself "organizied"—in addition to buying several guns, he cleverly fashions an arm-mounted slide mechanism that he can use to rearm quickly when necessary. (This is, in principle, no different from the gadgetmaking savvy shown by Spider-Man and Batman.) Perhaps, by this point, Travis has a death wish of his own, and is hoping to go out in the proverbial blaze of glory. We know he feels alienated and isolated generally: "Loneliness has followed me my whole life, everywhere. In bars, in cars, sidewalks, stores, everywhere. There's no escape. I'm God's lonely man." We know this feeling of loneliness has been greatly exacerbated by Betsy's rejection of him. (This would not be the same as Kersey's death wish, however. Kersey is *risking* death, maybe even inviting it, having lost his wife and daughter. He's quite content *not* to die, and even comes to rediscover meaning in his life, from the satisfaction of ridding the city of criminals.[8] Travis, on the other hand, tries to shoot himself after he is finished killing the criminals, failing only because he is out of ammunition.) But, even if Travis's means are unwarranted, his end is, in fact, a correct one. We see at the end of the film that the newspapers have painted him as a hero, and, ironically, he even earns Betsy's admiration for his deeds. In our last few glimpses of him, he seems lucid enough, although the film's conclusion leaves it an open question just how stable he really is.

## "We *Are* the People"

The ambiguity in Palantine's campaign slogan is used for comic relief, yet it raises an interesting question about Locke's skepticism about private justice.[9] The powers of the government come from the people, but, in delegating power, do we give up all our prerogatives? Assuming epistemological correctness, who has the right to pursue justice? If the answer is everyone, does that imply that Locke's argument about civil society is incorrect? If the answer *isn't* everyone, then who, and under what circumstances?

While Locke is surely right that we cannot expect objectivity from people serving as judges in their own cases, we *can* often know what justice entails. The bodega owner, for instance, is entitled to be protected against armed robbery. There are no police on the scene, and the bodega owner himself is powerless to repel the robber. Does that mean that private third parties are not entitled to assist? Travis is correct to intervene here, just as Batman or Spider-Man would under similar circumstances. Perhaps it is the lethal nature of his intervention that disturbs viewers who might prefer a less violent form of intervention. But, lacking superpowers, Travis really has no choice but to use his weapon.[10] Similarly, we can correctly infer that Iris needs rescuing. In this case, as noted, Travis does have a choice about the means of effecting the rescue, but his coming to see *that* she is in trouble is no different from how any decent person would think. If she cannot free herself, and, as Travis reminds her, the police cannot either, then the question is not so much who has the *right* to help as who has the *responsibility* to help. Contrary to Locke, the superhero's attitude is that it's everyone's right, if not duty, to fight crime—we *are* the people, and we must all do what we can to seek justice. This seems to be the case for Travis as well: a man who would not take it anymore, who will stand up against the scum. He, too, is the people.

What do we conclude about vigilantism, then? On the one hand, we do not want to countenance Klan lynchings or Travis's scheme to assassinate Palantine, but, on the other hand, neither do we want to approve of the indifference shown by Kitty Genovese's neighbors, who refused to intervene as she was attacked near her apartment.[11] A slogan like "let the police handle it" seems prudent in some cases yet morally obtuse in others. But it's not especially helpful either to formulate a rule such as "if you're a sane and prudent person, and can correctly identify situations calling for vigilantism, and can determine how to respond in a sensible manner, then you may proceed," for such a rule simply begs all the relevant questions. But one thing we can do is devote some time to contemplation and discussion of what is right and wrong. As Socrates put it, "It is the greatest good for a man to discuss virtue every day . . . for the unexamined life is not worth living for man."[12] At a minimum, we would then be able to recognize and confront the obvious badness we see before us rather than turning a blind eye. We can all stand up against the sick and venal. We *are* the people.

## Notes

I am grateful to Mark T. Conard for his helpful suggestions on this essay, and for many thought-provoking conversations about *Taxi Driver* over the years.

1. Charitably, perhaps Travis is reasoning in the following way: (1) Betsy is an angel; Betsy works for Palantine; therefore, Palantine is God. But (2) Betsy turns out to be "like the others," "living in hell"; thus, Palantine must be the devil. This isn't highly rational.

2. On Bernhard Goetz, see Suzanne Daley, "Man Tells Police He Shot Youths in Subway Train," *New York Times*, January 1, 1985.

3. See John Locke, *Second Treatise on Civil Government*, ed. Peter Laslett (Cambridge: Cambridge University Press, 1960), chap. 8.

4. Stan Lee and Steve Ditko, *Amazing Fantasy*, no. 15, 1962.

5. Of course, it would be impossible to rid the city of crime completely, but this can't be what makes Travis lose faith in Palantine, as Travis himself seems to understand, settling (á la Tolstoy?) for saving Iris.

6. I discuss this context for studying the ethics of vigilantism in "Superhero Revisionism in *Watchmen* and *The Dark Knight Returns*," in *Superheroes and Philosophy*, ed. Tom Morris and Matt Morris (Chicago: Open Court, 2005), 29–42.

7. The lapse of logic in this latter case was tragically repeated in reality, in John Hinckley's rationale for his assassination attempt on President Reagan in 1981.

8. An interesting question, not to be pursued here, is why audiences tend to find this attitude creepy in Kersey's case but heroic in Batman's. It might be that Batman apprehends without killing, but I suspect there's more to it, perhaps having to do with Kersey's story being more realistic.

9. Regarding the ambiguity of the campaign slogan, Betsy's coworker Tom (Albert Brooks) is seen arguing with the supplier about whether the campaign buttons should read "*We* are the people" as opposed to "We *are* the people," ultimately concluding: "*We* won't pay for the buttons."

10. The bodega owner's follow-up actions, however, are potentially controversial: he tells Travis to leave, and then sets about beating the (dead?) robber with a baseball bat. It's unclear whether this is part of the bodega owner's attempts to protect Travis or simply sadistic revenge taking.

11. Martin Gansburg, "Thirty-Eight Who Saw Murder Didn't Call Police," *New York Times,* March 27, 1964.

12. Plato, *Apology,* trans. G. M. A. Grube (Indianapolis: Hackett, 1975), 38 (Stephanus number).

# Goodfellas, Gyges, and the Good Life

*Dean A. Kowalski*

Through a careful analysis of Martin Scorsese's *Goodfellas* (1990), I intend to accomplish two interlocking goals in this essay. The first goal is to show how Henry Hill has some surprising affinities with the mythical character of Gyges, as depicted in Plato's *Republic*. Both men could satisfy virtually all their desires immune to public scrutiny or legal repercussion. As such, *Goodfellas* offers a novel way to explore the classic philosophical question: Lacking the negative social consequences of not doing so, why ought I to lead a morally good life? In fact, if I can continually get away with acting immorally, it seems that it is in my best interest *not* to lead a morally good life. The second goal of the essay is to explore and critically evaluate Plato's views about whether I ought to lead a morally good life. This is achieved by examining *Goodfellas*'s main characters: Henry Hill (Ray Liotta), Jimmy Conway (Robert De Niro), Tommy DeVito (Joe Pesci), and Paul Cicero (Paul Sorvino). As we will see, these four characters distinctively illuminate Plato's views on justice and the "unbalanced self"; however, they also, ironically, represent a serious objection to Plato's views. Near the end of the essay, a strategy is presented on Plato's behalf for dealing with this objection.

## Henry's Story

Scorsese opens *Goodfellas* with a shot of the thirteen-year-old Henry Hill peering across the street at the local cabstand, a legitimate front for the Cicero crime family. We hear an adult Henry (Liotta) reminiscing about his teenage years: "As far back as I can remember I always wanted to be a gangster. Being a gangster was better than being President of the United States. To me, it meant being somebody in a neighborhood of nobodies. They weren't like anybody else. They did whatever they wanted. . . . Nobody ever called the cops."[1] Throughout the film, and early on especially, Scorsese utilizes stop frames in addition to Henry's narration to tell his life story. These cinematic features act as photographs with captions, conveying critical moments in Henry's life.

The first cinematic snapshot of Henry captures the time he is beaten by his father for being truant from school. Henry has been spending all his time at the local cabstand; his part-time after-school job has become an all-day obsession. Henry shows up at the cabstand the next day with a black eye. He informs Tuddy Cicero (Frank DiLeo), the younger brother of Paulie Cicero, the Cicero family patriarch, that he can no longer run errands, lest his father kill him next time. Tuddy and his crew immediately find the Hills' postman. This leads to the second snapshot: the postman has his head in a pizza oven, with Tuddy explaining to him that not one more letter from the school will be delivered to the Hill residence. These first two stills depict Henry's adolescent years in the mob and suggest that his real family ties are with the Ciceros.[2]

The next three still frames represent Henry's rite of passage into Mafia adulthood. We first see Henry helping Tuddy firebomb cars at a rival cabstand by smashing windows with a tire iron and dowsing the seats with gasoline. We then see Henry running for safety, but not before a giant, fiery explosion dangerously lifts him off his feet. With Henry airborne, Scorsese stills the frame, and Liotta narrates:

> People looked at me differently. They knew I was with somebody. I didn't have to wait in line at the bakery on Sunday for fresh bread. The owner knew who I was with. He would come around from the counter no matter how many people were waiting. I was always taken care of first. Our neighbors didn't park in our driveway anymore even though we didn't have a car. At thirteen, I made more money than most grown-ups in the neighborhood. I had more money than I could spend. I had it all. One day, some neighborhood kids carried my mother's groceries all the way home. Know why? It was out of respect.

The subsequent two still frames introduce us to Jimmy "the Gent" Conway (Jimmy Burke in *Wiseguy*) as a mentor of sorts to Henry. Scorsese stills the frame the very first time Henry meets Jimmy. He also stills the frame after Henry's first arrest for selling Jimmy's bootleg cigarettes. Immediately after Henry's court appearance, Jimmy is there to congratulate him because, as Jimmy states: "You took your first pinch like a man and learned the two greatest things in life: Never rat on your friends, and always keep your mouth shut." And, although this advice proves to be ironic foreshadowing,

Jimmy leads Hill into the hallway, where all his "family" has assembled to congratulate him. In fact, Paulie exclaims: "You broke your cherry!" Henry is now a full member of the family.

We next see (and not merely hear) Liotta play Henry in 1963, a twenty-one-year-old man. He is handsome, well dressed, affluent, and respected. He relishes the life of a gangster. While having dinner with Tommy DeVito (Tommy DeSimone in *Wiseguy*), Henry narrates: "For us to live any other way was nuts. To us, those goody, good people who worked . . . for bum paychecks and took the subway to work every day and worried about bills, were dead. They were suckers. . . . If we wanted something, we just took it. If anyone complained twice, they got hit so bad, they never complained again." Soon after Jimmy, Tommy, and Henry steal $420,000 from Air France (without brandishing a gun), Henry meets Karen (Lorraine Bracco). Initially, she is not impressed with Henry. However, his connections, charm, and money win her over. Flashing rolls of bills, Henry and Karen never wait for a table, no matter how crowded the restaurant. One night at a show, Bobby Vinton sends a bottle of champagne to their table. Karen tells us: "There was nothing like it. I didn't think there was anything strange in all of this—you know, a twenty-one-year-old kid with such connections. He was an exciting guy." Henry and Karen are soon married. Both his birth and his mob families attend. Members of the latter present the newlyweds envelopes stuffed with hundred-dollar bills.

It is important to note that, because the Cicero family protects Henry, he conducts his "business deals" predominantly without fear of legal repercussion. Sometimes the police harass him, but rarely does anything come of it. In effect, he becomes invisible to the authorities. The one time he is convicted and sent to prison, he serves his time with Paulie and other gangsters. They enjoy separate quarters, home-cooked meals, and wine with dinner. Henry tells us: "When you think of prison, you get pictures in your mind from the old movies of rows of guys behind bars. But it wasn't like that for wiseguys. It really wasn't that bad. . . . Everybody else in the joint was doin' real time all mixed together living like pigs, but we lived alone. We owned the joint."

Henry has virtually free reign to do what he wishes, and he becomes connected, respected, and affluent doing so. He breaks the law and practices immoral behavior largely without consequence. If given the chance, who wouldn't lead a life like Henry's?

Perhaps some people might claim that Henry must conform to the Mafia's rules, that he must not cross the Ciceros. As such, Henry is not at liberty to do just anything he wants. Perhaps worrying about the mob is worse than worrying about the cops. However, by continuing his drug trade (started while he was in prison), Henry breaks one of Paulie's sacred rules of not dealing drugs. Narcotics officers eventually arrest Henry, and, while he is out on bail, Scorsese gives us one last still shot of him. Henry and Jimmy meet at a diner to allegedly discuss Henry's case. Jimmy asks Henry to help with a hit in Florida, but Henry knows that he will be the one getting whacked. Henry tells us that, at that moment, he knew that Jimmy and, presumably, others in the mob wanted Henry dead because they feared that he would "rat them out." Fearful for his life, Henry indeed turns on his Mafia family. He is granted clemency for doing so, and he and his family enter the witness protection program. Thus, Henry truly becomes invisible without ever having to face the consequences of his prior illegal and immoral behavior or the consequences of crossing the mob. So the question remains: If you can avoid the negative consequences associated with it, why shouldn't you lead an immoral life, especially if you can benefit greatly from doing so?

Before delving into Plato's answer to that classic philosophical question, let's return to the end of *Goodfellas*. The next to last scene is set in a courtroom. Henry is on the stand, testifying against Jimmy and Paulie. When asked, he points to both men. But then Henry gets up from the witness stand and addresses the camera directly. It's as if Scorsese allows Henry to tell the ending to his own story. Henry laments:

> You see, the hardest thing for me was leaving the life. I still love the life. We were treated like movie stars with muscle. We had it all, just for the asking. Our wives, mothers, kids, everyone rode along. I had paper bags filled with jewelry stashed in the kitchen. I had a sugar bowl of coke next to the bed. . . . Anything I wanted was a phone call away—free cars, the keys to a dozen hideout flats throughout the city. I'd bet 20–30 grand. I'd either blow the winnings in a week or go to the sharks to pay off the bookies. It didn't matter. It didn't mean anything. When I was broke, I'd go out and rob some more. We ran everything. We paid off cops. We paid off lawyers, judges. Everyone had their hands out. Everything was for the taking. And now it's all over. And that's the hardest part, there's no action. I have to wait around like everyone else. . . . I'm an average nobody. I get to live the rest of my life like a schnook.

This soliloquy is full of remorse and regret. Henry is not at all happy about turning on his mob cohorts, entering the witness protection program, and leaving behind his gangster lifestyle. In fact, he would be happier if he could return to that life. Plato, as we'll soon see, disagrees with Henry. He brazenly argues that it is *impossible* for a person to be happier leading an immoral life. The morally good person is always happier. Plato's position is clearly controversial. It is also deserving of careful exploration.

## Glaucon, Gyges, and Plato

In his great work the *Republic,* Plato is very concerned about whether there is any good reason for believing that we should *not* lead an immoral life if given the chance. Although the *Republic* covers a lot of philosophical ground (to say the least), Plato's primary project is to answer two questions: What is justice? What reasons do we have for leading a just (or morally good) life? He attempts this through an extensive dialogue between his great teacher Socrates and various interlocutors, most notably Plato's (historical) brother Glaucon.

Glaucon is troubled. He doesn't believe that a person benefits more by becoming unjust rather than just, but he is aware of many who do believe this. In fact, we might call it the *majority view* about justice. More specifically, those who hold the majority view believe that no one does the morally correct thing for its own sake; rather, they think that we act justly only because acting unjustly has consequences that are so much worse than acting morally. What troubles Glaucon so is that he has never heard the majority view sufficiently refuted. He hopes that Socrates can provide the refutation he seeks. But, before he can be convinced of Socrates' success, he must present the majority view as strenuously as he can.

Glaucon begins espousing the majority view by questioning whether people really want to become morally good. Rather, it seems that we choose to do good acts only because it is the lesser of two evils. Often doing the right thing inconveniences us, but, if we were to ignore our duties and act immorally, we would no doubt be found out. Acting unjustly invariably means having to pay for the consequences of our moral indiscretions. Paying the consequences is much worse than putting up with the minor inconvenience of acting morally. Thus, although doing the morally correct thing is not ideal for us, it is better than going to jail or acquiring a bad reputation. This is how doing the right thing is the lesser of two evils.

But what if the greater of the two evils were no longer a factor? Consider the following analogy with visiting the dentist. It seems natural to compare leading the life of a morally good person to making regular trips to the dentist's office: If you could be assured of never suffering from tooth decay, I'm sure you would never sit in that damnable chair. However, in fact, *not* visiting the dentist is bound to catch up with you eventually, especially once your teeth begin to rot and fall out. Therefore, even if it means periodically having your teeth mercilessly grated on with an iron hook, you are much better off putting up with the inconvenience of regularly listening to your dentist's lame jokes (as he savagely pierces your gums again with that miserable scraper). But imagine if you or I could eat and drink whatever we wanted without ever needing to brush, floss, or, especially, sit in the dentist's chair? In a world without tooth decay, cavities, or gum disease, dentistry would be a very lonely occupation. This plausible intuition opens the door for the majority to argue that, just as no one goes to the dentist for the fun of it, no one does the morally correct thing for its own sake. That is, if you or I could lead an unjust or immoral life without ever having to worry about paying the price for our misdeeds, it would seem irrational for us to behave justly. If we enjoyed the kind of freedom that Henry Hill enjoyed, why not lie, steal, and cheat? Glaucon didn't know about modern dentistry or mafiosos, but he did know enough to realize that the majority view might be on to something. If there are no prospects of going to jail or being executed, our best interests are served by doing *whatever* is required to satisfy our wildest desires.

In the *Republic,* Glaucon utilizes the mythical story of Gyges and two other thought experiments to articulate the majority view. While tending his flock, Gyges finds a gold ring. He places it on his finger and soon discovers that, when he turns the band one way, he becomes invisible and that, when he turns it the other way, he becomes visible again. On realizing this, Gyges seduces the queen, kills the king (with her help), assumes the throne, and thereby gains immediate access to great wealth and fame. He is able to accomplish this without damaging his reputation. In fact, it is presumed that Gyges has every appearance of being noble, generous, and kind.

This familiar fable allows Glaucon to pose a second thought experiment to Socrates. Building on the Gyges story, we are to imagine that there are two invisibility rings. One ring is given to a morally good person and the other to an immoral person. It seems plain to Glaucon that, before too long, we would have two unjust persons because "no one, it seems, would be so incorruptible that he would stay on the path of justice, or bring himself to keep away from other people's possessions, . . . when he could take whatever he wanted with impunity." So, on behalf of the majority view, Glaucon concludes that there "is strong evidence that no one is [morally good] willingly but only when compelled. No one believes justice to be a good thing when it is kept private, since whenever either person [given the invisibility rings] thinks he can do injustice with impunity, he does it."[3]

Glaucon believes that the majority view can be further established by discussing one final thought experiment. This thought experiment has two interlocking, main features. First, Glaucon proposes the possibility of a completely unjust or immoral person who is so resourceful that he is able to deceive everyone into believing that he is perfectly just or morally good. As Glaucon says: "We must allow that while doing the greatest injustice, he has nonetheless provided himself with the greatest reputation for justice. If he does happen to slip up, he must be able to put it right, either through his ability to speak persuasively . . . or to use force if force is needed, because he is courageous and strong and has provided himself with wealth and friends" (361a–b). In the second part of this thought experiment, Glaucon proposes the possibility of a perfectly just or morally good man who has been completely misunderstood by society. He has the reputation of being completely unjust, even though he is not unjust at all. As Glaucon describes:

> Let's now put the just man next to him [the completely unjust man described previously] in our argument. . . . We must take away his reputation. For a reputation of justice would bring him honor and rewards, so that it would not be clear whether he is being just for the sake of justice, or for the sake of those honors and rewards. We must strip him of everything except justice, and make his situation the opposite of the unjust person's. Though he does no injustice, he must have the greatest reputation for it, so that he may be tested with regard to justice by seeing whether or not he can withstand a bad reputation and its consequences. Let him stay like that, unchanged, until he is dead—just, but for all his life believed to be unjust. (361b–d)

The main point of the thought experiment is simply this: Which person would you choose to be? Glaucon fears that the answer is clear: No one, it seems, would choose to be the second man. If so, then Glaucon (perhaps to his own dismay) has gone a long way to establish the majority view. If we could get away with being like the first man, our best interests would be served by not acting in morally good ways.[4]

The intuitions driving these thought experiments serve to underpin the argument Glaucon espouses on behalf of the majority view. That argument can be recast, beginning with the following disjunction: either we act justly simply for its own sake, such that becoming a morally good person is its own unique reward, or we act justly only because of the negative consequences of acting unjustly (where this might include considerations involving the afterlife, should there be any).[5] If being a morally good person is its own reward and pursued for its own sake, then, regardless of whatever negative consequences are associated with leading such a life, we still have sufficient reason to act justly. But the interlocking thought experiments that Glaucon presents seemingly show that the benefits of being a perfectly unjust person who is believed to be perfectly just are too attractive to pass up and that the negatives of being a perfectly just person who is believed to be perfectly unjust are too severe to endure (see 361d–362d). If so, then the next premise of the argument is established: Justice is not its own reward or sought for its own sake. Therefore, the argument concludes that we act justly only because of the negative consequences of acting unjustly. Consequently, perhaps the majority view is correct and Plato mistaken. Without having to worry about getting caught, we would all act like Henry or Gyges; our lives would be better, and we would be far happier.

Both Henry Hill and Gyges had the opportunity to act as they pleased, without having to worry about the ramifications of their actions. They benefited greatly from acting unjustly. Gyges became a wealthy king, and Henry became "somebody in a neighborhood of nobodies." Furthermore, we can presume that, should either of them "slip up," as Glaucon said, both had the connections, charm, wealth, and power to "make things right again" (361a). This was often true of Henry. He often bought or talked his way out of any difficult spot he encountered, including those involving his wife and various mistresses. Accordingly, because both Henry and Gyges could operate in virtual anonymity without fear of paying the consequences of their moral indiscretions, and because the benefits of acting unjustly or immorally were great, it seems that neither had any reason not to act unjustly or immorally. The only possible response is that acting justly or being a morally good person is its own unique reward and, thus, that leading a morally good life for its own sake will actually (somehow) benefit you more. But the argument that Glaucon espouses makes this dubious. You will neither benefit more nor be happier than a person who is perfectly unjust but who is believed to be just. You are better off and happier being an undetected unjust person. Henry and his Mafia family would agree. Reminiscent of a tune that could have been included in the famed *Goodfellas*'s sound track, Billy Joel's 1977 "Only the Good Die Young," Henry might say: "I'd rather laugh with the sinners than cry with the saints; the sinners are much more fun."[6]

## The Just State and the Just Person

Most scholars believe that, by the point in the *Republic* at which Glaucon challenges Socrates to refute the majority view about justice, Plato is more likely providing his own views through Socrates than reporting what Socrates himself would answer. Thus, we can say that Plato (and not necessarily Socrates) attempts to answer Glaucon's challenge by constructing an elaborate analogy between the perfectly just state (or commonwealth) and the perfectly just person (see 368e–369a). Plato believes that the ideal society is made up of three classes of citizens: producers, guardians, and rulers.[7] Each class has a distinctive role to play in society. When each class successfully fulfills its role, the state is well ordered and harmonious and justice prevails. When justice prevails, happiness also prevails. But if any class fails to fulfill its distinctive role, then the state is not well ordered. It is disharmonious, and neither justice nor happiness prevails. Analogously, Plato believes that there is a threefold division within the self or person. This division corresponds to his belief that there exist three interrelated elements of human nature: appetitive, spirited, and rational. When each of these elements exhibits the characteristic it is fittest to exemplify, then the person is well ordered, and he enjoys harmony among his elements. Just as a well-ordered state is a just state, someone who enjoys harmony among his three basic elements is a perfectly just—or morally good—person. He is also truly happy. Disharmonious persons cannot be truly happy. Therefore, just as the citizens of a commonwealth have sufficient reason to work toward living in a just state, individual persons have sufficient reason to work toward becoming well ordered and harmonious.[8]

Plato initially discusses the appetitive and rational elements in conjunction. The appetitive element "feels passion, hungers, thirsts, and is stirred by other appetites." It thus corresponds to our basic wants and needs for water, food, and sex, among other things. This element drives us toward physical gratification and worldly possessions. But, more generally, it motivates us to act at all. The appetitive element is, thus, analogous to an engine; it is what keeps us moving throughout our day. The analogy with the producers in Plato's ideal society is this: just as the producers (laborers, doctors, merchants) provide the commonwealth with its daily necessities and services, the person cannot do anything, let alone survive, without the appetitive element. Consequently, Plato's analogy between the rulers and the rational element is straightforward: just as the rulers create judicious policies for the well-being of the state, our rational element is to determine sensible courses of action that we, as individuals, ought to follow. The rational element keeps the appetitive element in check by issuing sound (personal) policies to direct it to seek neither too much (lest we become lazy gluttons) nor too little (lest we become out-of-touch ascetics). Thus, these two elements function properly when the appetitive exemplifies moderation and the rational exemplifies wisdom (see generally 439d–e).[9]

Plato believes that the third element of human nature is analogous to the guardian class of the commonwealth. He calls this the *spirited element*. It cannot be reduced to the appetitive because "we often notice . . . that when appetite forces someone contrary to his rational calculation, he reproaches himself and feels anger at the thing in him doing the forcing [the appetitive element]" (440b). However, it is not identical to the rational class because "one can see it [spirit] even in small children: they are full of spirit right from birth, but for rational calculation, some of them seem never to possess it, while the masses do so quite late" (441b). Plato's analogy between the guardians and the spirited element is this: just as the guardians (police, national guard, army) are to act as the brave and loyal agents of the rulers, the spirited element is to provide us the courage to do as reason demands. It also explains the personal pride and satisfaction that we experience when utilizing our courage successfully. It further explains why we become angry or disappointed with ourselves when we cave to the appetitive element and act contrary to what our reason demands, as we do in reaching for that second piece of cake. Thus, this element functions properly when it exemplifies courage (which involves loyalty to oneself).

Accordingly, when the appetitive element functions properly, manifesting temperance, the spirited element functions properly, manifesting courage, and the rational element functions properly, manifesting wisdom, then a person becomes well ordered and, thereby, functions optimally. According to Plato, anything that functions optimally in this sense achieves the best overall state of affairs it can; it reaches the pinnacle of its existence. Therefore, persons who reach their pinnacle by becoming well ordered thereby become truly happy. But the fact that a person is temperate, courageous, and wise also means that she has become a just or morally good person. Thus, a just or morally good person is also truly happy. Furthermore, because being truly happy, reaching the pinnacle of our existence, is in our all-around best interest, each of us has good reason to become a morally good person. Anything short of harmony between the three elements thus means that the person cannot be truly happy. So anything short of being a just or morally good person is not in our best interests as it does not result in being truly happy. Therefore, unjust persons like Gyges or Henry Hill cannot be truly happy. If this is so, it is not in one's best interest merely to appear to be just while actually being perfectly unjust or immoral on the inside. This is the heart of Plato's response to Glaucon's challenge.

## *Goodfellas* and the Unbalanced Self

Plato attempts to dramatically reinforce how the malfunctioning of one's self leads to unhappiness with the following metaphor. He has us imagine a kind of mythical creature formed by combining different parts of familiar animals. For example, centaurs are the combination of the upper half of a human being with the lower half of a horse. But Plato's mythical creature is less familiar. He wishes us to combine three things—an animal with several tame and savage heads, a lion, and a human being smaller than the first two. Once we have mentally combined these "so that they somehow grow together," we are then to encompass them in a large human being that, from the outside, looks "like a single creature, a human being." Plato continues:

> When someone claims, then, that it profits this human being to do injustice, but that doing what is just brings no advantage, let's tell him that he is saying nothing other than that it profits him to feed well and strengthen the multifarious beast, as well as the lion and everything that pertains to the lion; to starve and weaken the [small, inner] human being, so that he is dragged along wherever either of the other two leads; and not to accustom the two to one another or make them friends, but leave them to bite and fight and devour one another. (588e–589a)

The multifarious beast with the several heads is the appetitive element, each head representing a different bodily desire or need. The lion, of course, is the spirited element. The small human being is the rational element—the proverbial voice of reason. According to Plato, for anyone who may appear just on the outside but actually be unjust on the inside, the appetitive and spirited elements have become dominant. Thus, the rational element—the element that is most closely associated with who we are as rational animals—has become enslaved. The person has become more like an animal and, in effect, has lost rational control of his or her own actions. One's voice of reason loses all its import. Sometimes, the appetitive element wins out, leading to the accumulation of greater wealth, pleasure, or power. Sometimes, in a few cases at least, the spirited element wins out by infusing sufficient disgust, shame, or anger to sway the person from feeding his overrun appetites. But, because the person is malfunctioning, which element wins out—and it may be a classic psychological struggle—is not up to her. In fact, nothing is up to her in the sense of being in rational control of what she does next. Indeed, it is tempting to conclude on Plato's behalf that such a creature has ceased being a person, insofar as she is no longer rational and persons are rational animals.[10]

It's also tempting to argue on Plato's behalf that the disharmonious person suffers from some sort of psychological turmoil. Plato claims that injustice is "a kind of faction among those three [classes or elements]—their meddling and interfering with one another's jobs; the rebellion of a part of the soul [self] against the whole in order to rule in it inappropriately . . . and that their disorder and wandering is . . . in a word, the whole of vice" (444b). Here, the other two elements overstep their proper place. The voice of reason goes all but ignored by the other two more powerful elements. Consequently, Plato might be interpreted as holding that the unjust person is always conflicted in his actions. The rational element knows what ought to be done, and wishes to accomplish it, but cannot because the appetitive and spirited elements have grown beyond its control. As such, the unjust person suffering from psychological turmoil or conflict cannot be truly happy.

The most obvious example of a disharmonious person occurs when the appetitive element overexerts itself and is no longer under the guidance of the rational element. Henry Hill provides stunning examples of this, especially as the story turns to the 1980s. Henry and Karen now live in an extravagant home, complete with an imported, black marble table and a custom, remote-controlled, wall-sized entertainment center. These luxuries are the result of Henry's booming drug trade. In fact, his drug operation has become so incredibly large and complex that he enlists the help of Jimmy, Tommy, Karen, Sandy (Debi Mazar), his current mistress, and Lois (Welker White), his old babysitter. However, Henry also snorts almost as much cocaine as he sells. With his cocaine addiction and the pressures of running his drug operation, he has become incredibly anxious and para-noid. He never sleeps and is constantly worried that someone or something is following him, including police helicopters. As Plato would say, Henry's appetitive element has overtaken his rational element. Thus, his lifestyle is evidence that he suffers from an internal imbalance. This would probably lead Plato to conclude that he is not happy, even though, akin to Gyges, he enjoys relative freedom from legal prosecution.

Furthermore, there is also some evidence that Henry's spirited ele-ment is causing him disharmony. We see Henry continuing with his drug operation, even though Paulie has directly ordered him to stop. This might represent hubris on Henry's part. He is overconfident to the point where he seemingly believes that he can traffic drugs without Paulie's knowledge or permission. We also see him attempting to spend time with his paraplegic younger brother, Michael (Kevin Corrigan). This might be an example of his spirited element rising up against his appetitive element. Arguably, Henry is moved by the pangs of not spending enough time with Michael, even though doing so will, no doubt, have (temporary) negative ramifications for his drug operations. With all the sources of tension in his life at the time, it seems that his (emotionally driven) choice to juggle one more thing is additional evidence that his voice of reason goes almost completely unheard. Thus, it seems plausible to contend that, at the beginning of 1980, his life is completely out of control. He has become a slave to both his appetitive and his spirited elements. As such, Plato would ask: How can Henry be serving his best interests, even if he continues to go undetected by the authorities?[11]

Plato's views on the ways in which the spirited element can malfunction are complex. For the most part, he seemingly believes that the interaction between the multifarious beast and the spirited lion is necessarily adversarial. Thus, it seems that Plato envisions the "noble lion" as *always* rising up against the many-headed beasts of our appetites. If so, then the spirited element malfunctions *only* when it acts akin to the "cowardly lion" and fails to curb a person's appetites for wealth, pleasure, or power. At times, however, Plato suggests that a person's spirited element can malfunction in other ways. On the one hand, he suggests that the lion may conspire with the multifarious beast, often against the wise counsel of the rational element. Jimmy Conway may be a prime example of someone whose spirited element serves his appetitive element rather than his rational element. After all, no wiseguy is more tenacious in obtaining contraband. As Henry tells us early on: "What Jimmy really loved to do was steal. He actually enjoyed it." On the other hand, Plato also suggests that the spirited element can exert its power against both the appetitive and the rational elements. For example, he claims that the spirited element explains why some people are simply stubborn or ill-tempered. These traits are to be "condemned because they inharmoniously increase and stretch the lion-like element" (590b).[12]

Certainly, Tommy DeVito is an example of someone with an overstretched spirited element. The difference between Tommy and Jimmy in this regard is that Tommy's spirited element tends to overexert itself (roughly) for its own sake and not for the sake of acquiring further monetary or otherwise appetitive ends. Two examples support this contention. First, consider the case where Tommy meets Billy Batts (Frank Vincent) in Henry's Suite Lounge nightclub. Batts has recently been released from prison after serving a six-year term. The trouble begins when Billy reminds everyone in the joint that Tommy used to shine shoes. Tommy reminds him that he isn't that little kid anymore. He now deserves Billy's respect. Sensing that Tommy is becoming unnerved, Billy throws more barbs Tommy's way. The bravado of the two Sicilians gets the better of them. In fact, Tommy becomes enraged. Although Henry convinces Tommy to "get some air," Tommy tells Jimmy: "Keep him here; I'll be back." When he returns, Tommy savagely beats Billy to a bloody pulp simply out of spite. He later kills Billy with his mother's kitchen knife. Second, consider Tommy's interactions with young Spider (Michael Imperioli) during two subsequent poker games. At the first game, Tommy complains that Spider purposely snubbed him by bringing everyone at the table a drink except him. Spider assures Tommy that it was a misunderstanding, and he heads back to the bar to fetch Tommy his Cutty and water. Tommy becomes incensed and insists that Spider dance over to the bar and back with his drink. To quicken Spider's steps, Tommy begins shooting his pistol at Spider's feet. A bullet pierces Spider's foot. At the next game, with his foot bandaged, Spider is again making sandwiches and drinks for Tommy, Jimmy, Henry, and their crew. When Tommy begins humiliating Spider again, Spider mutters an expletive about Tommy. The gang starts ribbing Tommy. Jimmy chuckles, throws Spider a hundred-dollar bill for his bluster, and then asks Tommy: "Are you gonna take that from him? What's the world comin' to?" Tommy's pride wouldn't allow it. He instantly whips out his pistol and fatally shoots Spider in the chest.

Accordingly, Henry, Jimmy, and Tommy are vivid examples of Plato's unbalanced or disharmonious person. Plato would conclude that each is unjust and, thus, that none of them can be as happy as the just person. However, Henry, Jimmy, and Tommy ironically seem to also represent a worrisome objection to Plato's view. In fact, the problem may appear to be rather obvious: Neither Henry, Jimmy, nor Tommy seems all that unhappy. Furthermore, Henry detests leading a life that seems more just. As his closing narrative indicates, he was clearly happier when he was living the unjust life of a gangster.[13] Moreover, none of these characters seem all that psychologically conflicted about their behavior. It isn't the case that any of them suffer from some sort of conscious turmoil as they conduct their "business." There is no evidence that any of them desire to act justly but can't owing to being enslaved by their respective appetitive or spirited elements. Rather, Henry seemingly wants to sell drugs, Jimmy seemingly loves to steal, and Tommy seemingly revels in being hot tempered. Therefore, the objection continues, because it seems that imbalanced persons (in Plato's sense) do not necessarily suffer from psychological conflict or turmoil, it is not necessarily the case that they are any less happy than the perfectly harmonious and just person. Therefore, the objection concludes, it is not necessarily in one's best interest to lead a just life. If so, then Plato's answer to Glaucon's challenge seems to be in jeopardy.

The objection to Plato's view being developed here is, perhaps, manifested most clearly in the case of Paul Cicero. Henry's initial description of Paulie is prophetic: "Paulie may have moved slow, but it was only because Paulie didn't have to move for anybody." As the Lucchese crime boss, Paulie is virtually untouchable. But, as the boss, he is akin to Plato's ruler. Paulie invariably makes careful decisions and lays down policies that he believes will best benefit himself and his "family." He is never psychologically conflicted; he always seems cool and collected. Nevertheless, he willfully participates in unlawful and immoral behavior. Perhaps the most striking example of this from the movie is when he becomes partners with Sonny the restaurateur (Tony Darrow). Paulie simply runs the place into the ground. When Sonny becomes bankrupt—primarily because Paulie keeps stealing from the restaurant—Paulie has the place burned to the ground for the insurance money. He does nothing except receive tribute for the protection he provides Sonny, and Sonny does everything he can to make ends meet. Paulie becomes rich, and Sonny becomes penniless. Because of Paulie's status, Sonny has no choice but to acquiesce. Paulie has everything anyone could ever want without having to worry about anything. As such, he doesn't seem to suffer from any unhappiness. What could Plato say in response to the examples of Henry, Jimmy, Tommy, and Paulie?

## Health and Happiness

The objection embodied in the *Goodfellas* characters may trade on differing senses of happiness, on the one hand, and an overly narrow conception of internal (psychological) conflict, on the other. In fact, the objection may involve forms of happiness and turmoil that Plato simply doesn't intend. But these potential rejoinders are best explored once we become more familiar with Plato's analogy between health and happiness.

For all organisms, including the commonwealth and the human being, happiness is a matter of being optimally healthy. An organism's being optimally healthy is a matter of its varied functions being brought into harmony or attunement with one another. So, for a biological organism, the heart must pump blood at the correct rate, neither too fast nor too slow. The kidneys must clean the blood at the rate it circulates, and the lungs must oxygenate it accordingly. Analogously, the state is healthiest when its "organs"—the societal classes—have achieved a harmonious arrangement between producers, guardians, and rulers, and a person is healthiest when the appetitive, spirited, and rational elements achieve harmonious interaction. Therefore, although it is a bit strange to say that a commonwealth or an animal can be happy in this sense, Plato is clearly committed to holding that a person cannot be truly happy unless she is optimally healthy.

Accordingly, perhaps the best response that Plato can make to the objection posed by the *Goodfellas* characters is to reinforce his analogy between justice and health. Returning to the *Republic:* "Life does not seem worth living when the body's natural constitution is ruined, not even if one has food and drink of every sort, all the money in the world, and every political office imaginable. So how—even if one could do whatever one wished, except what would liberate one from vice and injustice and make one acquire justice and virtue—could it be worth living when the natural constitution of the very thing by which we live [self, or inner person] is ruined and in turmoil?" It is clearly not in one's best interests to lead a life that continuously harms the body. This remains true even if the harm inflicted is due to pleasurable activities. One should not unceasingly smoke cigarettes even if it brings the smoker pleasure to do so. But, if this is true of the body, why can't it be true of the soul or inner self? If so, then it is clearly not in one's best interests to lead a life that continuously harms (or distorts) the inner self. And this is so even if the harm inflicted is due to pleasurable activities. One should not allow the appetitive element to satiate itself contrary to the dictates of reason, even if it brings great pleasure to do so. Thus, to ask whether it is in one's best interest to be a morally good person is like asking whether one desires a healthy body rather than one riddled with cancer. In many ways, Plato would say that Gyges or the main characters from *Goodfellas* suffer from "cancer of the soul." Henry's appetitive element grows out of control, enfeebling the other two elements. Tommy's spirited element is the cancerous culprit. And, arguably, Jimmy and Paulie are beset with both forms of the psychological disease. If no one would willingly choose to suffer from bodily cancer, no one would willingly choose to suffer from "soul cancer." In fact, merely raising the question seems, as Plato claims, "ridiculous" (445a–b).

The plausibility of Plato's analogy may, ultimately, rest on the distinction between *feeling* happy and *being* happy. Feeling happy involves a common-sense understanding of happiness that invariably refers to an inner, subjective state that a person (psychologically) experiences as pleasant. But, for Plato, being happy has more to do with how, objectively speaking, a certain being exists (or, perhaps, can be objectively described). Furthermore, Plato seems to believe that feeling happy does not entail being happy, and vice versa. Thus, one can feel happy without thereby being happy, and one can be happy without thereby feeling happy. The *Goodfellas* characters (including Paulie) are examples of the former, and Glaucon's perfectly just man who seems unjust is an example of the latter. Consequently, Plato is committed to the position that one can be mistaken about being happy. The possibility of error here is grounded in his belief that genuine happiness is a state of being and not necessarily a psychological state. Plato doesn't argue that being optimally healthy necessarily produces more pleasure than a life of pleasure seeking. Rather, he argues that being optimally healthy is *better* or more *valuable* than any pleasurable psychological state. Therefore, insofar as being optimally healthy is to be just, a person is happier being just rather than not because he or she achieves an optimally best state of being.

Nevertheless, it may seem preposterous to some that a person can be mistaken about what makes her happy. Indeed, some might complain that, in meeting Glaucon's challenge, Plato has merely changed the definition of *happiness* to suit his needs. But this may be a bit unfair, for two reasons.

First, Plato employs something akin to the (more or less) familiar distinctions between fleeting and lasting happiness, on the one hand, and baser and nobler happiness, on the other. Sexual gratification is an example of something that (often) provides us with fleeting and baser happiness. Developing and nurturing genuine, lifelong friendships is an example of something that (often) provides us lasting and nobler happiness. Moreover, we are apt to say that lasting and nobler forms (or sources) of happiness are more valuable or better than fleeting and baser forms (or sources). So, while the analogy is not perfect, it seems that Plato's sense of true or genuine happiness, as an optimally best state of being, is closer to those things that produce lasting and nobler happiness.[14]

Second, people are often mistaken in what will make them *lastingly* happy, just as we are often mistaken about what makes us healthy. Note that feeling healthy is not necessarily the same as being healthy, as in the case of suffering from high cholesterol. Further, people can be mistaken or ignorant about what they truly desire, exactly because they lack proper belief about what is actually in their best interests. The examples are endless: infatuated with a rather narrow appreciation of beauty, we drive ourselves to undereat and overexercise, only to face kidney failure and other ailments; completely smitten with a classmate, we leave our current lover only to discover our new partner is a cold, selfish, and uncaring person; blinded by the pending prestige and sizable raise, we believe we really want the promotion, even though it means spending even more time at work and even less time with family and friends. Analogously, if we can be ignorant of being healthy or what we truly desire, why not believe that we can be ignorant about what makes us happy, especially genuinely or truly happy? Consequently, Plato seems on firm ground in holding that Gyges is not truly happy, just as we would seem to be in holding that the characters from *Goodfellas* are not truly happy. By choosing to lead their lives by their appetitive or spirited elements, they fail to reach the pinnacle of human existence embodied in achieving optimal health and, thus, miss out on the chance to become truly happy. This is so even if Gyges or the *Goodfellas* characters don't *feel* unhappy (or if Glaucon's just man appearing to be unjust doesn't *feel* happy).

Nevertheless, Plato's answer remains controversial. After all, a terminally ill cancer patient who wishes to be healthy is clearly unhappy. He is no doubt suffering great physical and psychological pain and torment. But it isn't quite as clear that a person inflicted with Plato's "soul cancer" suffers psychologically. Paulie Cicero certainly doesn't. This insight invites the following questions: But if I am completely unaware of the fact that I am diseased and, thus, suffer no overt physical or psychological detriments from it, why should I care if I am unhealthy? What benefit will I gain by knowing that I am not healthy?

Such questions are difficult to answer, but not impossible. In fact, they may rest on an overly narrow understanding of psychological turmoil. According to Plato, just as a person's being happy doesn't necessarily require him to feel happy, his being psychologically conflicted may not require him to feel psychologically conflicted. Again, some might find this suggestion preposterous, perhaps even more outlandish than Plato's suggestion that a person can be mistaken about what makes him or her truly happy. Someone may ask: How can I possibly not be consciously aware that I am psychologically conflicted? But recall that Plato's sense of psychological conflict involves one's inner being and how it is malfunctioning. So just as a person might be unaware that she is neurotic—in fact, she may enjoy using a new bar of soap every time she washes her hands—a person can be unaware that her three elements are not in harmonious attunement.

Perhaps Plato would push this sort of response, arguing that the mere fact that one is not aware of being diseased (or malfunctioning) is itself an undesirable state of affairs. Even if a person is unaware of the fact that he suffers from an undesirable state of affairs, he remains better off having it removed. In fact, Plato would probably argue that being ignorant is an undesirable state of affairs that should always be avoided. In realizing that you are unhealthy, you are in a better position to make an informed decision about what is actually in your best interest. Therefore, if you are aware of what you ought to do, morally speaking, but fail to act on it, this must mean either that you do not genuinely know what morality requires of you or that you are somehow psychologically conflicted about acting on that knowledge. If the former, then you are ignorant of important truths. If the latter, then you suffer from a sort of inner conflict (either the more familiar sort or in Plato's more technical sense). Plato, most assuredly, would say that it would be better—intrinsically better—for you to be neither. If so, it is intrinsically better to lead the good life. Therefore, even if Gyges or the *Goodfellas* characters don't *feel* inner conflict in that they are not consciously aware of it, they have *become* conflicted in the sense of failing to fully grasp what morality requires of them. This failure is the outcome of either their rational elements having drastically atrophied (resulting in simple ignorance) or their appetitive or spirited elements having gone to extremes (resulting in ignorance caused by licentiousness, cowardice, or peevishness and the like). Consequently, even Gyges and the *Goodfellas* characters—like the rest of us—have sufficient reason to lead the good life.

## Notes

I am indebted to Mark Conard for careful commentary on earlier drafts of this essay. The editors have decided for stylistic purposes that the more familiar *GoodFellas* should appear as *Goodfellas*.

1. This piece of dialogue from the movie is taken almost verbatim from the book that inspired *Goodfellas*, Nicholas Pileggi's *Wiseguy: Life in a Mafia Family* (Boston: G. K. Hall, 1987), 4. However, as die-hard fans of *Goodfellas* are well aware, Scorsese's movie diverges occasionally from Pileggi's book. For instance, in the book the Ciceros are the Varios; I stick with the movie version of the story, referring to this family as Cicero.

2. This is confirmed in *Wiseguy*: "I [Karen, Henry's wife, played by Lorraine Bracco] had seen that Paulie was like a father to Henry, much more than Henry's real father, who he rarely saw and almost never spoke to. Henry was with Paulie almost every day" (Pileggi, *Wiseguy*, 94).

3. Plato, *Republic*, trans., and with an introduction by, C. D. C. Reeve (Indianapolis: Hackett, 2004), 360b, 360c. Readers should note that I follow the standard practice of using "Stephanus numbers," i.e., the margin page numbers added by the Stephanus family, early editors of Plato's work. The Stephanus numbers for the *Republic* run from 327 to 621, complete with subsections lettered a–e for each new section number. Thus, the very first Stephanus number for the *Republic* is 327a, and the last is 621c. Subsequent citations will be given parenthetically in the text.

4. Interestingly enough, Henry Hill well fits the description of the first man, especially in the case of his being released from prison on early parole. Unfortunately, *Goodfellas* all but omits this part of Henry's life; however, in the movie, Paulie does make it clear that he played a crucial role in Henry's early release from prison, and, thus, he strongly urges Henry to stop selling dope now that he is out.

*Wiseguy* gives us a much more detailed picture. Pileggi writes:

> On July 12, 1978 Henry Hill was granted an early parole for being a model prisoner. He had availed himself of the prison's self-improvement and educational programs [having earned an associate's degree while incarcerated]. . . .

> He had adjusted well to rehabilitation and had entered into community-service and religious programs created to assist inmates. He had been courteous and cooperative during interviews with prison personnel, social workers, and psychologists. He had appeared self-confident and mature. He had strong family ties and, upon release, he had been guaranteed a $225-a-week job as an office manager for a Long Island company near his home. (219)

But Pileggi is clear that Henry carefully orchestrated the arrangement. His rehabilitation was merely a facade:

> Of course the prison officials had no way of knowing how expertly Henry had manipulated and misused their system. Nor did they know that his new job was essentially a no-show affair that had been arranged for him by Paul Vario [Cicero]. . . . When he signed out of Allenwood [prison] for the last time, the Bureau of Prisons noted that his prognosis was good and that it was very unlikely he would ever return to prison again. . . . [But] after four years behind bars Henry had no intention of going straight. He couldn't even conceive of going straight. He needed to make money. For Henry, it was a simple matter of getting out and getting over. (219–21)

While in prison, Henry conveyed every appearance of being rehabilitated. He was courteous, cooperative, spiritual, and industrious, hallmarks of the morally good person. However, he was a bookie, sold drugs, bribed prison guards, lied, and pretended to be religious to gain additional weekend furloughs. That is, he furthered his interests—he got what he wanted most, being out of prison—by *appearing* to be a good person without actually *being* a good person. Thus, Henry is exactly the kind of person Glaucon describes: an unjust person who has connections, skills, and wealth sufficient to convince everyone that he is a just person. He has the reputation of being a morally good person, but this reputation is false.

5. Plato was aware that, to be as strong as possible, the argument must somehow address concerns about the afterlife. After all, some (like Adeimantus, Plato's other brother) might counter that, if (as the saying goes) the just person is rewarded in heaven, then he can still benefit in the long run by remaining perfectly just until the day he dies. As such, although the perfectly just person suffers on earth, he will be rewarded with the everlasting bliss of heaven, and, although the perfectly unjust person benefits for a while on earth, he will be sent to hell everlastingly. Plato's rejoinder (via Adeimantus) to this, in part, is that it seems possible that the Greek gods could be persuaded or bribed not to punish the perfectly unjust person in the afterlife (365b–d). As such, the perfectly just person still loses out because he forgoes the benefits of being unjust on this earth. After all, he could also bribe the gods.

It is a bit more difficult to apply this line of argument to monotheism because it is believed that an omnicompetent God could not be bribed. However, note that, if an individual leads a morally good life only because of the expected reward of heaven, not because she believes that leading a morally good life is its own reward, then she is still acting from self-serving motives. Thus, we cannot answer Glaucon by merely saying that we will go to hell if we become the perfectly unjust person.

6. The story behind the *Goodfellas* sound track begins with the surveillance tapes made by the FBI. The actual wiseguys (Hill, Burke, DeSimone, and others) knew that many of their cars were bugged. They often turned up the car radio extremely loud to drown out their conversations. Thus, many popular songs can be heard on the surveillance tapes, to which Scorsese acquired access. The tapes inspired him to incorporate the popular songs of the day into *Goodfellas.* Scorsese realized that the careful viewer could keep track of the chronology of the movie, from the 1960s to the 1980s, by which song was heard on the sound track.

7. The terms that Plato uses for the three societal classes are often translated as *producers, auxiliaries,* and *guardians.* For familiarity's sake, however, I call the auxiliaries *guardians* and the guardians *rulers.* This usage, I think, better captures the role that Plato intended for each class.

8. When discussing justice among people or within an individual person, Plato tends to use the Greek word *psyche,* and this has traditionally been interpreted as meaning "soul." Because the word *soul* now invariably carries religious import that Plato does not intend, most commentators urge us to interpret Plato's *psyche* as meaning "self" or "person."

9. It is a bit controversial whether Plato is committed to holding that moderation (or temperance) is exemplified only by the producers or the appetitive element. In fact, in some places (430e, 431e–432a) he seems to claim that temperance is something that pertains to the whole state and not just the producers or appetites. However, he also believes the temperance is primarily recognizing (and accepting) who should rule and who should be the ruled. In this way, *temperance* does best describe the producers and appetitive element because Plato clearly holds that the producers and the appetites are best ruled (431b–c). When they rule, the state or the person is not well ordered. For this sort of approach to understanding the role of temperance in Plato's system, see Julia Annas, *An Introduction to Plato's Republic* (Oxford: Oxford University Press, 1981), 115–18, esp. 116.

10. Plato would no doubt rely on his metaphysical theory of the forms when expressing this sort of argument. Assuming that the form of the person is the rational animal, Plato would argue that various human beings "participate in" or "approximate" this form in various degrees. Thus, those who are most rational better approximate the form than those who are least rational. Consequently, those human beings who (regularly) aren't rational at all, for whatever reason, don't participate in or approximate the form in any significant sense. Therefore, even though such individuals remain human, they fail to be persons because they fail to participate in the relevant form. Some philosophers hold a similar view without Plato's metaphysical underpinnings, with Kant being a notable example.

11. Of course, Henry is soon arrested on narcotics charges, presumably because his mule babysitter called for airline reservations on his home phone. Scorsese underscores this moment in Henry's life by providing us with a camera still of Lois with the

airline ticket in her hand calling from Henry's home phone. Just as the still of the Hill's postman in the pizza oven was significant in Henry's formative years in the mob, this shot of the ticket in Lois's hand represents the beginning of Henry's departure from his Mafia family. In any event, Henry again relies on his knack for becoming invisible by entering the witness protection program. Although it cannot be claimed that he always intended to turn on his Mafia family, it remains the case that Henry never really had to face the legal consequences of his actions.

12. For Plato's relevant views on the spirited element, see *Republic,* 440b, 590b–c.

13. Merely perusing the dust jacket of Henry Hill's *Gangsters and Goodfellas: The Mob, Witness Protection, and Life on the Run* (New York: M. Evans, 2004) will further attest to this. Interestingly enough, Hill claims that Pesci's Oscar-winning portrayal of Tommy was "toned-down" (225). *Gangsters and Goodfellas* has other insights and hindsights. It is interesting to compare Scorsese's interpretation of Hill's story with Henry's version.

14. But remember that, for Plato, being happy may or may not cause, or be associated with, pleasant psychological feelings. Again, for Plato, being happy is identified with a distinctive (objective) state of being that characterizes the whole entity and not merely its psychological (subjective) states. This is somewhat analogous to how a lifelong friendship is not always associated with pleasant feelings but the friendship remains inherently valuable nevertheless. Therefore, even though the friendship may sometimes not make you *feel* happy, your life is still better for cultivating it. In this technical sense, then, your life is happier for cultivating the friendship regardless of any pleasant feelings caused by or associated with it.

# Mean Streets
## Beatitude, Flourishing, and Unhappiness
*Mark T. Conard*

The history of philosophy, particularly ethics, contains a sustained debate and discussion about the nature of happiness, from Aristotle's *eudaimonia,* or "flourishing," to Aquinas's beatitude and Mill's hedonism. But there is comparatively little discussion about unhappiness, except as it's seen as simply the result of someone's having failed to achieve happiness. In this essay, I use Martin Scorsese's early masterpiece, *Mean Streets* (1973), as a springboard into a discussion of unhappiness. I don't presume necessarily to say whether the protagonist, Charlie (Harvey Keitel), is happy or unhappy. I simply want to use the film as a means to enter into a discussion about unhappiness, given the lack of attention to the latter in the philosophical literature.

First, why are philosophers generally so concerned with happiness, and what role does it traditionally play in ethics? There are several different definitions of *happiness,* as we'll see below, and most philosophers observe that, since people (generally) strive to achieve happiness, it must be a natural end for human beings, in the sense of an ultimate goal or desire (and many argue that it's, in fact, the highest good or supreme end for human beings). Consequently, on the one hand, becoming clear about what happiness is might aid us in being able to achieve it, and, on the other hand, since my pursuit of my happiness and your pursuit of your happiness might well conflict with one another (suppose, e.g., that we want the same prospective mate or house or job), there need to be some rules about how I can justifiably go about living my life and achieving my happiness. And that's what ethics generally is: the rules, principles, and guidelines for how I might legitimately (i.e., morally) go about living my life and striving to achieve happiness. And these rules and guidelines, then, often help us resolve interpersonal conflict, reduce the amount of suffering in the world, and make life a bit better for all of us.

We should note that what we're after here is a philosophical, *not* a psychological, definition or understanding of happiness and unhappiness.

That is, a psychological understanding of happiness or unhappiness would concentrate on subjective inner states or emotions, a feeling of contentment or discontentment, or what have you. Philosophers, on the other hand, are more interested in happiness as the end or goal of human action, whatever it is that we're trying to achieve in our lives, whether it's salvation in heaven, a life containing more pleasure than not, or flourishing. However, we should expect that a subjective feeling of contentment (or discontentment), an emotion, would likely follow from or be a part of the experience of happiness or unhappiness in most or all of the philosophical senses.

But why talk about or focus on unhappiness? First, unhappiness is worth discussing simply because it is such a prevalent feature of human experience, so prevalent, in fact, that there are those who argue that it is the natural state or condition of human beings, as we'll see below. Second, happiness in any philosophical (and probably psychological) sense often seems to be so elusive as to be unattainable, and, again as we'll see below, there are those who argue that, given the elusiveness or unattainability of happiness, it's simply cruel to perpetuate the idea that we're capable of attaining happiness and ought to spend our lives striving for it. If this is the case, then accepting that unhappiness is our lot in life might, in fact, be liberating and, paradoxically, lead to a sort of contentment.[1]

Before we can talk about unhappiness, we need to talk about its apparent opposite, happiness, and its various definitions. First, however, I want to discuss briefly Scorsese's film.

## Very Mean Streets Indeed

*Mean Streets* shows us a slice of life in New York's Little Italy during the early 1970s. It concerns four friends, Tony (David Proval), Michael (Richard Romanus), Johnny Boy (Robert De Niro), and Charlie. Tony owns the neighborhood bar where the friends hang out, Michael is a petty loan shark and mobster wannabe, and Johnny Boy is a wild and impulsive ne'er-do-well who likes to blow up mailboxes and shoot out windows from the rooftops. Charlie (the protagonist, as I mentioned) is a conflicted Catholic torn between his perceived duties to his friends, his own desires, and the mandates of his uncle Giovanni (Cesare Danova), the local mob boss who is grooming Charlie to become part of the world of the Mafia. Charlie has a strong sense of Catholic guilt, and, while he's skeptical of the church's ability to provide redemption and salvation, he is still plagued with the thoughts of sin and damnation. He also feels the need to protect Johnny Boy, to keep him out of trouble with the law, and to save him from any trouble with his many creditors, most notably Michael. Further, Charlie is having an affair with Teresa (Amy Robinson), Johnny Boy's epileptic cousin, and he has a strong sexual desire for one of the dancers at Tony's bar, Diane (Jeannie Bell). Giovanni has warned Charlie to stay away from both Johnny Boy and Teresa because of Johnny Boy's wildness ("Honorable men go with honorable men," says Giovanni) and because of Teresa's illness (she's "sick in the head"). And, since she's black, Diane is strictly taboo in the world of Little Italy.

Charlie is poised to take over a restaurant for his uncle since the owner has become unable to make his loan payments to Giovanni. However, Charlie's commitment to his friends seems to override his desire to please his uncle. Johnny Boy comes to show not just disrespect but utter contempt for Michael himself and for his financial obligations to him, creating a very dangerous situation (Michael is prepared to break Johnny Boy's legs, or worse). Charlie knows that Johnny Boy needs to lay low, so the two of them borrow Tony's car and, bringing Teresa along, head to the outer boroughs to keep safe. However, while they're driving through the unfamiliar streets of Brooklyn, Michael pulls up beside them, and a would-be assassin in the car (an uncredited Scorsese) shoots Johnny Boy in the neck and Charlie in the hand. The car crashes, and Teresa is thrown partially through the windshield. The film ends with the three of them, bloodied, in a dark alley. Teresa is being pulled from the wreckage, Johnny Boy staggers down the alley, blood seeping from his wound, and Charlie kneels on the ground cradling his wounded hand.

As I said, in order to talk about unhappiness, I discuss three traditional definitions of *happiness:* as beatitude, as pleasure, and as flourishing. I take these definitions in order.

## Unhappiness as Damnation

Beatitude is a religious conception of happiness; it is supreme bliss, which is to be achieved only after this life, in heaven, and with God. The great medieval philosopher Saint Thomas Aquinas (ca. 1225–74) distinguishes this ultimate happiness from a more mundane happiness that can be achieved in this life: "Happiness is twofold; the one is imperfect and is had in this life; the other is perfect, consisting in the vision of God." Further, he goes on to say that the earthly variety of happiness "does not consist in goods of the body, which goods alone, however, we attain through the operation of the senses"; rather: "The happiness of this life consists in an operation of the intellect." It's quite traditional for philosophers to separate human nature into these two halves, mind and body, spirit and flesh, intellect and appetite.

Indeed, we're all capable of sensual pleasures, such as those derived from food and sex, and we also enjoy more intellectual pleasures, such as those derived from learning, understanding, problem solving, etc. And it's also quite traditional for philosophers to disparage the former type of pleasures and extol the latter, as Aquinas does here. In any event, the earthly type of happiness, consisting in pleasures of the intellect, is itself only partial and incomplete, Aquinas says, since perfect, complete happiness consists in "the vision of the Divine Essence, which man cannot obtain in this life." He goes on to say: "Hence it is evident that none can attain true and perfect Happiness in this life."[2]

It's fitting to begin with happiness as beatitude since, as I mentioned, Charlie is a partially lapsed Catholic plagued by the prospect of the opposite of perfect happiness in the presence of God: damnation and the fires of hell, which would be the definition of unhappiness in this case, and a most extreme form of unhappiness it is. In the film, Charlie's thoughts are expressed in voice-over, sometimes by Scorsese, and sometimes by Keitel. The first line of the film, prior to the credits, is a voice-over by Scorsese that reveals Charlie's skepticism about the church's ability to provide the salvation necessary to make it into heaven: "You don't make up for your sins in church. You do it in the streets. You do it at home. The rest is bullshit, and you know it."

After the credits, each of the four principle characters is introduced. When we first meet Charlie, he's inside a church, kneeling at an altar. Scorsese's voice-over says: "Lord, I'm not worthy to eat your flesh, not worthy to drink your blood." In his first spoken line, Charlie repeats: "Not worthy to drink your blood." Then, in voice-over, Keitel reveals further Charlie's skepticism:

> OK, OK, I just come out of confession, right? Right. And the priest gives me the usual penance, right? Ten Hail Marys, ten Our Fathers, ten whatever. Now, you know that next week I'm gonna come back and he's just gonna give me another ten Hail Marys and another ten Our Fathers. I mean, you know how I feel about that shit. Those things, they don't mean anything to me. They're just words. Now, that may be OK for the others, but it just doesn't work for me. I mean, if I do something wrong, I just wanna pay for it *my* way, so I do my own penance for my own sins. What do you say, huh? That's all bullshit, except the pain, right? The pain of hell. The burn from a lighted match increased a million times. Infinite. You know, you don't fuck around with the infinite. There's no way you do that.

Charlie is skeptical of the church's ability to save him, wanting to find redemption on the streets, yet is likewise skeptical of his ability to be saved there—it's "all bullshit." That is, Charlie seems to be convinced of his own sinful, guilty nature and believes deep down that there is no salvation or redemption for him, that he's damned and, thus, doomed to supreme unhappiness. Several times during the film, Charlie holds his hand over an open flame, reminding himself of the pain of hellfire and, perhaps, preparing himself for what's to come.[3] As David Denby says, Charlie is "a suffering, masochistic Catholic, a man who constantly must sin to fulfill his sense of unworthiness."[4]

## Nietzsche on Religion and Unhappiness

Now, interestingly, someone like the nineteenth-century German philosopher Friedrich Nietzsche (1844–1900) would argue that religion is not the solution to Charlie's problem regarding happiness or unhappiness but, rather, part of the problem itself. That is, he argues that religion (and, particularly, Western, monotheistic religion) purposefully makes us feel reprehensible, sinful, and guilty, without the possibility of atonement, and is, thus, perhaps the greatest source of unhappiness known to mankind. In his *On the Genealogy of Morals*, Nietzsche claims, and not without good reason: "What really arouses indignation against suffering is not suffering as such but the senselessness of suffering." That is to say, human beings are resilient creatures; we can put up with a good deal of pain and suffering—life is full of it, of course—so long as there is some meaning or sense to it. It's meaningless, senseless suffering that we can't endure: "Man, the bravest of animals and the one most accustomed to suffering, does *not* repudiate suffering as such; he *desires* it, he even seeks it out, provided he is shown a *meaning* for it, a *purpose* of suffering." And, indeed, Nietzsche argues that this question or problem of the meaninglessness of suffering has been one of the great human problems since we first appeared on the earth: "The meaninglessness of suffering, *not* suffering itself, was the curse that lay over mankind."[5]

One of the inherent sources of suffering, Nietzsche argues, is our own animal instincts. That is to say, our animal and protohuman ancestors lived in the wilds by their violent instincts, hunting, defending themselves, etc. These creatures weren't reflective by nature; they had to act quickly, violently, and automatically in order to survive. When, however, at the dawn of human civilization, people came to live together in communities, we could no longer freely vent those animal instincts outwardly; we could no longer attack and kill at will since that would mean the very destruction of the community itself. But those animal instincts didn't simply disappear. So what happened to them? They were internalized, says Nietzsche: "All instincts that do not discharge themselves outwardly *turn inward*—this is what I call the *internalization* of man. . . . Hostility, cruelty, joy in persecuting, in attacking, in change, in destruction—all this turned against the possessors of such instincts." Consequently, we started gnawing at, eating at, torturing ourselves: "The man who, from lack of external enemies and resistances and forcibly confined to the oppressive narrowness and punctiliousness of custom, impatiently lacerated, persecuted, gnawed at, assaulted, and maltreated himself."[6]

This is a source of great internal suffering, and, as we saw, according to Nietzsche human beings need to make some sense of their suffering in order to endure it. So what meaning did we give to this suffering? We interpreted it as guilt and sinfulness: "This man of the bad conscience has seized upon the presupposition of religion so as to drive his self-torture to its most gruesome pitch of severity and rigor. Guilt before *God:* this thought becomes an instrument of torture to him. He apprehends in 'God' the ultimate antithesis of his own ineluctable animal instincts; he reinterprets these animal instincts themselves as a form of guilt before God."[7] Our internal suffering—that gnawing, nagging feeling we get (most of us anyway) when we feel like we've done something wrong, broken the rules, etc., the "sting of conscience"—is, says Nietzsche, essentially those internalized instincts. And religion tells us that this internal suffering we experience is a result of our natural sinfulness and guilt, our unworthiness before God.[8]

Let's make this clear. Human beings are animals—we are embodied and, thus, naturally have needs, wants, desires, lusts, instincts, etc., and, again, we suffer from this embodiment (not just because of internalized instincts, but also because of the very nature of desire and need, since to desire or want is, in a sense, to suffer [more about this below]). Religion then interprets this suffering as sinfulness. It tells us that we suffer because we're sinful and guilty. That is, it traditionally chastises and punishes us for being the kinds of creatures that we naturally are and can't help being, and it wants to convince us that we're sinful to a degree for which we can never atone (we're born into original sin; God sacrifices his only begotten son for our sins, but, of course, that doesn't absolve us of our guilt and unworthiness; it burdens us with an irredeemable debt for which we must do penance and reveals to us even more our wretched, sinful natures). But, again, this false interpretation gave us a meaning for this great suffering, which is what we needed in order to survive. We still suffered miserably—in fact, we suffered worse—but we could endure it because it was given a sense and a meaning.[9]

So—and returning to the problem—the church may not be the means to bliss and salvation that Charlie takes it to be. In fact, if we're to believe Nietzsche, it's one of the primary sources of suffering and unhappiness in his life, given that it makes him feel guilty and sinful just for being the kind of creature he is—that is, one that is embodied and that has animal desires—and sinful and guilty to a degree that can never be atoned for.

## Unhappiness as Pain and Suffering

One common understanding of happiness is to equate it with pleasure and the lack of pain and suffering. This is known as *hedonism,* and the theory goes back at least to Epicurus (341–271 B.C.). One modern and important proponent of hedonism is John Stuart Mill (1806–73), whose utilitarianism is one of the most important ethical theories in the history of philosophy. Utilitarianism "holds that actions are right in proportion as they tend to promote happiness." That is, to act morally is to produce the greatest happiness for the greatest number of people. And, Mill goes on: "By happiness is intended pleasure, and the absence of pain; by unhappiness, pain, and the privation of pleasure." In everyday language, we tend to associate hedonism with the pursuit of physical, sensual pleasures: food, drink, and sex. However, Mill makes the same distinction that Aquinas does between so-called higher- and lower-order pleasures: "Human beings have faculties more elevated than the animal appetites, and when once made conscious of them, do not regard anything as happiness which does not include their gratification." That is to say, animals are also capable of enjoying the pleasures of food, drink, and sex. Human beings, however, have intellectual, moral, and emotional faculties that animals don't; and, once we've experienced the pleasures associated with those higher faculties, we wouldn't be content with a life that contained only the lower-order pleasures (once we've experienced art, poetry, and love and compassion, e.g., we couldn't be content with a life in which we experienced *only* sensual pleasures). Defending hedonism, Mill says: "There is no known Epicurean theory of life which does not assign to the pleasures of the intellect, of the feelings and imagination, and of the moral sentiments, a much higher value as pleasures than to those of mere sensation."[10]

So, to reiterate and to be perfectly clear, according to Mill's version of hedonism, the definition of unhappiness is "pain, and the privation of pleasure," or, perhaps more accurately, the preponderance of pain and suffering over pleasure in one's life.

Let's note that Charlie has sources of pleasure, of both the lower and the higher orders. The lower-order pleasures include his sexual relationship with

Teresa, his (unconsummated) lust for Diane, and his bouts of heavy drinking with his friends. Among the higher-order pleasures we might include the apparent satisfaction he derives from helping people, following the example of Saint Francis.[11] Charlie also derives pleasure from his association with his uncle. This is hardly the sort of life that Mill had in mind (associating with gangsters), but the sense of respect, the feeling of belonging, and the idea of doing something mature and important are, clearly, all sources of deep satisfaction for young Charlie.

Now, while Charlie does have these sources of pleasure, it's important to note that his desires clash with one another. Charlie's relationship with Teresa and his lust for Diane are, clearly, in conflict with his desire to please his uncle, again because Giovanni has warned him to stay away from Teresa and because Diane is black and, thus, taboo.[12] Further, his desire to help people, and particularly to help Johnny Boy, with whom he feels a particular kinship, likewise conflicts with his longing to be a part of his uncle's world.

For Plato, this conflict of desire is virtually the definition of *unhappiness.* In his *Republic,* he argues that the human "soul" has three parts: the rational, the spirited/emotional, and the appetitive or desiring. For Plato, well-being, and, indeed, happiness in the sense of flourishing (discussed below), consists in having a well-ordered soul, one in which the rational part is in control. That is to say, we all have emotions, appetites, and desires, but the best life to lead is one in which our rational faculties are in control and decide for us which appetites to fulfill, which to deny, and in what manner. Further, the rational part should help us keep in control of our emotions, help us understand in what situations and for what reasons our emotions are properly roused, and also keep us from being overcome by those emotions. Socrates asks rhetorically: "Isn't it appropriate for the rational part to rule, since it is really wise and exercises foresight on behalf of the whole soul?"[13] The worst kind of life, real unhappiness, is, according to Plato, to be ruled by the irrational parts of the soul, whether the emotions, the appetites, or both. Think of drug addicts, alcoholics, compulsive gamblers, anyone ruled by his appetites and not in rational control of himself—that kind of person is the most unhappy. Last, the rational part helps us adjudicate between the demands of our appetites and desires, allowing us to have a well-rounded, satisfying life, in which those appetites, desires, and emotions don't conflict with reason or with each other. And this certainly seems to be Charlie's problem. It's clear that his soul is not balanced, that he's not ruled completely by reason, given that his desires are in conflict and that they tug him in different directions. Further, his emotions sometimes get the better of him, as when he slaps Johnny Boy around after the latter discovers his relationship with

Teresa and (perhaps jokingly) suggests that he might tell Giovanni about it. Charlie is, thus, unhappy in Plato's sense of the word.

## Unhappiness, Suffering, and Pessimism

There are those who argue for a hedonistic conception of happiness as pleasure and then go on to claim that happiness in this sense is unobtainable and, thus, that we are fated to a life of unhappiness (as pain and suffering). Freud, for example, seems to take this view. He says: "What do [people] demand of life and wish to achieve in it? The answer to this can hardly be in doubt. They strive after happiness; they want to become happy and to remain so. This endeavor has two sides, a positive and a negative aim. It aims, on the one hand, at an absence of pain and unpleasure, and, on the other, at the experiencing of strong feelings of pleasure." Freud is, here, clearly equating happiness with pleasure and the absence of pain, as did Mill. He goes on to conclude that the purpose of life is, thus, the "programme of the pleasure principle." But, he says: "There is no possibility at all of its being carried through; all the regulations of the universe run counter to it. One feels inclined to say that the intention that man should be 'happy' is not included in the plan of 'Creation.'" That is to say, our efforts at achieving pleasure are so often thwarted by the world around us that we can hardly hope to experience any kind of long-lasting pleasure. What's more, he says: "We are threatened with suffering from three directions: from our own body, which is doomed to decay and dissolution and which cannot even do without pain and anxiety as warning signals; from the external world, which may rage against us with overwhelming and merciless forces of destruction; and finally from our relations to other men."[14] That is, not only are we frustrated in our attempts to find pleasure, but we're also continuously suffering because of unavoidable circumstances and because of the nature of human life on earth. Consequently, unhappiness as suffering is the natural, if not necessary, condition of human beings.

Arthur Schopenhauer (1788–1860) takes this view as well but pushes it even further. Traditionally, philosophers have claimed that human nature is closely tied to reason—that it's reason that distinguishes us as the kinds of creatures we are and, thus, that it's reason that is our essence (as we'll see Aristotle argue below). Schopenhauer denies this and claims, instead, that our essence is what he calls *will*. The will is the ceaseless, driving force that we find in ourselves as our appetites and desires, hunger, thirst, the life force, and (especially for Schopenhauer) the sex drive. Consequently, it's our very nature to want and desire, and, says Schopenhauer, to desire is to suffer.

So life is perpetual suffering: "All striving springs from want or deficiency, from dissatisfaction with one's own state or condition, and is therefore suffering so long as it is not satisfied. No satisfaction, however, is lasting; on the contrary, it is always merely the starting-point of a fresh striving. We see striving everywhere impeded in many ways, everywhere struggling and fighting, and hence always as suffering. Thus that there is no ultimate aim of striving means that there is no measure or end of suffering." Further, Schopenhauer holds a hedonistic conception of happiness. He claims that happiness or pleasure is the satisfaction of our wants and desires but that happiness is "negative," meaning that it's only a release from pain and want, which are original or positive in the sense of being our normal condition: "All satisfaction, or what is commonly called happiness, is really and essentially always *negative* only, and never positive. It is not a gratification which comes to us originally and of itself, but it must always be the satisfaction of a wish. For desire, that is to say, want, is the precedent condition of every pleasure; but with the satisfaction, the desire and therefore the pleasure cease; and so the satisfaction or gratification can never be more than deliverance from a pain, from a want."[15] Thus, as for Freud, for Schopenhauer unhappiness as pain and suffering is the natural state or condition of human beings. This leads Schopenhauer to pessimism, which, in its most common form, is a negative evaluation of life, given the preponderance of pain and suffering over pleasure. That is to say, pessimism is the idea that, on the whole, life is not worthwhile. It would be better if we'd never existed.[16]

Given the impossibility of attaining happiness, Schopenhauer of course rejects the idea that happiness is the highest good or supreme end of human life. In fact, he argues that, insofar as it makes our lives that much more miserable, the idea is pernicious since happiness is presented as a goal that we ought to pursue but, ultimately, can never achieve: "Optimism is not only a false but also a pernicious doctrine, for it presents life as a desirable state and man's happiness as its aim and object. Starting from this, everyone then believes he has the most legitimate claim to happiness and enjoyment. If, as usually happens, these do not fall to his lot, he believes that he suffers an injustice, in fact that he misses the whole point of his existence; whereas it is far more correct to regard work, privation, misery, and suffering, crowned by death, as the aim and object of our life."[17] Given that unhappiness is our lot, it's cruel to lead people to expect that they can be happy and to try to convince them that happiness is the ultimate goal of their lives. As I mentioned above, for many philosophers happiness is the central concept in their ethics. For Schopenhauer, on the other hand, the key notion in ethics is *Mitleid,* which is usually translated as "compassion," but both *Mitleid* and *compassion* also mean "suffering with." That is, for Schopenhauer, morality begins with recognizing that the suffering (and, thus, the unhappiness) of others is the same as one's own and acting accordingly. Morality has nothing at all to do with the pursuit of happiness.

## Unhappiness as *Dysdaimonia*

One of the most important conceptions of happiness in the history of ethics is the ancient Greek notion of *eudaimonia.* This Greek word is often translated as "happiness," though this translation can be misleading since *happiness* can mean a kind of satisfaction (or pleasure, as we saw above) or a state like contentment and *eudaimonia* doesn't refer to these. Rather, a better translation would be something like "flourishing." That is, *eudaimonia* is happiness in the sense of doing well, faring well, or making a success of life.

*Eudaimonia,* or happiness as flourishing, is one of the central ideas of Aristotle's ethics. At the beginning of his *Nicomachean Ethics,* he notes that human beings are goal-directed creatures; we do things for a reason. Further, he argues that there must be some final end or goal that we're all striving for and that gives sense and meaning to all our other activities. And we have a name for this final goal or highest good: "As far as its name goes, most people virtually agree; for both the many and the cultivated call it happiness [*eudaimonia*], and they suppose that living well and doing well are the same as being happy."[18] In other words, ultimately why do we do anything? In order to flourish and make a success of our lives. As the highest and final good, happiness as flourishing doesn't lead to some further end. The question, Why do you want to be happy or flourish? is meaningless.

One of Aristotle's central concerns in *Nicomachean Ethics* is to determine what flourishing is for human beings, what it means for us to flourish. He believes that flourishing for any creature will have to do with that creature's essence or nature, what makes it the kind of thing it is, and he also believes that reason is the human essence, that it's what distinguishes us from other living things (in contrast to, e.g., Schopenhauer, as noted above). Consequently, human flourishing will have something to do with the utilization of our faculty of reason. Ultimately, then, he concludes that flourishing is a life of excellent activity guided by reason and in which we exercise the virtues (courage, temperance, justice, etc.) that are crucial for human flourishing because it's in acquiring and exercising them that we embody reason in our lives and, thus, utilize our characteristic function. That is, virtues are states of character or dispositions to act in a particular kind of way, specifically, to act in accordance with what reason dictates. For example, when you're facing a fearful situation, reason can tell you when you ought to stand and fight and when it's best to back down, given your sex, age, physical conditioning, etc. To have gained the virtue of courage means to have developed in yourself a disposition—a natural and automatic way of behaving—to act in accordance with what reason dictates. The courageous person doesn't have to stop and think about what dangers he should face; he just automatically faces them, and, thus, he's embodying reason in his life and actions. So, again, flourishing for human beings is a life of excellent activity—it's doing the things that we do (e.g., carpentry, learning, making music, athletics, etc.) and doing them excellently, to the best of our abilities—and a life in which the virtues are exercised.[19]

Unhappiness in this case we might call *dysdaimonia*, failing to flourish, failing to make a success of one's life. Aristotle seems to think that this happens in a great many ways, at least with regard to acting virtuously or acquiring the virtues: "Moreover, there are many ways to be in error.... But there is only one way to be correct. That is why error is easy and correctness is difficult, since it is easy to miss the target and difficult to hit it."[20] However, we might generalize and say that there are two basic ways in which one obtains *dysdaimonia*. First, one can fail to acquire the virtues, or, to put it positively, one can acquire vices. Aristotle describes virtue as a kind of mean, in the sense of average, between two extremes, each of which is a vice, a vice of excess and a vice of deficiency. So, returning to our example of fear, if one has the response to fear that reason dictates (and has, through habitually facing up to fearful situations, acquired the disposition to act in this way automatically), one has the virtue of courage. If, on the other hand, one experiences an excess of fear and is afraid of certain things that one ought not fear, then one has developed the vice of cowardice. If, on the other hand, one experiences too little fear, for example, rushing headlong into perilous situations, then one has developed the vice of rashness or foolhardiness. In acquiring and displaying the vices, Aristotle argues, one embodies irrationality in one's life and, thus, fails to flourish; one is unhappy in this sense.

The second way in which one might attain *dysdaimonia* is by attempting to flourish or be excellent at the wrong sorts of things. One might be tempted to ask Aristotle: If the best life is a life of excellent activity, doing the things that I do and doing them excellently, then what happens if I'm a murderer or a rapist—can I do these things excellently and flourish? Aristotle has a response to this:

Now not every action or feeling admits of the mean. For the names of some automatically include baseness—for instance, spite, shamelessness, envy [among feelings], and adultery, theft, murder, among actions. For all of these and similar things are called by these names because they themselves, not their excesses or deficiencies, are base. Hence in doing these things we can never be correct, but must invariably be in error. We cannot do them well or not well—by committing adultery, for instance, with the right woman at the right time in the right way. On the contrary, it is true without qualification that to do any of them is to be in error.[21]

We can, I think, safely argue that Charlie has come to *dysdaimonia* in both these ways. First, while he does display certain virtues—for example, generosity and loyalty to his friends—he displays more vices. For example, he exhibits intemperance when he drinks so much at a party that he passes out. We observe his deceitfulness in his interaction with his uncle Giovanni (when he lets Giovanni think he's keeping his distance from Teresa and Johnny Boy), with Teresa (when he's not truthful about his reasons for not wanting to continue seeing her), and with Diane (when he tells her he wants her to be a hostess at his new restaurant when really what he wants is to sleep with her). Further, I discussed above the fact that Charlie's desires are in conflict and that he seems to be pulled by them in different directions. In this way, he displays what the Greeks call *akrasia,* sometimes translated as "incontinence," but probably most often understood as "weakness of will." He's motivated by his nonrational desires, as opposed to being in rational control of himself. And this also leads to indecisiveness, which is, perhaps, Charlie's most salient feature. He desires salvation but doesn't want to have to follow the church's dictates to find it; he wants to follow in his uncle's footsteps but doesn't want to heed his uncle's admonitions to stay away from Teresa and Johnny Boy; he continues to sleep with Teresa even though he admits that he'll never be in love with her and knows that he should keep away from her; and he wants to seduce Diane, and even makes a date with her to have Chinese food, but stands her up at the last minute, knowing that a man in his position, up and coming in the Mafia, can't be seen with a black woman.

Last, Charlie has come to *dysdaimonia* because of his profession as a novice gangster and numbers runner. Surely, these would count on Aristotle's list of those sorts of actions about which we can never be right. That is, there certainly are rules of conduct and markers of success within the Mafia world of Little Italy. Anyone in that life knows what's expected of him, how he ought to behave, and what it means to flourish or be successful in that realm. So one can flourish as a gangster; however, Aristotle would argue, given the inherently base or ignoble nature of the profession and its activities, one would, thereby, fail to flourish *as a human being*.

*Eudaimonia,* or happiness as flourishing, is obviously quite different from hedonism, or happiness as pleasure. Indeed, Aristotle believes that it's a mistake to construe happiness as pleasure and to pursue pleasure as if it were the highest good.[22] However, he does believe that pleasure supervenes on *eudaimonia*: "Hence these people's life does not need pleasure to be added [to virtuous activity] as some sort of extra decoration; rather, it has pleasure within itself."[23] In other words, acting virtuously, living a life of excellent activity, is naturally pleasing. The person who lives this way doesn't have to pursue pleasure for its own sake.

Because of all this, *eudaimonia* may be a more attractive candidate for a definition or understanding of happiness than hedonism, insofar as it not only seems to describe more accurately the way people tend to live their lives but may also be more readily attainable than pleasure and an absence of pain. If that's so, then we may not be fated to unhappiness—at least in the sense of *dysdaimonia*. However, I want to end this essay with a discussion of another view of human beings, according to which unhappiness is a necessary part of our lives and experience.

## Unhappiness as an Ontological Condition

I mentioned above that, according to Freud, given a hedonistic conception of happiness, and given the preponderance of suffering in life, unhappiness seems to be the natural state or condition of human beings. Schopenhauer, as we saw, starts with the same premises and has a similar sort of view, but his conclusion is stronger than Freud's. For Freud, in other words, suffering and unhappiness are a kind of happenstance of our condition, and, if our condition could change, so would the preponderance of suffering, and, thus, we would no longer be fated to unhappiness. For Schopenhauer, on the other hand, this is an impossibility. Suffering and unhappiness are not just the accidental conditions we happen to find ourselves in; rather, they're necessary, given the kinds of creatures we are. For Schopenhauer, there seems to be something ontological about unhappiness—it seems to be a part of our essence or being.

I want to finish this discussion by talking about another view of unhappiness as ontological, one that isn't necessarily as pessimistic as Schopenhauer's and that dates back at least to Plato's *Symposium*. In that dialogue, Socrates and his friends are having a party to celebrate the victory of one of the characters, the playwright Agathon, whose tragedy has just won a competition. They decide that the topic of conversation for the evening will be the god of love, and so, over the course of the evening, each of them gives a speech in praise of love. One of the party guests is the great comedy writer Aristophanes, and his speech is one of the most memorable passages in all Plato's works.[24] He says that originally human beings were quite different, that at one time we had two heads, four arms, four legs, and two sets of sex organs and, thus, originally there were three sexes, not two: the double male, the double female, and the male/female. Given this original double nature, people were much more powerful and full of hubris, so much so that they made an attack on the gods. Displeased by this, Zeus devised a solution, a way to lessen the power of humans and teach them humility: he cut them all in half.

Afterward, each person felt the loss acutely and wanted nothing more than to be reunited with his former other half. Those who'd been half of the double male or double female sexes became gay men and lesbians, and those who'd been half of the male/female sex were now heterosexuals: "Now, since their natural form had been cut in two, each one longed for its other half, and so they would throw their arms about each other, weaving themselves together, wanting to grow together." And they were so sick with longing and so distracted, Aristophanes says, that they just wasted away and did or thought of nothing else. Feeling sorry for them, Zeus realigned their genitals (after being cut in half, the genitals were, apparently, on the opposite side from where we find them now) and created interior reproduction: "The purpose of this was so that, when a man embraced a woman, he would cast his seed and they would have children; but when male embraced male, they would at least have the satisfaction of intercourse, after which they could stop embracing, return to their jobs, and look after their other needs in life." This, then, is the nature of love: we wish to be reunited with our original other half: "Love is born into every human being; it calls back the halves of our original nature together; it tries to make one out of two and heal the wound of human nature." Aristophanes goes on to say: "'Love' is the name for our pursuit of wholeness, for our desire to be complete."[25]

This is one of the most beautiful and moving descriptions of love ever articulated, but it can also be understood as a theory of human nature. That is, on this view, there is a kind of gap or fissure at the heart of human nature (or, some say, human nature just *is* a gap or a lack), and this hole or emptiness can never be filled. We are forever incomplete; that's part of our essence or nature. In a sense, we *are* desire.

The French existentialist philosopher Jean-Paul Sartre (1905–80) holds a similar view. He talks about two different elements of human nature, *facticity* and *transcendence*. These terms refer to the fact that we're physical objects, we have bodies (our facticity), while at the same time we're subjects or selves, we have consciousness. Inanimate objects are pure facticity; they are what they are and can't be anything else. Sartre says that they're self-coincident. Everything that makes the desk a desk is present here and now. Nothing is missing. However, human beings aren't like that. We transcend our physical selves (to transcend is to be beyond, to be other than). That is, in no way is everything that makes me who I am present here and now in or as my physical body. My past, for example, is an important constituent of my nature, as is my future, since it gives meaning and sense to all that I'm doing. So it's the nature of subjectivity or consciousness to lack the self-coincidence that objects possess. There's something missing or lacking at the heart of consciousness, and this is demonstrated through human desire: "The existence of desire as a human fact is sufficient to prove that human reality is a lack. In fact how can we explain desire if we insist on viewing it as a psychic *state;* that is, as a being whose nature is to be what it is? A being which is what it is, to the degree that it is considered as being what it is, summons nothing to itself in order to complete itself."[26] Sartre's language here is complicated, perhaps unnecessarily so, but we can, I think, make sense of it. To treat desire as a "psychic state" is to treat it and us as if we were simply objects, things that, again, lack nothing and are whole and complete (they are what they are) since a state is something positive and whole. Sartre thinks desire, rather, points to the fact that we're by our very nature incomplete. We're missing something, and we're continually trying to fill that gap or lack—and that's precisely what desire is. Consciousness *is* desire, says Sartre. It's a kind of emptiness, always reaching out toward objects, grasping them in awareness, wanting to possess them, to be filled by them.

But, because that emptiness, that lack of self-coincidence, just *is* our nature and essence, this is an impossible goal. In fact, to be filled, to cease to be a lack or gap, would mean the destruction of consciousness and, thus, of ourselves. This is what happens in death. When we die, we become objects, pure facticity; we become self-coincident. So human nature is a perpetual, unfulfillable longing; this is the "wound of human nature," as Aristophanes puts it.

So, if we accept that to desire and to want is to suffer, and if we accept a hedonistic conception of happiness and unhappiness, then we can conclude that unhappiness is ontological in a sense; it's part of our nature, our essence. However, I don't think we need to be as negative and pessimistic as Freud and Schopenhauer about this. Yes, it's part of human nature to want, to desire, to long, and there's never any ultimate satisfaction or fulfillment of this desire, but there's something beautiful (if sad) and oh so human about the longing itself.

## Notes

1. In *Annie Hall* (Woody Allen, 1977), Alvy Singer (Woody Allen) tells Annie (Diane Keaton) that, in his view of life, people are divided into "the horrible and the miserable." The horrible includes the blind, the disabled, those with a degenerative illness, etc. The miserable is everyone else. So, he says, when you go through life, "you should be thankful that you're miserable."

2. St. Thomas Aquinas, *Summa Theologica*, vol. 1, *First Part of the Second Part (QQ. 1–114)* (New York: Benzinger, 1947), 597 (question 3, art. 3), 605 (question 4, art. 5), and 610 (question 5, art. 3).

3. "This literal playing with purgation symbolizes both Charlie's reckless and foolhardy 'playing with fire' by continuing to associate with Johnny Boy . . . and Teresa, as well as his anticipation of the painful Hell-fires . . . that he expects await him in the afterlife" (Michael Bliss, *The Word Made Flesh: Catholicism and Conflict in the Films of Martin Scorsese* [Lanham, MD: Scarecrow, 1998], 30). Some critics, however, see Charlie's wound in the hand at the end of the movie as his symbolic stigmata and read this as evidence that Charlie has found some sort of redemption. Les Keyser notes that this is Scorsese's view as well: "While critics have seen the ending of *Mean Streets* as an apocalyptic and despairing vision of God's terrible wrath, Scorsese intended a more hopeful lesson. In his vision Charlie's wound, a shot in the hand, is his 'stigmata,' Johnny Boy's neck wound is not fatal, and Teresa survives—for, as Scorsese envisions the narrative, 'they all learn something at the end of *Mean Streets,* only they have to get it from, again, the hand of God'" (*Martin Scorsese* [New York: Twayne, 1992], 40).

4. David Denby, "*Mean Streets:* The Sweetness of Hell," in *Scorsese: A Journey through the American Psyche,* ed. Paul A. Woods (London: Plexus, 2005), 36.

5. Friedrich Nietzsche, *On the Genealogy of Morals,* trans. Walter Kaufmann (New York: Vintage, 1989), 68, 162. I discuss the relationship between suffering and unhappiness below.

6. Ibid., 84–85.

7. Ibid., 92.

8. Interestingly, Freud borrows from Nietzsche this idea—that civilization requires the internalization of animal instincts and that these internalized instincts become what

we call *conscience*—without crediting him: "What means does civilization employ in order to inhibit the aggressiveness which opposes it, to make it harmless, to get rid of it, perhaps? We have become acquainted with a few of these methods, but not yet with the one that appears to be the most important. This we can study in the history of the development of the individual. What happens in him to render his desire for aggression innocuous? Something very remarkable, which we should never have guessed and which is nevertheless quite obvious. His aggressiveness is introjected, internalized; it is, in point of fact, sent back to where it came from—that is, it is directed towards his own ego. There it is taken over by a portion of the ego, which sets itself over against the rest of the ego as super-ego, and which now, in the form of 'conscience,' is ready to put into action against the ego the same harsh aggressiveness that the ego would have liked to satisfy upon other, extraneous individuals" (Sigmund Freud, *Civilization and Its Discontents,* trans. James Strachey [New York: Norton, 1961], 83–84).

9. I'll mention in passing that, according to Nietzsche, despite (or, perhaps better, because of) the terribleness of this internal suffering, the internalization of these instincts is what makes all higher culture and civilization possible. That is, our protohuman ancestors were not reflective, meditative people; they had no inner life (if you sat around and thought about things too much, you'd no doubt get eaten by tigers or bears). Only with the sublimation of these instincts, their being turned inward, do human beings develop an inner life, what we might call a soul; only then do people become interesting: "The entire inner world, originally as thin as if it were stretched between two membranes, expanded and extended itself, acquired depth, breadth, and height, in the same measure as outward discharge was *inhibited.*" Nietzsche goes on: "Let us add at once that . . . the existence on earth of an animal soul turned against itself, taking sides against itself, was something so new, profound, unheard of, enigmatic, contradictory, *and pregnant with a future* that the aspect of the earth was essentially altered" (*Genealogy of Morals,* 84, 85). It's only once we've begun torturing ourselves that the soul develops, we gain an inner life, become meditative; and it's only then that art, philosophy, religion, and, indeed, as I said, all higher culture and civilization become possible. Freud borrows this idea as well: "Sublimation of instinct is an especially conspicuous feature of cultural development; it is what makes it possible for higher psychical activities, scientific, artistic or ideological, to play such an important part in civilized life" (*Civilization and Its Discontents,* 51).

10. John Stuart Mill, *Utilitarianism* (New York: Meridian, 1962), 257.

11. Arguing with Teresa, Charlie tells her of his admiration for Saint Francis of Assisi, claiming that he "had it all down." Teresa reminds Charlie: "Saint Francis didn't run numbers."

12. Note, too, that those lower-order pleasures conflict with Charlie's religious beliefs and with his apparent desire for salvation, given the Catholic Church's prohibition against premarital sex and, we can presume, contraception. And this is part of what Nietzsche was talking about: Charlie has natural desires for sex and lusts after Teresa and Diane, while the church tells him that these desires are sinful and that acting on them will doom him to eternal damnation.

13. Plato, *Republic,* trans. G. M. A. Grube (Indianapolis: Hackett, 1992), 441e.

14. Freud, *Civilization and Its Discontents,* 25–26.

15. Arthur Schopenhauer, *The World as Will and Representation,* trans. E. F. J. Payne (New York: Dover, 1969), 1:309, 319.

16. "That human life must be some kind of mistake is sufficiently proved by the simple observation that man is a compound of needs which are hard to satisfy; that their satisfaction achieves nothing but a painless condition in which he is only given over to boredom; and that boredom is a direct proof that existence is in itself valueless, for boredom is nothing other than the sensation of the emptiness of existence" (Arthur Schopenhauer, "On the Vanity of Existence," in *Essays and Aphorisms,* trans. R. J. Hollingdale [New York: Penguin, 1970], 53).

17. Schopenhauer, *World as Will and Representation,* 2:584.

18. Aristotle, *Nicomachean Ethics,* trans. Terence Irwin (Indianapolis: Hackett, 1999), 1094a, 1095a.

19. There is more to Aristotle's account of *eudaimonia* than simply excellent activities and the virtues. Certain external goods, as well as friends and family, are all important in living the best sort of life. Aristotle says: "Nonetheless, happiness evidently also needs external goods to be added, as we said, since we cannot, or cannot easily, do fine actions if we lack the resources. For, first of all, in many actions we use friends, wealth, and political power just as we use instruments. Further, deprivation of certain [externals]—for instance, good birth, good children, beauty—mars our blessedness. For we do not altogether have the character of happiness if we look utterly repulsive or are ill-born, solitary, or childless; and we have it even less, presumably, if our children or friends are totally bad, or were good but have died" (ibid., 1099b). However, for the sake of brevity, I'm restricting my discussion of the ways in which one fails to achieve *eudaimonia* to the activities one pursues and the virtues.

20. Ibid., 1106a.

21. Ibid., 1107a.

22. "The many, the most vulgar, would seem to conceive the good and happiness as pleasure, and hence they also like the life of gratification. In this they appear completely slavish, since the life they decide on is a life for grazing animals" (ibid., 1095b).

23. Ibid., 1099a.

24. Keep in mind that, while Aristophanes was a real person, the *Symposium* is a work of fiction, these conversations probably never happened, and the words and ideas expressed are Plato's.

25. Plato, *Symposium,* trans. Alexander Nehamas and Paul Woodruff (Indianapolis: Hackett, 1989), 191a–193a.

26. Jean-Paul Sartre, *Being and Nothingness,* trans. Hazel E. Barnes (New York: Washington Square, 1956), 136.

**Part 2**

# RATIONALITY, CRIMINALITY, AND THE EMOTIONS

# The Cinema of Madness
## Friedrich Nietzsche and the Films of Martin Scorsese
*Jerold J. Abrams*

> The best things we have come from madness, when it is given as a gift of the god.
>
> —Plato, *Phaedrus*

## The Director and the Madman

Martin Scorsese is the greatest director alive. Every film scholar knows that. And everyone knows that his films are about violence, criminals, gangsters. At least, that's the stereotype—and, really, it's not far wrong. Yes, there are a few exceptions: *The Age of Innocence* (1993) stands out, and so does *Alice Doesn't Live Here Anymore* (1974). But the paradigm cases are about violence, typically gang violence: *Mean Streets* (1973), *Taxi Driver* (1976), *Raging Bull* (1980), *Goodfellas* (1990), *Cape Fear* (1991), *Casino* (1995), *Gangs of New York* (2002), and *The Departed* (2006). Inevitably, aficionados leave it at just *Mean Streets* and *Taxi Driver*: the early masterpieces. That's my view too. And future film scholars will, no doubt, look back as well and claim that Scorsese simply defines the genre of gangster cinema, just as Hitchcock simply is suspense cinema, Fellini is carnival, and Eisenstein is Russian montage. But as these film scholars proceed to write so many books on the history of cinema, establishing all the various Platonic forms of film, it is important that something doesn't get lost in the equation of Martin Scorsese and Paul Schrader with gangster/criminal cinema. And that something is Scorsese's cinema of madness. In particular, I mean Scorsese's (and Schrader's) masterful explorations of the philosophical idea of madness—madness in the sense in which Plato meant it in the *Phaedrus* and the *Ion* and Nietzsche in virtually everything. No mere marginalia in the middle works or footnote to some Picassoan Blue Period, the idea of madness runs through the entirety of Scorsese's cinema: from the early works like *Mean Streets* and *Taxi Driver,* to the middle works like *The Last Temptation of Christ* (1988) and *Cape Fear,* up through the more recent *Bringing Out the Dead* (1999) and *The Aviator* (2004). All along it's been right there, actually in two forms. The first form of madness in Scorsese's works is primitive and destructive but not intellectually creative. For example, Johnny Boy Civello (Robert De Niro) in *Mean Streets* is just a wild and dangerous punk. And it's the same thing with Tommy DeVito (Joe Pesci) in *Goodfellas:* true, he's more intelligent and conniving than Johnny, but still he's basically a nutso destructive gangster out only to maximize his own gain. We like these guys because we know that their fatal flaw of destructive madness must, ultimately, destroy them too. But they're hardly complex and, at the end of the day, not particularly interesting. Far more interesting, I think, is the second form of madness we find in Scorsese. This is a more complex form of madness, destructive like the first, but also intellectually creative. It's the kind of madness you find in the madman in Nietzsche's *Gay Science* and Zarathustra in his *Thus Spoke Zarathustra,* both of which set out to destroy something and to create something new as well. In this category belong Max Cady (Robert De Niro) in *Cape Fear* (who is, in fact, a constant reader of Nietzsche's works), Travis Bickle (Robert De Niro) in *Taxi Driver,* Jesus (Willem Dafoe) in *The Last Temptation of Christ,* to some extent Frank Pierce (Nicolas Cage) in *Bringing Out the Dead,* and certainly Howard Hughes (Leonardo DiCaprio) in *The Aviator.*

## Nietzsche's Madman

Now, it's no secret that some of history's greatest philosophers hold madness rather than reason to be the great fountain of consciousness—not in the many, mind you, but in the few, the geniuses.[1] Remember the epigraph to this essay, from Plato's *Phaedrus:* "The best things we have come from madness."[2] And remember too those first lines of Homer's *Odyssey,* so close to Plato's heart: "Sing to me of the man, Muse." And then just down the page: "Launch out on his story, Muse, daughter of Zeus, start from where you will—sing for our time too."[3] This is precisely what Plato has in mind with his own analysis of madness. The poet or philosopher channels a demon spirit that renders him temporarily mad and an instrument of the demon's art. Two thousand years later, Nietzsche would say the same in the section of *Daybreak* entitled "Significance of Madness in the History of Morality," where he cites Plato directly:

"It is through madness that the greatest good things have come to Greece," Plato said, in concert with all ancient mankind. Let us go a step further: all superior men who were irresistibly drawn to throw off the yoke of any kind of morality and to frame new laws had, *if they were not actually mad,* no alternative but to make themselves or pretend to be mad—and this indeed applies to innovators in every domain and not only in the domain of priestly and political dogma:—even the innovator of poetical metre had to establish his credentials by madness.[4]

For Plato and for Nietzsche—and, I think, for Scorsese too—the madman is the archetypal creator of civilization. And, likely, Plato and Nietzsche suspected themselves at least a little mad in some way or another. Indeed, for Nietzsche, it's well known that he went permanently mad in 1889. But that's not exactly the kind of madness Plato and Nietzsche mean. They don't necessarily mean clinical disorders like schizophrenia, paranoia, narcissism, mania, depression, obsessive-compulsive disorder, and so many variations and combinations of these, although, of course, these can and often do play an important role in philosophical and poetic madness. Certainly, many a mad genius has many of the properties described in these medical categories (as we will see shortly in Scorsese's *The Aviator*). But while important—sometimes instrumental—they are neither necessary nor sufficient for the specific kind of madness Plato and Nietzsche have in mind.

Nietzsche's concept of madness, in particular, is distinctly philosophical and seems to have the following properties: (1) massive intelligence; (2) deep artistic creativity; (3) isolation and a feeling of radical separation from regular people; (4) a sense of being far greater than the herd; (5) the feeling of an inner demon forcing its art to the surface of one's mind;[5] (6) the ability to see the contingency and flux of nature and values (here today gone tomorrow); (7) the ability to imagine and entertain alternative value schemes (Nietzsche calls this "revaluation of values"); (8) overrichness in "will to power," the ability to will one's own creative revaluation; (9) bravery, first, to sound out the hollowness of previous idols and values and, then, to determine new ones, in other words (Nietzsche's), "to philosophize with a hammer." Taken together, these traits produce a higher philosophical state of mind, one infused with all the frenzy of poetic imagination and all the razored intellect of logical positivism. And when civilization proceeds down its natural path to decadence, as it always seems to do, it's always the madman who steps in and goes mad for the rest of us, to set the will of millennia on new tracks.

As an elite madman himself, Nietzsche found few peers in his own day, which is why he so often speaks in the second person to the future, directing himself to those few and rare individuals to come. It's as though he were whispering to fellow mad friends of the future, those who know, those with secret knowledge, when he says things like: We special ones, we "dwell in the little world of exceptions," in "the evil zone," and "in spite of that fearful pressure of 'morality of custom' under which all the communities of mankind have lived." For, throughout history, novelty has been repressed in favor of the rule. But, in spite of this, "new and deviate ideas, evaluations, drives again and again broke out." In fact, madness is, according to Nietzsche, the very fountain of culture: "Almost everywhere it was madness which prepared the way for the new idea, which broke the spell of a venerated usage and superstition." We need it to be this way. That's how sea changes in history occur—not by social movements but by genius, mad genius—and the genius knows this too. He knows that if he weren't really as mad as he is—well then, he'd simply have to fake it. For we do and always have demanded, and probably always will, that a young god or demon, even a master philosopher, first show us his ID proving to us that he is truly a madman: that he came from a horrible land of drugs and muses and is *never* going back.[6]

After *Daybreak,* with his definition of the madman in hand, Nietzsche proceeds to *The Gay Science,* where he gives the madman flesh. In a section entitled "The Madman," Nietzsche writes: "Have you not heard of that madman who lit a lantern in the bright morning hours, ran to the market place, and cried incessantly, 'I seek God! I seek God!'" Hearing this, the people are surprised and mock him: "Why, did he get lost? said one. Did he lose his way like a child? said another. Or is he hiding? Is he afraid of us? Has he gone on a voyage? Or emigrated? Thus they yelled and laughed." But the madman isn't really looking for God. In fact, *he's* the one doing the mocking. For, while the crowd no longer believes in the God of old, they have not yet conceived the consequences of their secularism. So the madman continues: "'Whither is God?' he cried. 'I shall tell you. *We have killed him*—you and I. All of us are his murderers.'" Now, of course, Nietzsche doesn't mean deicide literally. Rather, it's science and secularism that have "killed" God, that have decentered the old medieval worldview. Notice how Nietzsche has Galileo in mind: "What did we do when we unchained this earth from its sun?" For now we stray "through an infinite nothing" and all the coldness of space. "God is dead. God remains dead. And we have killed him." So what should we do? asks the madman: "How shall we, the murderers of all murderers, comfort ourselves? . . . Is not the greatness of this deed too great for us? Must not we ourselves become gods simply to seem worthy of it? There has never been a greater deed; and whoever will be born after us—for the sake of this deed he will be part of a higher history than all history hitherto."[7]

Readers of Nietzsche will recognize in this madman passage a prototype Zarathustra and his almost identical message. After the death of God, nihilism and darkness follow because all our values are loosed and decentered. New tablets must now be written; indeed, we must become gods, or at least godlike, in order to be worthy of our deicide. We must will a new kind of man, a man beyond man, what Nietzsche calls the *overman*. And it is the function of the madman to light the way and offer us a start.

## *Cape Fear*

That Scorsese is deeply interested in Nietzsche's views on madness and values and power will come as no surprise to anyone familiar with his 1991 remake of J. Lee Thompson's *Cape Fear* (1962). For, here, the antagonist/protagonist, Cady, is a reader of Nietzsche and, as it turns out, a psychopathic killer who has raped a girl. Well, maybe, maybe not. After all, his defense attorney, Sam Bowden (Nick Nolte), buried evidence that the girl was promiscuous, evidence that would have acquitted Cady, and they both know it. Now, after studying Nietzsche in prison for the last fourteen years (we see *The Will to Power* among his books), Cady's coming after Sam, which is not exactly revenge. As a Nietzschean, Cady knows that revenge is for the little people, an ideology of the weak. Higher men want to show their wrongdoers how much help they've actually given them. The most powerful man thanks his attacker for enhancing his power. That's Cady's aim, to show Sam and his family what he's become.

Naturally Sam wants no part of this and hires a private investigator to spy on Cady:

> PRIVATE INVESTIGATOR: You know where he was today? He was at the public library reading *Thus Spoke Zarathustra* by Friedrich Nietzsche. He's this German philosopher. He said that God is dead—
> SAM: God is dead, right.

Frustrated by all this, and being an educated man, certainly worried enough to know what kind of consequences might follow from a man who, like Cady, believes that he is "beyond good and evil," Sam takes a more drastic course of action. He hires three thugs to beat up Cady in a back lot, while he watches. But they're no match for Cady, who takes them out in double-quick time and then speaks to Sam, who he knows is cowardly hiding behind a dumpster: "I'm better than you *all!* I can outlearn you. I can outread you. I can outthink you. And I can outphilosophize you. And I'm gonna outlast you. You think a couple of whacks to my good ol' boy guts is gonna get me down? It's gonna take a hell of a lot more than that, counselor, to prove you're better than me. I am like God, and God like me. I am as large as God, he is small as I. He cannot above me nor I beneath him be. Silesius, seventeenth century." Cady cites Silesius here, but he might just as easily have quoted Nietzsche's madman passage in *The Gay Science* or any page of *Zarathustra.* He sees himself as a new god, something above ordinary men, greater in every way than Sam. He says the same to Sam's daughter, Danielle (Juliette Lewis), after she throws boiling water in his face, which doesn't even faze him: "Are you offering me something hot? Let's get something straight here. I spent fourteen years in an eight-by-nine cell, surrounded by people who were less than human. My mission in that time was to become more than human. You see?"

Well, do we? Is Cady a Nietzschean madman, perhaps an overman? Lawrence S. Friedman thinks neither. In *The Cinema of Martin Scorsese,* he writes: "*Untermensch* rather than *Übermensch,* Cady turns out to be less than human, not more, despite his claim to superman status."[8] I must say that I'm not entirely satisfied leaving it at that. There's more to Cady than simply an underman, a tool, or a savage. I prefer to think of him as a failed madman, but still perhaps something more than human. He has, after all, overcome a great deal in prison. After being jailed unjustly and being raped and tortured, he has taught himself not just to read but to read the hardest books and now wills himself to become something new. He has uncovered a noble lie in the Platonic sense—just as Zarathustra claims to—about his godlike judge, Sam Bowden (that he buried the truth), and is prepared to overcome him, indeed, all the various lies by which society lives.

Moreover, Cady acts from an inspired and educated madness and treats his crimes as philosophy and art. He even dresses the part and, with a flare like Sherlock Holmes's, meets his nemesis with elegance, to "teach" the so-called master, the man, the lawyer, about "loss." And, dark as Cady is, we hate Sam, the man of society, even more because he's getting away with his own crimes. Still, we'd forgive him that if only he treated his crimes as art as well, as the very definition of his character. Cady is simply unafraid of his crimes; he sees them as being beyond good and evil. He's someone unafraid of becoming what he is and unafraid to mete out equivalence, not because the attorney has it coming, and not because it's right, but because it's art, and because it's "education." So this is not a revenge story but the criminal's own story, which he's making up as he goes along. And while at times we will casually call him evil, perhaps even a devil—as though it's so simple—he's more complex than that, and Nietzsche would agree. After all, as Nietzsche puts it: "I guess that you would call my overman—devil."[9]

## *Taxi Driver*

In an earlier incarnation of the Scorsese/Nietzschean madman, De Niro is more sympathetic but certainly less mad and far less creative. *Taxi Driver*'s Travis Bickle is a war veteran driving a cab in New York City. Naturally, Bickle talks to himself, driving around the city: "Loneliness has followed me my whole life. Everywhere. In bars, in cars, sidewalks, stores, everywhere. There's no escape. I'm God's lonely man." He lives at the bottom of a city of skyscrapers, in the dregs, surrounded by crime. New York is a kind of Dantean inferno feeding on the weaknesses of weak people, turning them into zombies. Total scum, and it all needs to be washed off the face of the earth. No exceptions. Travis says this to Senator Charles Palantine (Leonard Harris), a candidate for president, who gets into Travis's cab: "This city here is like an open sewer, ya know, it's full of filth and scum. Sometimes I can hardly take it. Whoever becomes the president should just really clean it up, ya know what I mean? Sometimes I go out and I smell it. I get headaches, it's so bad, ya know. It's like, they just never go away, ya know. It's like I think that the president should just clean up this whole mess here. He should just flush it right down the fucking toilet."

Bickle himself, of course, is hardly above the sewer. In fact, he's half in and half out of this inferno, and he wants out completely. So, as a mode of escape, he fixes on a beautiful and classy woman, Betsy (Cybill Shepherd), and asks her for a short date. She agrees. Pie and coffee. It's here we see Bickle's keen intelligence: he's able to see right through her, knows her soul, that she's lonely too, and now she's completely disarmed. Bickle's intelligence is that of the hunter; it's what he learned in Vietnam, but it has its limits, and we see them when he takes Betsy for a second date to a porno flick. She rejects him, of course, a rejection that sends him over the edge.

Now he is thrust headlong deeper into isolation and beyond the fold of civilization. It is here that his mind starts working overtime. As Travis says in voice-over: "The idea had been growing in my brain for some time: *true* force. All the king's men cannot put it back together again." This is Bickle's will to power, his will to revaluate the values of society. If society will not accept him, then he will make society a reflection of his will. Now, in front of a full-length mirror, examining himself covered in guns, imagining his confrontation with the old law, preparing to overturn the scum on the streets of New York: "You talkin' to me? You talkin' to me? You talkin' to me? Then who the hell else are you talkin' to? You talkin' to me? Well I'm the only one here. Who do you think you're talking to? Oh yeah? Huh? OK." Guns out. Prepare to die.

Travis has accepted himself as completely beyond society. And he is resculpting his body, which may seem everyday on the surface of things but is clearly a reflection of his mind's own transformation: "There will be no more pills, no more bad food . . . no more destroyers of my body. From now on it'll be total organization. Every muscle must be tight." He is readying himself, not just to stand outside the law, but to murder at will, in the name of his own madness and new values, the pimp, the hotel manager who supports the pimp, even Palantine (if need be). Travis is preparing to bring the new law. For so long he used to meditate: "Someday a real rain will come and wash all this scum off the streets." Now that day is coming in the form of Travis Bickle. He begins by killing Sport (Harvey Keitel) and then saves the underage prostitute Iris Steensma (Jodie Foster). And, to our surprise, society celebrates the renegade who simply would not take it anymore, revealing the decadence into which New York had fallen. And while at the end Travis is still driving a cab, after recovering from severe gunshot wounds, we know that it's not over. He's only just beginning. And he knows that we'll accept him as a madman because it's time.

### *The Last Temptation of Christ*

Twelve years after *Taxi Driver*, Scorsese would develop the same themes of the madman, the free criminal, and the prostitute's savior, only this time in the context of religion. An adaptation of Nikos Kazantzakis's novel of the same name, *The Last Temptation of Christ* is not a factual account but a semifictional interpretation of the Gospels.[10] It begins with Jesus lying on the ground in an open field, wrecked and exhausted, with his voice-over narrating: "The feeling begins. Very tender. Very loving. Then the pain starts. Claws slip underneath the skin, and tear their way up. Just before they reach my eyes, they dig in. Then I remember." Now cut to Jesus, a carpenter, pounding something, what we do not yet know. Still the same voice-over: "First I fasted for three months. I even whipped myself before I went to sleep. At first it worked. Then the pain came back. And the voices. They call me by name. Jesus." Five minutes into the film, you know that this is no ordinary "greatest story ever told": apparently, Jesus is going mad, and, as a carpenter, he's making crosses.

At the time, this was about as controversial as movies got. And some may blame artists for an irresponsible aestheticism, but the view that madness is intrinsic to the incarnation of God is hardly limited to the poets and imagemakers. It is discussed by philosophers as well, to the effect that Christ simply must have experienced madness by sheer immersion in the absolute depths of the human condition. The French philosopher (and Nietzsche scholar) Michel Foucault makes the same point in his *Madness and Civilization:* "Christ did not merely choose to be surrounded by lunatics; he himself chose to pass in their eyes for a madman, thus experiencing, in his incarnation, all the sufferings of human misfortune. Madness thus became the ultimate form, the final degree of God in man's image, before the fulfillment and deliverance on the Cross." And further: "Madness is the lowest point of humanity to which God submitted in His incarnation, thereby showing that there was nothing inhuman in man that could not be redeemed and saved."[11]

Foucault's point is important because, typically, we think of Jesus as a noble among savages come to redeem them. His companions are thieves and beggars, prostitutes and lepers, the lowest of the low of society. And, in almost Homeric heroic fashion, Jesus endures beautifully and with the grace of a superman everything those prostitutes and beggars could never even think to handle. He has all virtues and all the strength of will. So then the question: What makes him like us anyway? Foucault's answer, and certainly Scorsese's as well, is plainly madness.

Indeed, Jesus experienced not only absolute physical suffering but absolute mental suffering as well, and that really is what makes Jesus a peer to the loonies and addicts. But what makes him a peer to the madmen and the gods is that now he must somehow come out the other end of his insanity in order to be in full possession of the secret of Nietzsche: that a mad god must go far beyond the herd, into the desert of the Jews in pure isolation, or deep in a faraway cave like Zarathustra. Here he'll see reality in flux and values as unstable and, through wild, mad visions, revaluate the law that holds a people captive and corrupts them. Once in possession of this secret knowledge, hallucinations remain: still the snakes and the lions and the flames speak to him. But the tables have turned: now he's in control of them.

Jesus explains this turn in his madness: "I used to think that God was angry too. But not anymore. He used to jump on me like a wild bird and dig his claws into my head. But then one morning he came to me." What has changed in Jesus is the nature of his possession. Once God possessed him, dug in his claws like a devil. Now Jesus possesses himself. Now he *is* that god, a mad god of love and violence, prepared to come with an ax and call it

Truth with a capital *T*. But, of course, in speaking of truth, a mad god never speaks in syllogisms or transcendental deductions of pure practical reason. His vision is no Euclidean morality, axiomatic from a priori principles and pure intuitions. The law is no text and no equation, but nothing other than the wild visions of Jesus himself, not necessarily rational by any means, but pure love forged in crazy nights and so many hallucinations. And when it's all said and done and omniscience is unfolding, he gives this truth: that the old god is dead and I am now God.

> JESUS: When I say "I," Rabbi, I'm saying "God."
> RABBI: That's blasphemy.
> JESUS: Didn't they tell you. I'm the saint of blasphemy. Don't make any mistakes. I didn't come here to bring peace. I came to bring a sword.

And as this new, mad, blasphemous god, he is also a new law: "*I* am the end of the old law and the beginning of the new one." Here, Jesus is revaluating the old law: "Mourners will be blessed. You'll have God to comfort you. You won't need men to do it. And the meek? They're the ones who will be blessed. And the suffering, they'll be blessed too. And the peacemakers and the merciful and the sick and the poor and the outcasts, you'll all be blessed because heaven is yours." And not only will the last be the first, but the first will also be last, as Jesus says, turning to a man laughing at his sermon: "And believe me, believe me. Those who are laughing now will be crying later. Those whose stomachs are filled now will be hungry later. And the rich will be poor forever." Here, Jesus is in full Nietzschean form as he completes his massive revaluation of all values.

And, certainly, in speaking words such as these Jesus is one of Nietzsche's primary models. For example, in *Zarathustra* Nietzsche writes: "The *creator* they hate most: he breaks tablets and old values. He is a breaker, they call him lawbreaker. For the good are *unable* to create; they are always the beginning of the end: they crucify him who writes new values on new tablets; they sacrifice the future to *themselves*—they crucify all man's future."[12] Here, of course, by *good* Nietzsche means the herd and really thinks they're bad: they're good only insofar as they call themselves good, while they see the madman and the overman as dangerous and evil, a man who claims himself to be god but is really to them more of a devil. This is precisely the god that Kazantzakis has in mind, precisely the one Schrader and Scorsese put to the screen: a mad Nietzschean god of revaluation.

As a final point, note that Kazantzakis, Schrader, and Scorsese also understand their own Nietzschean revaluation of the story of Jesus. After all, so much has been reversed. Jesus is neither omniscient nor omnipotent as a god; he makes mistakes regularly. He's not always so eloquent, and his intended aims in speaking to crowds often and frustratingly go awry. He rebels and makes crosses in a rage against God. Indeed, he takes no small part in crucifying his fellow man. He's insane and barely makes it as a messiah, only by a hair's breadth. His last temptation almost gets the best of him. Lucifer has him, while Jesus enjoys multiple wives for a good many years—all this in his mind on the cross—he simply can't save himself. And it's Judas who will not betray him. Dante may in *The Divine Comedy* put Judas at the bottom of hell and have him devoured for eternity by Lucifer, but, for Kazantzakis, Schrader, and Scorsese, it is Judas who saves God.

### Bringing Out the Dead

The theme of the outsider who sees visions and spirits and lives between worlds, like good and evil, light and dark, life and death, is repeated in Scorsese's 1999 film *Bringing Out the Dead*. Frank Pierce is a burned-out paramedic who works the night shift, works on the dying, knows what takes place in the transition between life and death, and lives there himself—on the edge. He even knows what the dead enjoy: "Do you have any music?" asks Mary Burke (Patricia Arquette) as he tries to revive a flatliner. This ability to stand at the intersection of life and death, to see both sides and will people back from the dead, naturally makes Pierce feel like a god: "Saving someone's life is like falling in love. The best drug in the world. For days, sometimes weeks afterwards, you walk the streets, making infinite whatever you see. Once, for a few weeks, I couldn't feel the earth—everything I touched became lighter. Horns played in my shoes. Flowers fell from my pockets. You wonder if you've become immortal, as if you've saved your own life as well. God has passed through you. Why deny it, that for a moment there—why deny that for a moment there, God was you?" But what kind of god? Certainly not an all-powerful one. A contingent god at best. In fact, he's a kind of wraith trapped among ghosts and other midway demons. Each night he sees them, the ghosts, people he tried and failed to save who've come back to haunt him. Pierce accepts that: "These spirits were part of the job." But he can't control them, and, as the nights roll on, it's getting worse: "Rose's ghost was getting closer."

Of course, it's only natural that Pierce wants out, wants to escape from the horrible ritual of murder and drugs and his front row seat at death in the streets. Like Jesus, he'd do anything to escape. He tries but fails in this, just as he fails to revive so many souls. There's no way out, and, somehow, he knows this too. No one will fire him, no matter what he does, no matter how many ghosts he sees, no matter how much he drinks, no matter how crazy he appears. As many sick days as he's taken, as many insults as he's hurled at his boss, as many failures in the field as he's racked up, it simply doesn't matter. Besides, it's all a sham anyway: he'd never quit if he could. He's compelled from a force within him, a kind of divinely inspired madness. He's got that "total unfreedom" that Nietzsche mentions, that "convulsion and froth of the epileptic" that "mark the madman as the mask and speaking-trumpet of a divinity."[13]

Yes, indeed, Pierce has the mask and the gift. Problem is he can't go all the way, for two reasons. First, he believes in the institutional world he serves, which is one reason you could never rename the film *Taxi Driver: Part II* even though so much is the same—New York isolation, the madman, a civil servant, a nighttime driver who moves passengers from place to place, insomnia, existential pain—only this time it all takes place in an ambulance rather than a taxi. For, ultimately, Pierce and Bickle are worlds apart, especially when it comes to what they see and what they will. Travis wills revaluation through "true force," while Pierce wills the status quo. His job, as he sees it, is not to change people; it's not even to save them; it's merely "to witness": "I realized that my training was useful in less than 10 percent of the calls, and saving someone's life was rarer than that. After a while, I grew to understand that my role was less about saving lives than about bearing witness. I was a grief mop. It was enough that I simply showed up." Of course, it's true that, in the end, Pierce (like Bickle) saves a woman (saves Mary), but this is a temporary fix. Sure, he takes her from a drug den for a day, but what about the rest of her days? And what about his?[14]

What makes Frank Pierce a failure as a Nietzschean madman is his softness. He sees ghosts and refuses to guide them. He hears the ghosts speaking to him but never musters the courage to go in with them. The one moment he's close, when he takes the drug "Red Death"—note the reference to Edgar Allan Poe's short story "The Masque of the Red Death"—he's close, but he fails. The ghosts horrify him all over again. He runs away with Mary over his shoulder and reenters his impotent land of witnessing. Jesus was there once, too, and so was Travis Bickle, even Max Cady—all of them. They all got to this point, a hard point in madness, where reality starts melting and so does the self. The key turn here is revaluation, and it's this turn that Pierce can't take. He calls himself a god, but he lacks the hammer of the gods to reshape the metaphysical twilight that surrounds him. All he can do is watch, exhausted, beaten.

## *The Aviator*

Howard Hughes in *The Aviator,* by contrast, really is a madman. Hughes doesn't fit in, but he doesn't care. He's brilliant and wealthy, and he'll show *them* how it's done. He depends on polite society to maintain not a facade but a certain herd stability so that a select few like him can change us. Think of his view as Nietzsche's: "A people is a detour of nature to get to six or seven great men.—Yes, and then to get around them."[15] Hughes sees himself as one of those six or seven, and probably he *was* one of them: after all, he revolutionized the flight industry, was the world's first billionaire and a master filmmaker, and built the biggest plane in the history of aviation.

Part of the source of Hughes's genius is his obsessive-compulsive disorder—I say *part* because Hughes is unique in *any* population. Still, it's an important part. Hughes is attacked by obsessions, uncontrolled thoughts that emerge spontaneously, excessive worries that he knows are neither rational nor beneficial. It's the future coming to destroy him. Everything is dirty; everything is disorganized; visions and phantoms are everywhere. Naturally, this breeds a certain paranoia, and, certainly, Hughes is paranoid, a condition made worse by his failed hearing: he thinks people are always talking about him.

So he compulsively works without stopping, engineering the external world, every facet of it, to tame the monster with management and organization, innovation in technique, and repetition against difference. By performing his own unique rituals, he'll colonize time and keep the obsessions from taking over completely. He wants his chocolate chip cookies just so: with the chips medium size and not too close to the perimeter of the cookie. Otherwise, all hell breaks loose. And he takes his meal at the club the same way always: New York–cut steak, then twelve (exactly twelve) peas lined up in three symmetrical columns of four, a quarter of an inch between any two peas, and a bottle of milk with the cap still on so the bottle is airtight. No exceptions. Now enter Errol Flynn (Jude Law), who has just stolen a pea from Hughes's plate, thinking it's nothing, everyone's having a good time—what's mine is yours and so on. But Hughes starts to twitch and frown and try to deal with the disaster, and, of course, he can't stay a minute longer. Katharine Hepburn (Cate Blanchett) understands, but Errol Flynn has no idea, so he just jokes and calls Hughes a "madman," having no clue how right he really is.

Hughes trusts Kate, so he confides in her that he knows what's coming: "You know, sometimes I . . . I get these feelings, Katie. I get these ideas, these . . . crazy ideas about . . . things that may not . . . things that may not really be there. Sometimes I truly fear that I'm losing my mind. And if I did, it would . . . It'd be like flying blind." Faced with this horror, he has no choice but to work even harder, to build bigger and even more efficiently: continue to beat the monster into submission, a battle, of course, he must, ultimately, lose. But, in the meantime, he'll go faster than anyone else on earth. Indeed, he'll be the first to fly around the world, from New York to New York, in four days, during which time, in the air and over the radio, he also negotiates and purchases Trans World Airlines.

As Scorsese puts it: "His obsession of speed really is the idea of trying to capture on film the sensation of what it is to be a god. Because you're like a god. You're flying up there. You're flying through the clouds. You're flying, you know. No one can touch you."[16] It's the same with Hughes's love of film: escape, protection. He's in the cockpit of his own private theater, a safe god alone and away from people, where he can contemplate the images of reality from afar, considering their rearrangements in peace. And *that* really is the key to Hughes's madness: the limits of reality simply don't exist for him and may, therefore, be reshaped in any way. The so-called laws of culture and being are there only to be broken and remade, revolutionized and revaluated, and Hughes is the man to do it.

The best sequence of the film is the maddest and near the end. Hughes has locked himself away in a screening room, naked, alone, isolated. He's talking to himself. Film images reflect against the walls—and not just the wall with the screen. The entire room is a system of film screens. And the depth of the room is changing, seems to shift this way and that. He's still living on bottles of milk, but now he's collecting the bottles after the milk is gone and lining them all up against one of the walls, some filled with his urine. Another row of milk bottles full of milk glows blue as colors flash around the room of his mind. What is real and what is unreal are unknown to us or to him. The room is his mind from so many perspectives, in so many hallucinations, with so many bottles in rows. And we can have no idea when we go just outside the room whether this is real either, whether Juan Trippe (Alec Baldwin), Noah Dietrich (John C. Reilly), and Kate are really there trying to get through, speaking through the door, or just the voices in his head. And the moment we think it might be real, cut to Hughes flash-forward. Suddenly he's aging: longer hair and a beard. And the screening room is padded—the kind of room they put the crazies in. He babbles to himself and spells out methodically (slowly) "Q-U-A-R-A-N-T-I-N-E," the same way his mother taught him to when she was also telling him: "Howard. You are not safe." So he's quarantined himself from himself—deep down inside himself. Steadily, the analogy to Scorsese's Jesus is coming into view: a mad superman, naked, a revaluator of all values, being tortured to death by his madness. And then we see it explicitly: crucified in his own white cinematic armchair, a film god with long hair and a beard, as white light explodes from the camera projector like a magnificent halo behind his head.

The vision of the madman as filmmaker must be something close to Scorsese's heart. For here is a mature work about flying high into the heights of hallucination and one's mind, like a screen reversing all reality, like a cognitive camera obscura, ideas upside down on the back of the inner eye, received upright and then twisted and transformed—and put back there on an external screen for all to see and see differently. Scorsese, here, says a great deal about film as art, about film as divine madness.

## Madness and the Criminal Mind

There is no question that an understanding of the character of the madman is essential to an understanding of Scorsese's work as a whole, perhaps even equally as important as an understanding of the character of the gangster—here briefly returning to the distinction between gangster and madman with which we began. Certainly, the gangster and the madman are Scorsese's favorite protagonists, each representing alternative approaches to the criminal mind, the man who stands outside society. But it is essential that we keep the two apart. For the madman is the free criminal, the criminal of self-consciousness, who must make the turn away from society toward himself in order to rearrange the reality of his world. In reality, gangsters, by contrast, are rarely madmen—and almost never in Scorsese.

Gangsters are technicians, not visionaries, rarely isolated, and never bent on creatively revaluating the values of humanity. In fact, the gangsters of *Casino* and *Goodfellas,* even *Mean Streets* and *Gangs of New York,* all want the ordinary values to remain in society. They want the code of the herd to stay steeled in place, precisely as the condition for the possibility of their own violations. They don't want the straight world to operate any differently than it already does. Their very livelihood depends on America's going about its business so that they, the gangsters, can go about subverting it. And they do so in collectives: after all, gangsters run in gangs, often quite respectable on the surface, sometimes somewhat respectable in depth. They run businesses, attend social functions, raise families, participate in politics, and are usually very nationalistic about America. To put the point another way, gangsters still have a herd mentality. They may see themselves as slightly above other human beings, but they have little interest in changing those other human beings.

But none of the madmen discussed here are anything like that. Of course, as has been mentioned, the madman craves reinsertion into society but knows he can't have it, being beyond the boundaries of society. He's condemned to stand outside it, like a sage or a hermit. And, even there, hermits and sages rarely revaluate values. In fact, they don't really *do* anything to society from their isolated perspective. For the madman, however, it is precisely his job to stand far enough outside the fold to invert the order of being, to turn it inside out a hundred times and never come up with the same reality.

## Notes

I am very grateful to Mark Conard and Elizabeth F. Cooke for comments and conversation on an earlier draft of this essay. I am also grateful to Elizabeth F. Cooke, Chris Pliatska, and Karen Hoffman for conversations on Scorsese's cinema. Of course, any mistakes that remain are my own.

1. See Plato, *Ion*, 534b–e, trans. Paul Woodruff, in *Plato: Complete Works*, ed. John M. Cooper (Indianapolis: Hackett, 1997), 942. The more common view is found in the *Republic*, where Plato banishes the mad poets for being mad, for being irrational in a polis built to reason. But Plato has more interesting things to say on madness in the *Phaedrus* and the *Ion*, where he is less given to censorship, totalitarianism, and eugenics.

2. Plato, *Phaedrus*, 244a, trans. Alexander Nehamas and Paul Woodruff, in ibid., 522.

3. Homer, *The Odyssey*, trans. Robert Fagles (New York: Penguin, 1997), 77.

4. Friedrich Nietzsche, *Daybreak: Thoughts on the Prejudices of Morality*, trans. R. J. Hollingdale, ed. Maudmarie Clark and Brian Leiter (Cambridge: Cambridge University Press, 1997), 13–14.

5. As Nietzsche puts it: "Something that bore so visibly the sign of total unfreedom as the convulsion and froth of the epileptic, that seemed to mark the madman as the mask and speaking-trumpet of a divinity" (ibid., 14).

6. Ibid., 13–14.

7. Nietzsche, *The Gay Science*, in *The Portable Nietzsche*, ed. and trans. Walter Kaufmann (New York: Penguin, 1954), 95–96.

8. Lawrence S. Friedman, *The Cinema of Martin Scorsese* (New York: Continuum, 1998), 163.

9. Friedrich Nietzsche, *Thus Spoke Zarathustra: A Book for All and None*, trans. Walter Kaufmann (New York: Modern Library, 1995), 144.

10. Nikos Kazantzakis, *The Last Temptation of Christ*, trans. P. A. Bien (New York: Simon & Schuster, 1960).

11. Michel Foucault, *Madness and Civilization: A History of Insanity in the Age of Reason*, trans. Richard Howard (New York: Vintage, 1988), 80, 81.

12. Nietzsche, *Zarathustra*, 212–13.

13. Nietzsche, *Daybreak,* 13–14.

14. I am grateful to Karen Hoffman for conversation on this point.

15. Friedrich Nietzsche, *Beyond Good and Evil: Prelude to a Philosophy of the Future,* trans. Walter Kaufmann (New York: Vintage, 1989), 87. Similarly, Nietzsche writes: "Basic errors of biologists hitherto: it is not a question of the species but of more powerful individuals. (The many are only a means)" (Friedrich Nietzsche, *The Will to Power,* trans. Walter Kaufmann and R. J. Hollingdale [New York: Vintage, 1968], 360–61).

16. Martin Scorsese's comments are included on the DVD of *The Aviator* (released by Warner Bros. in 2005). With regard to size, nowadays we think of giant planes as pretty standard, 747s and so on. But Hughes was the first to build on this scale: the Hercules was 220 feet long and five stories high with eight huge engines and a wingspan longer than a football field. There was simply nothing like it. Hughes was also the first to fly it.

# The Age of Innocence
## Social Semiotics, Desire, and Constraint
*Deborah Knight*

This volume is dedicated to the topic of Martin Scorsese's philosophy as it can be appreciated through his films. Now, plainly, Scorsese is a filmmaker, not a philosopher, so there is a sense in which the term *philosophy* is being used as an honorific here. Equally clearly, narrative fiction filmmaking is a very distinct sort of practice, one that is not directly assimilable to the practice of philosophy. Although it has recently been argued that at least some fiction films *do* philosophy, that they can be profitably understood as *philosophizing,* I do not find this view persuasive.[1] Fiction films do not operate by means of reasons and arguments; rather, they operate by means of narratives that feature the contextualized actions of characters and are interpretable in terms of their style as well as their major themes and motifs. That said, it is not hard to construe some films—perhaps even many films—as illustrating some philosophical point or other. Consider the number of science fiction films that ask the question, What is it to be human? Or the number of westerns and gangster films that from their different directions ask, What is justice? Or again the number of European art cinema films that seem to owe a debt to Sartrean existentialism. But I would argue that the questions such films raise are better thought of as indicating some of their films' central themes, rather than as doing philosophy. Lately, defenders of the idea of film as philosophy have argued that it is appropriate to treat films as analogous to philosophical thought experiments.[2] My view is that the disanalogies are more significant than the putative analogies.[3] So, even if there are apparently philosophical questions that arise with regard to Scorsese's films, I recommend that we treat them as an opportunity for thematic analysis. Few works of fiction, it seems to me, are best thought of as *doing* philosophy, although perhaps there are exceptions, for instance, the works of Jorge Luis Borges.[4] But, since many works of fiction look thematically at topics that are central to philosophy, I think it desirable that philosophers not overlook such works when dealing with these issues. So, while I do not hold that we should treat fiction films generally, or Scorsese's films in particular, *as* philosophy, we can, nevertheless, profitably look for philosophical themes *in* Scorsese's films. The purpose of this essay, therefore, is to analyze certain philosophical topics and themes that emerge in *The Age of Innocence* (1993).

To anticipate, my argument is that, in *The Age of Innocence*, as in many other works from Scorsese's oeuvre, we are witness to a singularly cinematic examination of a highly codified social milieu. In particular, Scorsese attends to the dynamic tension between the constraints on individual aspiration imposed by this milieu and the desire of at least some key figures to escape these imposed constraints. Scorsese's investigation involves a combination of his signature camerawork and editing, the film's highly detailed and minutely observed mise-en-scène, and the striking role of the film's omniscient voice-over narrator (Joanne Woodward). As we see often in Scorsese's work, a central figure—whether an insider, such as a Joe Pesci character, or an outsider, in this case the Countess Ellen Olenska (Michelle Pfeiffer)—throws into sharp relief the unspoken rules and conventions of an insular social group. Both the unspoken rules and conventions and the more public display of wealth and position combine to form what I call the *social semiotics* of *The Age of Innocence*—the complex mixture of signs and codes that govern the actions of the members of New York's "polite society." I imagine that Scorsese was motivated to adapt Wharton's novel precisely because of the opportunity it gave him simultaneously to investigate this highly conventional world and to unmask its pretensions and rigidity.

## The Countess Olenska as Catalyst

*The Age of Innocence* is a sumptuous film, both visually and narratively rich. At the heart of the story is a powerful social elite organized around a combination of inherited prestige, wealth, and family connections. Especially important are the connections achieved through marriage between different prominent families. The narrative principally tracks three characters caught in a romantic triangle: Newland Archer (Daniel Day-Lewis), a young lawyer and member of a very respectable New York family who has a great love of culture and the arts; his fiancée, May Welland (Winona Ryder), a young woman born into the upper echelons of New York society who, in contrast to Newland, is unconcerned with anything either cultural or intellectual and whose primary ambition appears to be to make a good marriage; and May's disgraced elder cousin, the Countess Olenska, who, after several years in Europe, returns to New York after the failure of her marriage to a Polish count. Clearly, as everyone involved realizes without it needing to be said, the alliance of the Archers with the Wellands counts as a positive way of reinforcing family lines and social power. Equally clearly, Madame Olenska, who has drawn everyone's attention to the failure of her marriage by returning to New York, is no longer able to participate in the organization and reorganization of prominent family lines by means of marriage, given that she has already married outside her social circle, and also given that, within New York society, divorce is tantamount to scandal.

I just said that Ellen is an outsider, but this point needs qualification. Ellen grew up in New York with Newland and May—in fact, she recalls that Newland once kissed her as a child, although she loved the other boy, who was not interested in her. But Ellen's parents, described as nomads and as continental wanderers, took her out of the New York social cocoon at an early age. Thus, her return after a long absence as a separated woman is disruptive, and she becomes the focus of considerable speculation and gossip. Although Newland assures her that she is "among friends" in New York, we know that he is mistaken.

In any significant romantic triangle, there is typically a clear contrast between at least two of its members, and we see this with Ellen and May. In fact, Ellen is the antithesis of May: intelligent, independent minded, sexually experienced, interested in the arts and culture, and alive to the artifices of both European and New York society. She is a woman with ideas and opinions, something Newland is initially not entirely prepared to deal with. She is, moreover, a woman willing to initiate action, particularly with respect to Newland, inviting him on two significant occasions to call on her, requests that would be unseemly except that she is May's cousin and, thus, in an extended sense, almost a member of Newland's own family. Ellen operates as independently as a woman within the constraints of her society can, and she is not afraid of being to a certain degree unconventional. Indeed, her ultimate downfall can be ascribed to the fact that, although she recognizes the conventionality of her family's social circle, she is blind to many of its explicit conventions. Newland is attracted to the controversial side of Ellen's behavior. He is also, as the narrator remarks, "amused by the smooth hypocrisies of his peers." Thus, Newland realizes that, when Ellen's actions are judged to be controversial, it is very often as a result of the hypocritical views of those who sit in judgment. For instance, Larry Lefferts (Richard E. Grant) is openly critical of Ellen's past, which is rumored to include an extramarital relationship with her husband's secretary, despite the fact that Lefferts himself enjoys a reputation as a successful philanderer.

Realizing that the countess is the focus of cruel gossip, and believing that he is helping May and her family, Newland tries to rehabilitate the countess in the eyes of New York society. As a lawyer, he agrees to act on her behalf in negotiating a divorce from her husband, although his primary role here, on behalf of his law firm, is to show the countess that it is far more scandalous in America for disaffected couples to divorce than simply to agree to live apart. The more time Newland spends with Ellen Olenska, the more he finds himself attracted to her. Of course, as a gentleman, he believes that he cannot break his engagement to May, even if he has fallen in love with someone else. Indeed, in an attempt to counter his own growing romantic preoccupation with Ellen, he unexpectedly pursues May to her family's winter retreat in Florida to urge that their marriage be moved forward. Here, May is unexpectedly direct, demanding to know if there is someone else. Newland lies to her, and she agrees to his suggestion. Marriage does not diminish Newland's attraction to the countess, although his sense of obligation to his wife and to the society that she represents constrains his actions. The film's greatest irony, as it will eventually turn out, occurs when Newland ultimately understands that everyone, including May, takes it for granted that he and the countess have been lovers, although their relationship has never been consummated. To protect May, and with the help of the most powerful family in New York, the van der Luydens (Michael Gough and Alexis Smith), Newland's own social circle ultimately arranges to ship the countess back to Europe in order to preserve the seemliness of the rigid social status quo that she has, often quite unintentionally, violated.

### *The Age of Innocence* and Scorsese's Oeuvre

When we recall the number of Scorsese's films that are set in the past, including such recent ones as *Gangs of New York* (2002) and *The Aviator* (2004), or deal with events that are retold retrospectively, we see that, despite its superficial differences, *The Age of Innocence* is very much thematically consistent with many of his other films. As with other Scorsese films, *The Age of Innocence* positions its central characters in a quite particular social group, then, in turn, positions that social group in its period setting. This done, Scorsese's approach to his subject is often ironic, using the period setting to expose the hypocrisies of the society and even of the central characters themselves.[5] With *The Age of Innocence*, Scorsese appears initially to be dealing with material that is quite unlike what we think of as his primary concerns. In Newland, we have the antithesis of the extremely angry central male characters we find in, for example, *Taxi Driver* (1976), *Raging Bull*

(1980), *Goodfellas* (1990), or *Casino* (1995). Yet, while *The Age of Innocence* might seem far removed from these worlds, it is, in fact, connected to them in important ways. The society in which Newland, May, and Ellen move is just as codified and conventionalized as the one Henry Hill (Ray Liotta) encounters with the Mafia in *Goodfellas* or Howard Hughes (Leonardo DiCaprio) encounters in the Hollywood depicted in *The Aviator.* In *The Age of Innocence,* as elsewhere in Scorsese's oeuvre, the central characters' thoughts, hopes, and actions are scrutinized by a surrounding social group whose values are the dominant values and whose decisions will inexorably win out, whatever the central characters might themselves hope for. While it is true that *The Age of Innocence* is a period film—and was, in fact, a period novel since Wharton set it in the 1870s when she wrote it in 1920—the point of the period setting is to underline the ironic insight that it affords into the events of the narrative. In fact, the very title of the novel and film is ironic since innocent is precisely what this age described by Wharton and re-visioned by Scorsese is not. Rather, the character of the age is small-minded, self-regarding, pompous, judgmental, and rule bound.

Consider how the main themes of *Goodfellas,* for example, parallel those of *The Age of Innocence.* Both stories are told retrospectively, both films show how the central protagonists are defeated by the social struc-tures and expectations in which they are mired, and both films focus on male protagonists who realize too late the true meaning of the situations in which they find themselves. It is hard to miss how completely Newland and Ellen, in attempting to comply with the dominant moral conventions of their society, fail to achieve personal happiness and also fail in any way to loosen the social constraints that deny them whatever happiness might have been available to them. Late in the narrative, after following Ellen to Boston, Newland complains that she has given him a glimpse of what he calls a "true" life. But, having glimpsed a true life that he is unable to live, he is forced to realize that the life he is actually leading is a false one. Life lived in conformity with dominant social conventions—the very conventions that keep them apart—has become for Newland a false life. He asks how such a life can be endured. Ellen replies simply: "I am enduring it." For, after all, they are both obligated by the expectations of their society to lead lives that are false to their own feelings and desires.

## Ironic Observation

Scorsese does not exhibit a single approach to subject matter or style in his film oeuvre, but certain themes and motifs appear often. One that figures prominently in *The Age of Innocence* is the camera's fascinated examination of the fictional world of the characters, suggesting the degree to which their actions are to be explained in terms of the details—social, economic, familial, and other—that regulate their lives. In *The Age of Innocence,* we see every sort of material object or possession in the lives of the central characters. The film begins at the opera, with Scorsese's camera focused on details of attire, notably decorative objects such as jewelry, gloves, boutonnieres, pocket watches, and the thematically significant opera glasses. Collectively, these details introduce us to the social class of the film's characters. Close attention is paid to attire and the question of its appropriateness. May worries that her American gowns might make her look ridiculous during her honeymoon in London, while, earlier, Ellen begs off attending the ball following the opera held by Julius Beaufort (Stuart Wilson) and his wife, Regina (Mary Beth Hurt), believing her European dress is not smart enough for stuffy New York society. The camera seems fascinated by furnishings and decor, observing the wall coverings and furniture and, perhaps most especially, the art displayed in all the major townhouses. It is equally attentive to the formal portraits hung in the Beauforts' and van der Luydens' houses as it is to the paintings of dogs hung in the home of May's dog-fancying grandmother, Mrs. Manson Mingott (Miriam Margolyes). Art, like attire, tends to raise the question of just what is considered proper. The decision by Julius Beaufort, who himself has a dubious past and "passes" as an Englishman, to hang a large painting of female nudes by the (real-life) contemporary French artist Adolphe Boug-ereau (1825–1905) in plain sight in his crimson drawing room is thought to reveal his lack of taste. Of course, the real target of the film's irony here is not Beaufort, who, in fact, shows himself to have a European sensibility about art, but the New Yorkers who reveal themselves to be "squares" made uncomfortable by the painting's sexual content.

Indeed, the location and decor of houses function as indices of characters' lives and values. Ellen is told she must move from her rented house because the neighborhood is not fashionable enough. When she asks Newland why the family wants her to move, he points out that it is not enough for a neighborhood to be respectable, which hers is. But he admits that decisions about what counts as fashionable tend to be made by people who have little else to occupy themselves. We can conclude that it is some social whim rather than any sort of good sense that results in such a judgment. Another example of the pressure of idiosyncratic social decorum on individual choices is Mrs. Manson Mingott's house, situated in the neighborhood of "the Central Park," as the narrator describes it—at that time, a part of the city very far north of the fashionable areas preferred by the Archers and the Wellands. To make matters worse, the Mingott house is still considered "controversial" because it is built of pale cream stone rather than brown.

## Social Semiotics

From the initial moments of the film, we realize just how much value is placed on material objects and, in particular, on how they call attention to a character's social position, taste, and interests. Like Wharton, Scorsese understands the semiotics of New York society. Unspoken and almost automatic judgments are made on the basis of what sort of cutlery or plate you use on a given occasion, the street where your house is located, whom you receive and at what time—even how you enter a room or move around in it. Throughout, the film is replete with floral and culinary motifs. Scorsese's visual style makes tangible the degree to which even the close-up of Newland's hand adjusting the position of the gardenia in his lapel is significant. In this social milieu, all such choices constitute signs to be read and deciphered. To mention only two sequences that emphasize this attention to material detail, consider the range of information we discover in the sequence dealing with Mrs. Mingott's plans to host a dinner to introduce Ellen to New York society—an invitation that New York society unanimously declines—and the following sequence, which involves the comparably exhaustive examination of the preparations of the van der Luydens, who, to redress the slight to Mrs. Mingott's family by the snubbing of Ellen, compel New York society to attend a dinner that she has been invited to as a guest. Scorsese documents the range of choices made by both Mrs. Mingott and the van der Luydens, choices about flowers, cutlery, cuisine, footmen, the exact plates for the place settings. These are all decisions made with a view to impressing their New York peers. But, finally, it is not these decisions about what to serve and what to serve it on that are most significant. Rather, what matters is that Mrs. Mingott, considered the "dowager empress" of New York society, is unable to compel society to attend a dinner for Ellen Olenska. As the narrator observes, New York is a "hieroglyphic world." Its "arbitrary signs" are not subtle. The unanimous rejection of Mrs. Mingott's invitation is clearly not subtle. Rather, as the narrator suggests, it is "an eradication."

The participation of the van der Luydens in Ellen's subsequent rehabilitation is a telling instance of the influence of hierarchy within a social elite. The refusal by all the best society to attend Mrs. Mingott's party offends Newland because of the attitude it expresses both about Ellen and, by extension, about May's family. We can infer that he is upset on behalf of May and on behalf of Ellen, given his ties to both. Thus, along with his mother, he decides to seek redress through the most powerful and influential family in New York. One might just get away with snubbing Mrs. Mingott. After all, she is as unconventional as New York society is prepared to accept, despite her blood ties to so many of its members. But to snub the van der Luydens would be tantamount to removing oneself from New York society altogether. As the film's narrator acerbically remarks: "When the van der Luydens chose, they knew how to give a lesson." The lesson that they choose to give is that Ellen should be accepted back into society because she has the support of her family despite her adventures in Europe.

Another theme that recurs in Scorsese's oeuvre concerns the way in which social groups often operate by means of very complex conventions of observation and judgment. It is hardly surprising, for example, in his gangster films, that a sensible gangster would want to be acutely aware of what others in his milieu are doing. To fail to be scrupulously attentive means that one could end up dead, as we see, for instance, in *Goodfellas* and *Casino*. Newland Archer's social group is equally intent on observing, speculating, deducing, gossiping, and making judgments, even though, as the film's narrator archly observes, their social harmony "could be shattered by a whisper." Even Archer is not immune to these tendencies, thinking ill of the Beauforts and Lefferts of his world, while some of the most extended gossip we encounter in the film concerning Ellen Olenska comes from Newland's mother (Siân Phillips) and sister (Carolyn Farina) when Sillerton Jackson (Alec McCowen) dines with the Archers. As the narrator relates, Archer's family holds on to "the old ways." They are, thus, caught between defending someone who is related to Newland's fiancée and being keen to know all the most recent damning gossip about her.

That everyone is busy observing and judging is made quite clear in the film's opening scenes at the opera. In New York, a night at the opera is also a night that affords the opportunity to observe others and gossip with friends; only occasionally do some prominent members of the audience bother to attend to what is occurring onstage, using their opera glasses to range over the audience instead of watching the stage. Little wonder that the decision by May's mother, Mrs. Welland, to bring her niece Ellen to the opera with May is considered by both Lefferts and the old gossip, Jackson, to be pre-eminently worthy of discussion. As Jackson says to Lefferts: "I didn't think the Mingotts would have tried it out." (Here he is referring to the Mingott clan, as Mrs. Welland is Mrs. Mingott's daughter.) When the question arises as to whether Ellen Olenska will be brought to the Beauforts' annual ball, to be held later the same evening, it is agreed that, if that happens, the talk will be of little else. Newland overhears their remarks and thinks it would show support for May and her mother if he paid them a visit in their box. This marks his first meeting with the adult Ellen Olenska. For Newland, simply entering Mrs. Welland's box is intended to serve as a sign, a reprimand of sorts, to Lefferts and Jackson. As with material possessions, so with actions: in Archer's world, one's actions are often intended to mean something, and, even if they are not so intended, it is a fair guess that they will be interpreted as meaning something.

The one character who appears not to have a proper grasp of this social semiotics is the countess herself. Although she grew up in the same circle as May and Newland, her time in Europe has made her less than fluent in the unwritten codes of New York society. She discovers that New York society is a labyrinth when she thought it was "all straight up and down like Fifth Avenue, all the cross streets numbered and big honest labels on everything." Thus, Ellen is in a distinctly awkward situation. On the one hand, she is plainly aware of how rule governed and conventional New York society is. On the other hand, she is unable always to recognize the rules she ought to be following. One might say that Ellen is inclined to treat the various rules as arbitrary conventions rather than urgent matters of propriety. She suffers, as she says, from having been too independent. She does not willfully break the rules of her extended family; rather, she is often unaware that there is a rule she should be observing. So, despite the power of the van der Luydens and the efforts of Newland and Mrs. Archer to persuade them to help counter the snubbing of both Ellen and Mrs. Mingott, Ellen arrives casually and late to the van der Luydens' dinner. It appears simply not to occur to her that her behavior is disrespectful, not only of the van der Luydens, but of their cousin, an English duke, who was supposed to be the real focus of the evening. If this were not bad enough, after an extended conversation with the duke, whom she had previously known in Europe, Ellen does the unthinkable: she stands up and walks across the drawing room to sit beside Newland, where they engage in animated conversation. To leave the guest of honor is itself a violation of social norms, but, in addition to that, in New York society women are expected never to initiate such an action, certainly not to seek out the company of another male guest. By crossing the room to join Newland, Ellen violates a rule and is observed and judged by everyone present. To compound the situation, Ellen tells Newland that the duke is the most boring man she has ever met, and, instead of censuring her, Newland laughs with delight at her frankness. Her failure to recognize what counts as either correct or incorrect plagues Ellen and is already signaled when, at the beginning of the film, on being reintroduced to Newland in Mrs. Welland's opera box, Ellen casually reaches out her hand for Newland to kiss. An awkward pause indicates that he is unable or unwilling to kiss Ellen on the hand, perhaps judging the gesture to be too intimate. Finally, he takes her hand to shake. A gesture that in Europe Ellen would have given no thought to means something altogether more in America. It is noteworthy that the characters who most regularly use this gesture are associated with Europe, for instance, the van der Luydens' cousin the duke. Julius Beaufort kisses on the hand not only Ellen but old Mrs. Mingott as well.

## The Meaning of Signs

The social semiotics that characterize New York society are typified by any number of conventionally recognized actions and signs. Perhaps it is not surprising that Newland's developing relationship with Ellen comes to be characterized by a set of signs as well, but ones that are private to the two of them. Since theirs is a new relationship, a certain difficulty ensues in determining just what counts as a sign and also what counts as correctly interpreting it. A case in point concerns the flowers that Newland and Julius Beaufort both send to Ellen. The evening after the van der Luydens' dinner party, Newland visits Ellen at her house. She becomes sad during their conversation and starts to cry, in response to which Newland sympathetically puts his hand on hers and calls her by her first name. Afterward, on his way home, he stops at a florist to arrange for his daily bouquet of lilies of the valley to be sent to May. While there, he decides to send a bouquet of yellow roses to Ellen. Later, he tells May he has done so, asking if what he has done is right, and she says that of course it is. Not long after, Ellen is in a box at the theater along with the Beauforts, Larry Lefferts, and Sillerton Jackson. Newland has a seat in the orchestra. He is summoned by Regina Beaufort to join them. The play they have been watching features the tearful parting of lovers. Quietly, Ellen says to Newland, seeming to be referring to the characters onstage: "Do you think her lover will send her a box of yellow roses tomorrow?" Thus, Ellen opens the possibility that she and Newland could be lovers, with the bouquet of yellow roses being the sign. When Newland goes later to look for yellow roses, there are none in New York, so the meaning of this sign is left in limbo. Sometime later, Ellen finds a large bouquet of red roses and a card from Beaufort awaiting her at home when she returns with Newland to continue the discussion about divorcing the count. Ellen dramatically insists that her maid take the bouquet to a family down the street, recognizing that, in Newland's eyes, accepting red roses from Beaufort would signal that she might, in fact, be his mistress.

A less dramatic example of the role played by significant motifs can be seen the day Newland goes out to the country, hoping to arrange a seemingly coincidental meeting with Ellen. Driving up to the house where she is staying, he initially walks into the garden, where he sees a parasol that has been left behind. Imagining it to be Ellen's, he gently picks it up and kisses it. The irony here, quickly revealed, is that it is not Ellen's parasol at all but rather one that belongs to a girl from the same house who thanks Newland for finding it for her. A much more important motif is the key that Newland sends to Ellen after they have determined, late in the film, that she will come to him "one time" and then go home to Europe. Newland arranges for the key to be delivered to Ellen, but it is returned in an unopened envelope with no explanation. The question becomes, What does this action mean? Why has Ellen seemingly changed her mind? Newland can only speculate. It is not until several days later that he discovers the meaning of what Ellen has done. May has told Ellen that she is pregnant, although, when she does so, May does not yet know for certain. The belief that her cousin might be pregnant causes Ellen to change her mind about consummating her relationship with Newland.

The social semiotics of New York society have the effectiveness they do in the film because of the film's overall narrative structure, a structure that draws our attention to the various social forces that govern the actions of the central characters, notably, Newland and Ellen. Granted, this is something that Scorsese inherits from Wharton, but how he uses it to illustrate the society's stringent and often hypocritical conventions is what makes the film so powerful. I will discuss the film's coda, set many years after the end of the main events of the film, in a moment. But the structure of the body of the film goes roughly like this. At the beginning of the film, in response to the nasty gossip of Lefferts and Jackson, Newland aims to teach them a lesson by going across to speak to Mrs. Welland, May, and Ellen in their opera box. His action is duly noted by Lefferts and Jackson, who clearly recognize Newland's intention, although they decline to take the lesson. Later, the van der Luydens' lavish dinner to which Ellen is invited is meant as a lesson for their social peers: a lesson in how to host a dinner party and a lesson about how their peers should treat Ellen and her extended family, including Mrs. Mingott, the Wellands, and, indeed, even the Archers. I would argue that these two scenes frame the action of the beginning of the film. What frames the end of the main action of the film is the farewell dinner for Ellen, which is arranged by May under the pretext that she is simply doing what is right to honor her beloved cousin. What May and everyone else in their elite social circle are doing is analogous to attending a funeral to make sure the dear departed is really dead. The farewell dinner is the public way of signifying the general satisfaction felt by everyone that Ellen is going to be returned to Europe. When Newland realizes this—when he realizes not only that it is quite false that Ellen is "among friends" but that, worse yet, he is judged to be on the same level as the other adulterers, Lefferts and Beaufort—he realizes that May and their circle have, in fact, conspired to teach him a lesson. At the end of the evening, after Newland has offered to escort Ellen, the van der Luydens intervene to take Ellen home in their carriage. Whereas initially the van der Luydens had been central in rehabilitating Ellen, now they are equally central in orchestrating her return to Europe. Lefferts and Jackson pass Newland, smug and satisfied since they are fully aware of the lesson that Newland has been taught.

I said that I would return to the film's coda and, in doing so, have more to say about the semiotics of Newland's relationship with Ellen. Here, I want to focus on just two sequences of the film. The first occurs a year and a half after Newland's marriage to May, when he imagines that he has gotten over what he himself describes as "the madness of Madame Olenska." Everyone is in Newport, even obese Mrs. Manson Mingott. Newland and May visit her grandmother, with whom Ellen is staying. It turns out that Ellen is not in the house, and Mrs. Mingott directs Newland to go out onto the property to search for her. She is by the water, having walked out to the end of a pier to watch the sunset. Newland discovers her but does not go to greet her. Rather, he waits at some distance for a sign from Ellen. As the narrator tells us: "He gave himself a single chance." A boat is passing on the water, and Newland determines that Ellen must turn to acknowledge him before it passes a nearby lighthouse. She does not turn, and he goes back to rejoin his family, claiming he was unable to find her. Later, he learns that the two of them were working with contrary strategies. Ellen explains that she knew full well that Newland had arrived and so had gone to the end of the pier explicitly to encourage him to seek her out. This episode is something Newland remembers years later, during the film's coda, which takes place in Paris. May has died in the interim, and Newland is in Paris briefly with one of their sons. Newland is astonished to learn that his son has actually contacted the countess and arranged for them to visit her late one afternoon at her flat. Father and son arrive at the small square in front of the countess's building. Newland does not go up directly with his son. Instead, he sits on a bench and determines which windows must belong to her. While doing so, he recalls the moment in Newport but imagines a different outcome, namely, Ellen turning with a welcoming smile to greet him. By this time, he realizes, his son will have made it to the top floor and told Ellen that Newland is still downstairs in the square. Newland is willing Ellen to give him a sign, to come to her balcony and wave him up. She does not come. Rather, a servant closes her curtains against the late afternoon sunlight. Newland walks away. In the end, he would rather live with his memories of Ellen than meet her again at a time when, as a widower, he would, in fact, be able, if he chose, to rekindle their romance.

## What May and Ellen Represent

Newland is originally torn between May and Ellen because of what each of them represents. Newland chooses May because she is an insider, someone who is completely emblematic of his society. Yet, at the same time, he is bewitched by Ellen in large measure because she is an outsider. He finds himself caught between wanting to belong within his social elite and wanting to flee from it. The paradoxical upshot is that he can do neither success-fully. Newland cannot fully belong to his social elite because he has enough imagination to wish it were otherwise, thus violating its most important unspoken rule, to accept it as it is. Nor can Newland abandon it because it has indelibly shaped everything he is and knows and values. In many ways, it is Newland himself who represents the innocence referred to by the film's title. May, whom he believes to be without imagination or power, ultimately takes control of their marriage, while Ellen, whom he knows full well to pos-sess imagination, is unable, owing to her love for him, to effect any change in either of their circumstances that could potentially bring them together. In short, Ellen is unable to encourage him to hurt those he would have to hurt if he were to abandon May for her. Thus, ironically, the status quo is preserved by the combined machinations of society and the inability of either Newland or Ellen to violate its conventions.

In representing a society that operates by unspoken codes and rules, it is Scorsese's skills as a filmmaker and his inspired use of Joanne Woodward's laconic delivery of the omniscient narrator's observations that combine to help us understand the film's main themes. Scorsese's film style, especially the sorts of visual observation I have described, and the omniscient narrator's description of actions and motivations combine to illustrate the social semi-otics of New York society. The central characters reveal themselves through their actions, as interpreted by the camera, and what is not shown is told to us by the narrator, who is clearly detached from the characters in question. The narrator's first observation—"It invariably happened as it always hap-pened in those days, in the same way"—goes a long way toward situating us in relation to this fictional world, where decorum is maintained by means of repetition and the ritualization of social action. Taken together, the actions of characters and the details of the film's mise-en-scène cannot be understood independently of the codes and conventions that regulate behavior in this social group. Characters' actions and the details of setting, costume, and so forth function as signs within a broader system that governs individual behavior. So, while it is true that the meaning and significance of any given code or convention may be assigned and is, in that sense, arbitrary in its construction (e.g., the preference for brown as opposed to cream-colored stone), such codes are central to our understanding of the society that assigns them their meaning and value. My reason for devoting so much attention to the details of the film is to illustrate how Scorsese positions us to judge the characters and their actions. As previously mentioned, the film begins at the opera, establishing the notion of behavior as performance, a recurring motif. The characters of *The Age of Innocence* observe and judge one another. Scorsese takes this sort of observation and judgment to a higher level. Where the Leffertes, the Jacksons, and, indeed, even the Archers of this world judge one another, Scorsese's film judges them.

## Notes

1. The idea that films philosophize is defended in, e.g., Thomas Wartenberg, "Beyond *Mere* Illustration: How Films Can Be Philosophy," *Journal of Aesthetics and Art Criticism* 64 (2006): 19–32. Others have presented arguments that are closely aligned with the position Wartenberg is defending, e.g., Noël Carroll, "The Wheel of Virtue: Art, Literature, and Moral Knowledge," *Journal of Aesthetics and Art Criticism* 60 (2000): 3–36. A contrary view, which I find quite persuasive, is offered in Paisley Livingston, "Theses on Cinema as Philosophy," *Journal of Aesthetics and Art Criticism* 64 (2006): 11–18. Others who would argue against the idea that narrative fiction films can be philosophy include Peter Lamarque and Stein Haughom Olsen, *Truth, Fiction, and Literature* (Oxford: Clarendon, 1994).

2. Again, see Carroll, "The Wheel of Virtue," and Wartenberg, "Beyond *Mere* Illustration."

3. See my "*The Third Man*: Ethics, Aesthetics, and Irony," in *Ethics in Film*, ed. Ward Jones and Samantha Vice (Oxford: Oxford University Press, forthcoming). For related thoughts on disanalogies between philosophical thought experiments and films, see Murray Smith, "Film Art, Argument, and Ambiguity," *Journal of Aesthetics and Art Criticism* 64 (2006): 33–42.

4. Philosophers including Martha Nussbaum and ethical critics of literature including Wayne C. Booth regard many works of literary fiction as contributing to debates in moral philosophy. See, e.g., Martha Nussbaum, *Love's Knowledge: Essays on Philosophy and Literature* (Oxford: Oxford University Press, 1990), and Wayne C. Booth, *The Company We Keep: An Ethics of Fiction* (Berkeley and Los Angeles: University of California Press, 1988). I argue against ethical criticism in "Intersections: Philosophy and

Literature; or, Why Ethical Criticism Prefers Realism," in *Literary Philosophers? Borges, Calvino, Eco,* ed. Jorge Gracia, Carolyn Korsmeyer, and Rodolph Gasché (New York: Routledge, 2003), 15–25.

5. Scorsese appears in a cameo role in *The Age of Innocence,* as the photographer hired to take the wedding photographs of Newland and May. This is a very short scene, but thematically rich. The photographer creates an image with a recognized social significance, to publicly record their marriage to one another. Yet, like everything else in this society, the wedding photograph is a carefully staged event. And it records only the external aspects of that event. It tells us nothing about the real circumstances of Newland's marriage to May, especially in terms of its impact on his inner life and his conflictedness with respect to his love for Ellen. In the film, Scorsese puts himself in the role of recording the triumph of New York society's traditional expectations over the reality of Newland's situation. Little wonder that, a bit later in the film, the narrator remarks that Newland feels "buried alive under his future." The role Scorsese has given himself seems to be totally neutral—the photographer records events as if they were self-evident. His role as filmmaker is just the reverse, exposing the conventions of the society and actions he observes.

# *After Hours*
## Scorsese on Absurdity
*Jennifer L. McMahon*

Martin Scorsese is best known for films like *Taxi Driver* (1976), *Raging Bull* (1980), *Goodfellas* (1990), and *Mean Streets* (1973). These films are classic Scorsese to the extent that they foreground dramatic themes with which the director is clearly preoccupied, namely, themes of violence, corruption, and moral decay. While these films do have tremendous allure, this essay focuses on a film for which Scorsese has received less acclaim, one that is also in a genre not commonly associated with him. The film is *After Hours* (1985), the genre comedy.[1] In this essay, I argue that, through the highly palatable medium of comedy, *After Hours* successfully reveals the unpalatable truth that, at any moment, humans are vulnerable to the appearance of absurdity.

### The Philosophy of the Absurd

Before I can illustrate how *After Hours* reveals the existential truth of absurdity, it is necessary to offer some background on the concept of absurdity itself. After all, while most are familiar with the word *absurdity,* not all are familiar with its philosophical usage. While absurdity can be found in other types of philosophical writing, it is seen most frequently in the works of existential philosophers. Indeed, absurdity is one of the most prominent themes in existentialism, one that is addressed—though sometimes by a different name—in the works of such well-known existential philosophers as Friedrich Nietzsche, Søren Kierkegaard, Jean-Paul Sartre, and Albert Camus. With only the rare exception, existentialist philosophers contend that existence is absurd, in other words, that existence lacks any discernible order, meaning, or purpose.

While there is disagreement between the religious and the secular branches of existentialism regarding the ultimate nature of absurdity, both factions agree that humans experience their existence as being absurd.[2] As such, both see awareness of absurdity as characteristic of the human condition. Interestingly, though the differences are greatest between secular and religious existentialists, even existentialists within the same general category do not all view absurdity in the same way. For example, Jean-Paul Sartre and Albert Camus define *absurdity* differently (though compatibly).[3]

For Sartre, absurdity is a state of affairs. Existence is absurd because it lacks any inherent design, meaning, or end point. In *Being and Nothingness* and elsewhere, Sartre links the notion of absurdity to the notion of contingency. For Sartre, existence is absurd primarily because it is contingent (e.g., unnecessary). To say that existence is contingent is to say that it has no reason for being, that it could have been other than it is, indeed, that it did not have to be at all. According to Sartre, when one acknowledges the contingency of existence, one immediately apprehends its absurdity, and this realization of absurdity causes anguish. He states: "The essential thing is contingency." But at the same time he describes absurdity as the "key to existence."[4] Sartre states that, on recognizing contingency and its consequent, absurdity, "all the guard rails collapse": "[I realize that] I do not have nor can I have recourse to any value against the fact that it is I who sustain values in being. . . . In anguish I apprehend myself . . . as not being able to derive the meaning of the world except as coming from myself."[5]

Rather than characterize absurdity as a state of affairs, Camus contends that absurdity is a "feeling." For Camus, the feeling of absurdity emerges only within the context of a particular relation. He asserts that the feeling of absurdity "springs from a comparison." Specifically, "the absurd is born of [the] confrontation between the human need [for order] and the unreasonable silence of the world." Thus, instead of claiming that existence itself is absurd (in a manner similar to Sartre's), Camus states: "This world in itself is not reasonable, that is all that can be said. But what is absurd is the confrontation of this irrational and the wild longing for clarity whose call echoes in the human heart. The absurd depends as much on man as on the world." Likewise, where Sartre attributes the revelation of absurdity primarily to the discovery of contingency, Camus asserts that a variety of things can disclose the absurd. Principally, he cites awareness of one's mortality, the repetition of a "mechanical life," the "primitive hostility" of nature, and the strangeness of individuals (even ourselves).[6]

Though Sartre and Camus hold different views of absurdity, both agree that humans normally deny absurdity because of the discomfort it creates.

As mentioned previously, Sartre argues that awareness of absurdity causes anguish. He asserts that our "essential and immediate behavior with respect to anguish is flight" and that we try to "veil the enormous absurdity of existence."[7] When man discovers that "he is alone, without gain, without a past, with an intelligence which is clouded, [and] a body which is disintegrating . . . he . . . carefully buil[ds] up, furnishe[s], and pad[s] his nightmare."[8] In *Being and Nothingness,* Sartre enumerates the various veils and forms of "distraction" that individuals use to flee the truth of the human condition, classifying these behaviors under the generic term *bad faith.*[9]

Like Sartre, Camus believes that most people try to deny absurdity. Though he contends that an awareness of absurdity can strike at any moment, he recognizes that, when it does, most people do whatever they have to do in order to suppress it and that most do so successfully. This victory comes at a price. As indicated, Camus believes that the absurd is born of a relation. Indeed, he envisions the absurd as an equation. For Camus, absurdity is produced when one combines a rational agent possessing rational hopes and expectations with an arational world that cannot fulfill the aspirations of the rational agent. In order to eradicate absurdity, one must annihilate one of the necessary terms of the equation. In "An Absurd Reasoning," Camus devotes most of his attention to the radical "solution" of suicide. However, he also contends that the more standard response to absurdity is psychological denial, which he deems "philosophical suicide." As Camus explains, philosophical suicide can be achieved in a variety of ways, the common feature being a "negation of human reason." Whether one holds tight to the illusion of an ordered universe, takes a religious leap of faith, or just keeps busy so as to avoid thinking about the nature of existence, one is committing philosophical suicide, a solution to absurdity achieved via "a sacrifice of the intellect" and a "masking [of] the evidence."[10]

While both Sartre and Camus acknowledge that denial of absurdity can assuage feelings of anxiety, neither regards it as a permanent or ideal solution. Denial is not the preferred response to absurdity largely because it leaves individuals vulnerable to, and ill prepared for, the reappearance of the absurd. For both authors, absurdity is an existential fact. As such, it can be eluded, but not annihilated. Despite subtle differences in the ways in which they characterize absurdity (and more pointed differences on other existential matters), Sartre and Camus are alike in an important respect. Specifically, in their literary works, both illustrate how susceptible individuals are to the menace of absurdity and how powerful the revelation of absurdity can be. In this respect, their works bear a striking similarity to Scorsese's *After Hours.*[11]

## Portraits of Absurdity

Arguably, one could draw comparisons between *After Hours* and any number of works of existential fiction. The mindless repetition that characterizes the daily life of *After Hours*'s protagonist echoes that seen in Camus' *The Myth of Sisyphus*. Indeed, Camus states there that "the workman of today works everyday . . . at the same tasks" and that "[his] fate is no less absurd" than that of Sisyphus eternally rolling his rock.[12] Certainly, the first scene of Scorsese's film suggests that Paul Hackett (Griffin Dunne), the protagonist, finds his occupation as absurd as Sisyphus's plight. The melancholy expression that Paul wears, coupled with the plaintive tones and somber melody of Mozart's Symphony in D Major, makes this point quite clearly. Similarly, the focus on alienation and persecution in *After Hours* mirrors that found in Camus' *The Stranger* and *The Plague* as well as works like Dostoyevsky's *Crime and Punishment* and *The Brothers Karamazov*. When reading reviews of *After Hours*, one finds numerous references to the works of Kafka, not surprising given the prominence of similar themes and the fact that some of the film's dialogue is taken directly from Kafka's *Between the Law*.[13] Regardless of which work springs to mind, *After Hours* is replete with existential elements and even alludes to works that are part of, or associated with, the existential movement.[14] In what follows, I focus exclusively on Sartre and argue that *After Hours* closely resembles the novel *Nausea* and the play *No Exit*.

The first point of similarity between *After Hours* and *Nausea* is a similarity with respect to their protagonists. Both *After Hours* and *Nausea* focus on ordinary individuals. Indeed, their protagonists are almost antiheroes by virtue of their mediocrity. *After Hours*'s protagonist, Paul Hackett, is a nondescript computer programmer who works in Manhattan. Like a drone in the hive, he is one of countless many who spend their days confined to the windowless cubicles symbolic of the modern office. Similarly, apart from his shocking red hair, there is nothing special about Sartre's protagonist, Antoine Roquentin. He is an academic without renown, living in an ordinary town, who toils away day after day at his scholarly research. Indeed, the only unusual thing about Paul and Roquentin is the circumstances they confront. As audiences are witness, their lives are subject to a sudden transformation. Without warning or any clear insight as to the cause, their lives shift from being painfully ordinary to being positively absurd. I examine these transformations momentarily. However, by virtue of their emphasis on mundane individuals, both *After Hours* and *Nausea* illustrate that even the most ordinary person is vulnerable to an "overthrow" by the absurd.

*After Hours* and *Nausea* are also comparable in that their protagonists have markedly similar experiences. Specifically, while both are ignorant of the cause, Paul and Roquentin watch as their lives transform quite suddenly from mediocre to macabre. Moreover, both are catapulted into the absurd by an event that, under most circumstances, would seem innocuous.

Paul's sojourn into the absurd begins with a chance personal encounter. After work, Paul goes to a coffee shop to read and relax. Comfortably ensconced at a table reading Henry Miller's *Tropic of Cancer,* his attention is diverted by the query of another customer. Having noticed what Paul is reading, Marcy (Rosanna Arquette) asks him about the book. The two begin a flirtatious exchange that ends with Marcy giving Paul her phone number. Though fairly ordinary, their exchange affords glimmers of the absurd. For example, Marcy is strangely inquisitive. Moreover, she comments that she is staying with a friend in SoHo, an artist known for her absurd creations, namely, plaster renditions of bagels with cream cheese. To viewers, it seems clear that Paul finds Marcy captivating in large part because of her quirky behavior and unusual associations. As the film's opening scene makes clear, he is exhausted by the status quo and is looking for an escape into something exotic, something other than his humdrum life.

Like Paul's, Roquentin's discovery of the absurd also has humble origins. His saga begins when Roquentin picks up a stone on the beach and, to his surprise, finds himself overwhelmed with feelings of disgust and fear. Although he initially passes off his experience with the stone as "ridiculous" and a "passing moment of madness," he is soon subject to far more disturbing situations. For example, he shakes the hand of a friend and reports in horror that it feels like a "fat, white worm." Later, he seizes a doorknob and is terrified when it seems to take hold of him, to capture him with a "sort of personality." Later, he sits at the bar and for over half an hour is afraid to look at his glass of beer. Needless to say, these experiences lead Roquentin to question whether he is "insane."[15]

Just as Paul's and Roquentin's initial brushes with absurdity are catalyzed by a seemingly innocuous contact, so too do their experiences become increasingly absurd, even surreal.[16] Paul's encounter with absurdity is foreshadowed when he meets and then calls Marcy. Indeed, it is in pursuit of Marcy that Paul happens unsuspectingly into the world of the absurd. Absurdity is evident in *After Hours* in any number of examples. These examples build on, and relate to, one another in such a way as to create the comic effect of the film. The first event in the comic sequence occurs when Paul takes a taxi to meet Marcy in SoHo. Intent on completing some personal grooming, Paul sets the money for his fare, a twenty-dollar bill, on the partition between the front and back seats. A rush of wind blows the bill out the window. We discover that apart from ninety-seven cents in change, this is the only money Paul has. Arriving at the apartment of Marcy's friend Kiki (Linda Fiorentino), Paul's monetary misfortune transforms into an absurdity when he discovers that his twenty-dollar bill has attached itself to Kiki's life-size papier-mâché sculpture of a male figure, a figure that is, as Paul remarks, reminiscent of Munch's *The Scream.*

Things become more absurd as the evening continues. Though things don't go too badly between Paul and Marcy at first, allusions to serious burns, the discovery of a suspicious tube of cream, and Marcy's references to a past rape she enjoyed soon incline Paul to decide that things are too strange for him. He exits without telling Marcy. As he departs, absurdity strikes again as Paul, attempting to return home, enters the subway terminal to find that the base fare has—without his knowledge—increased to a dollar fifty (remember that he has only ninety-seven cents).

Unable to get home, and seeking refuge from the pouring rain, Paul enters a bar and meets an amiable bartender—and boyfriend to Marcy—Tom (John Heard). Tom is willing to loan Paul the money to get home. Here, absurdity is made evident again as Tom cannot open the register and, in sending Paul to get the key from his apartment, inadvertently leads Paul to become the prime suspect in a rash of burglaries.[17] The pace quickens from this point on as the absurdities compound. Consider these examples: On his way back to the bar, Paul sabotages what he assumes is the robbery of Kiki's statue. On returning the statue (a physically comic scene), Paul finds Kiki tied up, presumably by the thieves, only to learn that the robbery was a legitimate sale and that he has interrupted Kiki in a sadomasochistic tryst. After extricating himself from that awkward situation, Paul discovers that Marcy has committed suicide (presumably at his unannounced departure), calls 911, and, with Kiki now absent, politely posts signs that read: "Dead person here." On returning to the bar and finding it closed, Paul takes refuge at the apartment of retro waitress Julie (Teri Garr), who seems strange but likable, until we see her bed surrounded with mousetraps and learn that she has placarded the neighborhood with posters identifying Paul as the serial robber.

After taking leave of Julie, Paul meets, then narrowly escapes from, Gail (Catherine O'Hara), who, after agreeing to give him a ride home in her ice-cream truck, sees Paul's face on one of Julie's wanted posters. She blows the whistle (literally) on Paul to the neighborhood watch, a group that is now turned vengeful mob. The absurdity of the evening then finds its completion when, in an attempt to elude the marauding band of "conscientious" citizens set on his apprehension, Paul consents to let himself be made into a papier-mâché figure. Although he eludes the mob, Paul finds not escape but entrapment at the hands of an artist, June (Verna Bloom), who decides to keep him captive. In the film's last absurd and deeply comic twist, the enpapered Paul is stolen by the true serial thieves, Neil and Pepe (Cheech Marin and Tommy Chong), who, in their rush to escape, take a corner too fast and lose Paul out the back of their dilapidated van.[18] Released on impact, Paul emerges from his papier-mâché prison to find dawn breaking and himself in front of the doors of his office. He shakes the dust from his suit and enters the office as the closing credits roll.

Like Paul, Roquentin is also subject to the onslaught of the absurd and the transfiguration of his existence. Though the attack in *Nausea* is not as swift or satirical as that in *After Hours,* it is every bit as severe. As mentioned previously, the encounter with absurdity begins when Roquentin picks up a stone and feels powerfully and surprisingly "alarmed." Unable to shake what he describes as a "sort of nausea," he states: "Something has happened to me . . . it came cunningly, little by little . . . now it's blossoming." According to Roquentin, what begins as "a crowd of small metamorphoses accumulat[ing] in me" soon turns into a "veritable revolution." Unsure what is happening, and "afraid of what will be born," he decides to try to determine the "exact extent and nature of [the] change" affecting him.[19]

Unfortunately, his attempts to analyze things rationally do not offer Roquentin any reprieve from his unsettling situation. Instead, things becomes worse as he is attacked by absurdity from all quarters. As he states, his life takes on a "jerky, incoherent aspect" and becomes increasingly surreal. Indeed, he says that he feels as if he is "surrounded by cardboard scenery which could quickly be removed." It seems as if "anything can happen."[20]

The first thing that happens is that Roquentin's relationships to objects are compromised. Rather than retaining their normal appearance and use, objects take on a life of their own. For example, a small statuette appears to be "full of lymph," and a seat cushion looks like the bloated belly of a dead animal. In the famous scene at the root of the chestnut tree, common tree roots are perceived as "obscene [and] monstrous masses." As his life takes on a strange, hallucinogenic quality, Roquentin cries: "Things are divorced from their names. They are there, grotesque, headstrong, gigantic, and it seems ridiculous to . . . say anything at all about them. I am in the midst of things, nameless things, defenceless." He laments "the inconsistency of inanimate objects," objects that normally "fix the limits of probability" but now "[fix] nothing at all." He states: "Objects should not touch because they are not alive. You use them, put them back in place, you live among them: they are useful, nothing more. But they touch me, it is unbearable. I am afraid of being in contact with them as though they were living beasts."[21]

In an effort to escape his disturbing encounters with objects, Roquentin tries to be "close to people," stating that he is "resolved to take refuge in their midst . . . in case of emergency." However, he finds no consolation. Just as his experiences with objects have been compromised by his nausea, so too have his relationships with people. Rather than fulfill his expectation of solace, his encounters with people exacerbate his feelings of anxiety and dread. Watching people walk down the street, Roquentin notes their "inhuman" and "mechanical" appearance. Instead of offering kinship and comfort, people frighten him, appearing as "flabby masses which move spontaneously." A particularly powerful example of the change affecting his relationships occurs when he tries to find consolation in the bed of his lover, only to recoil in horror when her genitalia seem transformed into a feral garden replete with "ants . . . centipedes and ringworm."[22]

Horrified at the various metamorphoses to which he is witness, Roquentin attempts to escape into himself. This too is unsuccessful. When he looks into the mirror to get his bearings, he finds not comfort but that "nothing human is left," only "insipid flesh blossoming and palpitating with abandon." He describes what he sees as being "at the fringe of the vegetable world."[23] Later, when he sees his hand resting on the table and finds that it looks disturbingly like a crustacean, he is so unnerved he stabs himself in the hand.

Ultimately, the overwhelming feeling of nausea that affects Roquentin not only alters his experience but also leads to an increase in his understanding. As readers discover, the visceral feeling of nausea to which he is subject is the prelude to an unwanted existential revelation. As Roquentin states one of the first times he is overwhelmed with nausea: "Posed before me was a voluminous, insipid idea." Though he initially tries to evade this idea, he ultimately finds it inescapable. Near the end of the novel, he confronts his nausea and the truth that he has been trying to avoid: "I had found the key to Existence, the key . . . to my own life, . . . [It is] absurdity." Although he admits that "existence usually hides itself," during the famous scene at the root of the chestnut tree it "unveil[s] itself" to him. He states: "[Existence] had lost the harmless look of an abstract category: it was the very paste of things. . . . The diversity of things, their individuality, were only an appearance, a veneer. This veneer had melted." During this existential epiphany, Roquentin discovers that "the world of explanations and reasons is not the world of existence." He realizes that "every existing thing is born without reason . . . and dies by chance." As he sinks down on a bench, stupefied at his discovery, he states: "I knew it was the World . . . suddenly revealing itself, and I choked with rage at this gross, absurd being."[24] Perhaps even more explicitly than Paul, Roquentin comes to recognize that existence is absurd.

Like *After Hours, Nausea* escalates to a fevered pitch and has a conclusion that is anticlimactic. Despite having declared at the base of the chestnut tree that he hates "this ignoble mess," which is "mounting up, as high as the sky, spilling over, filling everything with its gelatinous slither," Roquentin ultimately concludes that the revelation of absurdity has not robbed him of the will to live. Rather, he has come to know "the real secret of existence," namely, the fact that, while existence is without reason, it is at the same time a "perfect free gift," a "fullness which man can never abandon." At the end of the novel, having "learned all [he] could know about existence," Roquentin accepts absurdity, admits nausea as his "normal state," and, like Paul, simply goes on with his life.[25]

Although there are important differences between Sartre's Roquentin and Scorsese's Paul, there are numerous important parallels, parallels that are significant with respect to the theme of absurdity. As mentioned previously, both Paul and Roquentin are painfully ordinary. By focusing on a normal person and that individual's encounter with the absurd, both Sartre and Scorsese make it clear that no one is immune from the absurd. Instead, like Camus, they emphasize that the absurd can strike anywhere, "at any street corner."[26] Similarly, to the extent that both characters are led into the absurd by a chance event, Sartre and Scorsese make it clear that existential crises—and epiphanies—can be catalyzed as easily by ordinary as by extraordinary events.

Another important parallel lies in the experiences that Paul and Roquentin have. Just as their lives are transfigured by their encounter with absurdity, they themselves are transformed. Roquentin states: "Something has happened to me. I cannot doubt it anymore."[27] Similarly, the straitlaced Paul becomes belligerent, screaming at Marcy: "Where are those plaster of paris paperweights, anyway? I mean that's what I came here to see. . . . That's what I want to see now! Because as we sit here chatting there are important papers flying rampant around my apartment!" Not surprisingly, as their experiences become increasingly strange, Paul and Roquentin become more and more agitated. As events compound to a point where they become threatening, both characters experience not only despair, hopelessness, and hostility but also persecution.

The theme of persecution is particularly important as it is made prominent in both works with notable chase scenes. In *After Hours,* Paul runs through the deserted streets, narrowly escaping the members of the local neighborhood watch, who have turned into a vigilante mob. Similarly, a terrified Roquentin is pursued through the streets of Bouville by the "thing," ostensibly a monstrous personification of his nausea. With these scenes of persecution, Sartre and Scorsese show not only that absurdity can engender powerful feelings but also that people actively try to escape it.

Another parallel between Paul and Roquentin lies in their response to absurdity. Though one can argue that Roquentin's epiphany is more certain than Paul's, it seems evident from Paul's commentary and behavior that he too has formally acknowledged the absurd and unpredictable nature of existence. Interestingly, as profoundly as Paul and Roquentin are affected by absurdity, neither one is shattered by it. Though they look into the abyss and are shaped by the encounter, neither one is lost. Both pick themselves up, brush themselves off, and go on with life.[28] To the extent that *Nausea* and *After Hours* conclude with their protagonists pressing on in the face of the absurd, both illustrate that admitting absurdity need not be fatal. Indeed, insofar as Paul and Roquentin both embody a sort of stoic resolve, *After Hours* and *Nausea* show that, while the encounter with the absurd is "bound to leave traces," "lucidity in the face of existence" can be achieved.[29]

A final similarity between Paul and Roquentin will also serve as a point of transition to the third and final work to be discussed here, namely, Sartre's *No Exit.* In *After Hours* and *Nausea,* both Paul and Roquentin experience feelings of estrangement. Specifically, as their experiences become increasingly unusual, they find it harder and harder to relate to other people. Because the circumstances they face are so incredible, they do not think it possible—or wise—to try to explain their predicament to others. Unable to share their experiences, both come to feel more and more isolated. Indeed, as things progress, others come to represent both a source of salvation and a threat. As Camus indicates, the discovery of absurdity is not only disturbing but also alienating, causing the individual to feel like a "stranger." Both Paul and Roquentin illustrate this point clearly. Similarly, both illustrate the fact that individuals often seek refuge from absurdity in their associations with others. Roquentin repeatedly goes to the bar to take comfort in human contacts. Likewise, Paul's sole goal is to find someone to take him home and away from absurdity.

## The Revelation of Absurdity

Importantly, there is a message about others that is made very evident in *After*

*Hours* that is not foregrounded in *Nausea*. While it can be found in *Nausea*, this message is seen far more clearly in Sartre's play *No Exit*. In *After Hours*, relationships with others are the primary vehicle for absurdity. This is not the case in *Nausea*. While Roquentin's relationships with others are tainted by absurdity, his discovery of absurdity issues from another source. However, in *No Exit*—as in *After Hours*—others are the principal mechanism for the revelation of absurdity. Others function in this way to the extent that the relationships that obtain between characters not only epitomize absurdity but also catalyze the main character's discovery of absurdity.

It should already be quite evident that in *After Hours* the theme of absurdity is conveyed predominantly through Paul's relationships with others. While there are occasions where the absurd is made manifest through objects, as in the scene where Paul's money flies out the window, it is more frequently the case that it is revealed through interpersonal associations. Virtually every personal encounter Paul has embodies the absurd. Though it seems fairly normal at first, Paul's relationship with Marcy comes to exemplify the absurd. From her bizarre choice of bedtime reading—Paul finds next to Marcy's bed a medical textbook with descriptions and illustrations of disfiguring burns—to her unusual ex-husband, Marcy is phenomenally strange.[30] Likewise, Marcy's roommate, Kiki, is highly unusual. When she falls asleep during Paul's provocative massage, it is a comic surprise. Similarly, when the wistful June takes Paul into her apartment, viewers hardly anticipate that he will become her prisoner. Perhaps it is this feature of surprise that makes the characters Paul meets such successful mediums for the conveyance of absurdity. Literally no one behaves as one would expect. Instead, it is as if Paul has been transported into his own personal twilight zone, where nothing, and no one, is quite normal.

In *No Exit*, Sartre invokes the same pattern. Set in hell, the play functions as an allegory illuminating the absurdity of the human condition.[31] The cast is composed of three main characters—Garcin, Inez, and Estelle. The play opens shortly after their deaths, with these individuals being transported and ultimately confined to a small, overheated, badly decorated room from which there is no exit. The play opens and closes in the same "horrible" room. Once together, the characters discover that the company of others is both intolerable and inescapable.[32] Indeed, it is from this play that the famous quotation "Hell is other people" is taken.[33] Clearly, Garcin, Inez, and Estelle abhor one another. Indeed, the play contains little other dialogue than the three bickering and baiting one another.

Like *Nausea* and *After Hours*, *No Exit* illustrates that we often look to others as bastions of hope in the midst of absurdity. In particular, it illustrates that we often try to use others as a means to escape absurdity, hoping that our relationships with them will offer us a sense of meaning and justification. This point is made evident in *No Exit* when Estelle tries to seduce Garcin in order to bolster her sense of self-worth by demonstrating that she is the desired female. Taking Garcin's arm, Estelle pleads: "My poor darling! Look at me. Please look. Touch me. Touch me." Then, taking his hand and placing it on her neck, she says emphatically: "[Trust] me." Disgusted with the display, Inez shouts: "Trust away! She wants a man—that far you can trust her—she wants a man's arm round her waist, a man's smell, a man's eyes glowing with desire. And that's all she wants."[34] Moments later, Inez herself succumbs to temptation and tries to steal Estelle away from Garcin.

No Exit is also like *After Hours* in that it illustrates that others can be threatening harbingers of absurdity. Just as Paul's security is threatened by the vengeful mob, Garcin, Estelle, and Inez threaten each other. Shortly after they find themselves together, Inez declares: "[You] see how simple it is. Childishly simple. Obviously, there aren't any physical torments. . . . We'll stay in this room together, the three of us, for ever and ever. . . . Each of us will act as the torturer of the two others." As we see, the torture to which the characters are subject is not primarily the result of actual acts of violence. Rather, it issues from their simple mutual presence. Inez cries: "To forget about the others? How utterly absurd! I feel you there in every pore. Your silence clamors in my ears. You can nail up your mouth, cut your tongue out—but [I] cannot prevent your being-there."[35] She goes on to liken being with others to being an insect caught in the burning rays of the sun.

Just as it is primarily Paul's relationships with others that advance the theme of absurdity in *After Hours,* so is it the relationship between Sartre's threesome that achieves this end in *No Exit.* For example, just as Paul has no underlying relationship to any of the characters he meets, Sartre's characters have no historical connection to one another. They embody absurdity to the extent that their placement together is arbitrary.[36] More important, once together, the play's characters both exemplify and catalyze the discovery of absurdity. Their territorial skirmishes over the deplorable sofas, their patently obvious seductions, their bumbling refusal to escape, all are comic and absurd. After trying unsuccessfully to kill one another (unsuccessful because they are all already dead), the three show that they have realized that their situation is absurd, stating: "[It's] all useless . . . how funny . . . let's get on with it."[37]

## Alternative Approaches to Absurdity

Having discussed various parallels between *After Hours* and two well-known literary works by Sartre, I must now examine a critical difference. As I have argued, *After Hours, Nausea,* and *No Exit* all make a point about absurdity. However, they do it rather differently. While not without its comic moments, *Nausea* is clearly not a comedy. It is a serious, even disturbing work. In this respect, it is like most other pieces of existential literature. Though many of these works offer character sketches or scenes for comic relief, few are comedies.[38]

*No Exit* is more difficult to characterize. While tackling weighty subjects, it takes a tone that is typically humorous. In this respect, it is very much like *After Hours,* which—albeit dark—is a clearly a comedy. This difference in tone begs the question: What medium is the best vehicle for existential revelation? Admittedly, there may be no decisive answer. Though it has always been popular, comedy has always been viewed by philosophers as an inferior means for transmitting truth.[39] Even existential philosophers who tend to challenge many traditional assumptions manifest this trend. For example, while existentialists lament their philosophy's being characterized as gloomy, they bear the bulk of the responsibility for this to the extent that they tend to favor a sober style over a comic one.[40] However, one finds reason for this preference in *The Plague.* There, Camus states through his narrator that with "fear serious reflection [begins]."[41]

Elsewhere, I have argued that there is a method in the morbidity so evident in existential literature.[42] Put simply, existentialists generally prefer to paint existence in alarming (rather than amusing) terms in order to command our attention. Their opinion is that the truths that they are attempting to reveal are so unpalatable that an ordinary person simply will not acknowledge them unless forced to do so. By portraying things in extreme terms, they attempt to capitalize on shock value in order to force their message on an unwilling—or at least resistant—audience. In short, existentialists like Sartre are likely trying to further their message by playing on their audiences' fascination with fearful spectacle.[43]

Certainly, existentialists like Sartre have had success with this methodology. It works because, as Edmund Burke states, "there is no spectacle [humans] so eagerly pursue, as that of some uncommon and grievous calamity . . . [which] always touches with delight . . . all this antecedent to any reasoning by an instinct."[44] The contemporary theorist of horror Noel

Carroll agrees that, whether by instinct or for some other reason, "[people] do seek out horror fictions for the purpose of deriving pleasure from sight and descriptions that customarily repulse them."[45] While not horror fictions in the manner of *Frankenstein* or *Psycho,* existentialist fictions often portray existence in horrifying terms. One could hardly describe some of the scenes in *Nausea* as anything but horrific. For example, Roquentin speculates: "What if something were to happen? . . . For example, the father of a family might go out for a walk, and, across the street, he'll see something like a red rag, blown towards him by the wind. And . . . he'll see that it is a side of rotten meat, grimy with dust, dragging itself along, . . . a piece of writhing flesh rolling in the gutter, spasmodically shooting out spurts of blood. . . . [Then] someone else might feel something scratching in his mouth. He goes to the mirror, opens his mouth: and his tongue is an enormous live centipede . . . [that] he will have to tear . . . out with his own hands."[46] Clearly, the vision painted is terrifying.

However, as *No Exit* suggests, Sartre commands a powerful response from audiences with an alternative approach. Arguably, with *No Exit,* Sartre adopts what many see as the stylistic opposite of horrific spectacle, namely, comedy. In *After Hours,* Scorsese makes the same choice. From an analysis of these two works, it is clear that comedy can also be an effective tool for the revelation of our existential condition. Interestingly, these works appeal to their audiences in a manner not dissimilar to the way horror appeals to its audience. Specifically, *After Hours* and *No Exit* also play on their audiences' fascination with grim spectacle. Not unlike many other comedies, these dark comedies rely on the portrayal of misfortune in order to achieve their comic effect. After all, there really isn't anything funny about being stranded in SoHo in the middle of the night, with no money, no way home, and a violent mob intent on your apprehension. Eternal damnation is even less amusing. *After Hours* and *No Exit* transform these undesirable situations into hysterical works of fiction. By modifying people's relation to something that would otherwise upset them, they allow their audiences to experience amusement rather than discontent. Specifically, by incorporating factors like comic dialogue and physical humor and, importantly, by preserving the audience's critical distance from the subject matter, they create a sense of levity in conjunction with a subject that might otherwise be tragic.

Dark comedies like *After Hours* and *No Exit* elicit an effect that is both similar and dissimilar to that elicited by horror. Clearly, the genres are different in that the overarching goal of horror fiction is to generate powerful feelings of fear and dread. While dark comedies purposively generate significant levels of discomfort, their principal intention is to compel a sense of amusement. However, horror fictions and dark comedies are alike in that they tend to draw on our perverse interest in the misfortunes of others. Whether the root of our attraction to horror fiction is a result of the adrenaline rush it engenders, the way it piques our curiosity, its use of spectacle, its ability to facilitate a cathartic release, or the simple fact that humans enjoy representation, works in this genre are a perennial favorite with audiences.[47] Dark comedies are equally popular. Like that derived from horror, the pleasure that we derive from them is complex. While not engendering the same adrenaline high as horror fiction, dark comedies also appeal to curiosity, capitalize on our attraction to spectacle, and stimulate catharsis. In particular, I would argue that, by inspiring us to laugh, dark comedies like *After Hours* help us give voice to and manage existential anxiety. Just as films like *After Hours* help us see the nature of the human condition, they also help us see the humor in it. By doing this, they can help us maintain perspective and psychological balance. Dark comedies show us some of the things that scare us most, things we might not usually want to view. By making these things funny, they foster a sense of psychological autonomy from things that might otherwise exert considerable conscious or unconscious influence. By showing us things we find unpleasant and finding ways to help us laugh about them, they can help individuals vent some of their anxieties about existence. This is extremely important to the extent that people are often discouraged from expressing, or even acknowledging, these anxieties.[48] By creating an opportunity for individuals to come to terms with certain existential facts, these works can help us realize not only that humans can live on in the face of sobering truths but also that they can live well.[49]

With respect to *After Hours,* it is through the events that affect the film's protagonist, Paul, that the film shows in a humorous manner that, on the most ordinary of days, amid the most average of circumstances, existential absurdity can be revealed. Like *Nausea, After Hours* illustrates that "we [are] a heap of living creatures, irritated, embarrassed at ourselves, we [haven't] the slightest reason to be [here] none of us, each one, confused, vaguely alarmed, [feels] in the way."[50] Like *No Exit, After Hours* illustrates that it is often others who disclose the absurd. While some existentialists might contend that adopting a comic form might carry with it the risk of losing an audience's appreciation for a work's content, I contend that there are occasions when sobering truths are assimilated more successfully when measured out in smaller—and sweeter—doses. Just as horrific portraits play on our fascination with grisly spectacle, comedy has a natural appeal. Humans like to laugh. Though there are occasions where laughter is not appropriate or productive (in an epistemic or moral sense), in certain contexts it can be both enlightening and empowering. Though Camus maintains that "seeking the truth is not seeking what is desirable,"⁵¹ *After Hours* illustrates that, if the truth can be conveyed in a palatable form, its receipt need not be repugnant. Clearly, people may well be resistant to the disclosure of absurdity. However, they will likely be less so if this truth is conveyed in a savory form.

## Notes

1. While Scorsese received best director honors for *After Hours* at the 1986 Cannes Film Festival, commentators repeatedly report that the film has been "overlooked" (Scott Weinberg, review of *After Hours,* January 15, 2003, http://ofcs.rottentomatoes.com/click/movie-1032180/reviews.php?critic=movies&sortby=default&page=1&rid=833530) and "underrated" (Mubarak Ali, "Old New York Nightmare," http://www.lumiere.net.nz/reader/item/216).

2. There are two general schools of existential thought: atheistic and religious. From the perspective of atheist existentialists, existence is absurd; there is simply no underlying order or meaning to existence. However, from the point of view of the religious existentialist, existence is not necessarily absurd; it is only experienced as such. Generally speaking, religious existentialists maintain that humans experience their existence as absurd because their limited intellect renders them incapable of apprehending the ultimate order or meaning of the universe, an order that cannot be perceived or proved but must be taken as a matter of faith.

3. Though any number of existentialists might be considered, for the purposes of this essay I focus on Sartre and Camus. I have selected Camus because he offers one of the most explicit discussions of absurdity. I have selected Sartre because there are important parallels between two of his literary works and *After Hours.*

4. Jean-Paul Sartre, *Nausea* (New York: New Directions, 1964), 131, 129. It should be noted that the passages cited are uttered by Sartre's main character, Roquentin, not Sartre himself. However, to the extent that Sartre acknowledged in interviews and his autobiography that he was Roquentin and makes analogous claims in his philosophical works, it seems safe to assume that the views expressed are Sartre's own.

5. Jean-Paul Sartre, *Being and Nothingness* (New York: Washington Square, 1956), 77–78.

6. Albert Camus, "An Absurd Reasoning," in *The Myth of Sisyphus and Other Stories* (New York: Random House, 1955), 5, 22, 21, 16, 10, 11, 11.

7. Sartre, *Being and Nothingness,* 78, and *Nausea,* 111.

8. Sartre, *Nausea,* 69.

9. Sartre, *Being and Nothingness,* 79.

10. Camus, "An Absurd Reasoning," 5, 31, 31, 28, 37.

11. At this juncture, it is necessary to pause for a moment to acknowledge the

philosophical debate concerning the heuristic value of fiction. Since the time of Plato, philosophers have debated whether fiction can educate. For most people, the claim that one can learn from fiction is likely uncontroversial. For philosophers, however, it is not. Obviously, it is beyond the scope of this essay to examine the philosophical debate about fiction in any detail or provide an exhaustive argument for the use of fiction. However, since the subsequent argument presumes that important philosophical truths are being conveyed through fiction, it must be noted that not all philosophers would accept this premise. For further discussion of the traditional opposition to fiction and arguments supporting its heuristic value, see Martha Nussbaum, *Love's Knowledge* (Oxford: Oxford University Press, 1990); David Novitz, *Knowledge, Fiction, and Imagination* (Philadelphia: Temple University Press, 1987); Wayne Booth, *The Company We Keep* (Berkeley and Los Angeles: University of California Press, 1988); Susan Feagin, *Reading with Feeling* (Ithaca, NY: Cornell University Press, 1996); and Jenefer Robinson, "L'éducation sentimentale," *Australasian Journal of Philosophy* 73, no. 2 (June 1995): 212–26.

12. Camus, *The Myth of Sisyphus,* 90.

13. Critics who liken Scorsese's *After Hours* to the works of Kafka include Roger Ebert (*Chicago Sun-Times,* October 11, 1985), Mubarak Ali ("Old New York Nightmare"), and Christopher Null (http://www.filmcritic.com/misc/emporium .nsf/ddb5490109a79f598625623d0015f1e4/81dd54bbd4c0c0b388256ac8006bd0af? OpenDocument).

14. For example, the protagonist both views and is, ultimately, made into a statue resembling the subject depicted in Edvard Munch's *The Scream.*

15. Sartre, *Nausea,* 2, 4, 2.

16. Commentators confirm this reading. For example, W. M. Frohock argues that *Nausea* takes the form "we identify . . . as surrealist" ("The Prolapsed World of Jean-Paul Sartre," in *Critical Essays on Jean-Paul Sartre,* ed. Robert Wilcocks [Boston: G. K. Hall, 1988], 165). John Fletcher describes *Nausea* as "a surrealist work" ("Sartre's *Nausée*: A Modern Classic Revisited," in ibid., 181). Likewise, James Plath describes *After Hours* as "a surreal excursion" (http://www.reel.com/movie.asp?MID=14&PID=10114813& Tab=reviews&CID=18#tabs), and Eric Henderson says that the film offers "a dreamlike, surrealist sense of encroaching hysteria" (http://www.slantmagazine.com/film/film_ review.asp?ID=1203).

17. To the extent that no one in New York City would give a perfect stranger the key to his or her apartment, this act is itself representative of absurdity.

18. In his review, Vincent Canby questions the casting in *After Hours,* remarking that Cheech and Chong "don't . . . seem to belong" (*New York Times,* September 13, 1985). However, it is my contention that Cheech and Chong are ideal for the roles of Neil and Pepe. Their appearance furthers the theme of absurdity precisely because one wouldn't expect individuals whose personalities are, as Canby puts it, "an immediate reflection of West Coast drug culture" to play the roles of serial thieves in New York City.

19. Sartre, *Nausea,* 127, 11, 4, 5, 5, 5, 1.

20. Ibid., 5, 76.

21. Ibid., 5, 125, 127, 125, 76, 76, 10.

22. Ibid., 8, 24, 111, 24, 59.

23. Ibid., 17, 17, 100.

24. Ibid., 5, 129, 127, 127, 129, 133, 134.

25. Ibid., 134, 135, 131, 133, 135, 157.

26. Camus, "An Absurd Reasoning," 9.

27. Sartre, *Nausea,* 4.

28. Paul literally brushes himself off. At the end of the film, after escaping his papier-mâché prison, he brushes the dust off his clothes and goes back to work.

29. Albert Camus, *The Plague* (New York: Random House, 1948), 259, and "An Absurd Reasoning," 4.

30. As Marcy explains to Paul, her ex-husband was obsessed with *The Wizard of Oz.* Indeed, his fascination was so great that, when he and Marcy had sexual intercourse, he used to scream out: "Surrender Dorothy!"

31. To the extent that Sartre was an atheist who did not subscribe to a belief in hell, his choice of setting is necessarily symbolic. For Sartre, humans are mortal beings who are confined to the empirical world. Though we might wish for them and take great pains to imagine them, there are, in his view, no other planes of existence to which humans have access. Sartre finds hell an appropriate symbol for existence to the extent that humans cannot escape existence and find much of it intolerable.

32. Various restrictions are present that exacerbate this effect. The quarters are cramped and hot. Confinement to a single room effectively denies the characters a reprieve from one another. Moreover, the inhabitants of hell cannot sleep. They lack eyelids and the opportunity that they offer to close the "shutter" for even a moment (Jean-Paul Sartre, *No Exit and Three Other Plays* [New York: Vintage, 1946], 5). These details are significant to the extent that they emphasize an important theme, namely, the essentiality and inescapability of what Sartre calls "being-for-others" (*Being and Nothingness,* 399). The characters themselves acknowledge their dependence on one another when, on the door's opening, all refuse to leave the room and, later, when they exclaim: "We're inseparables" (Sartre, *No Exit,* 42).

33. Sartre, *No Exit,* 45.

34. Ibid., 39, 40, 41.

35. Ibid., 17, 22.

36. The relationships are arbitrary in that none of the characters are specially selected by virtue of some relationship in life (e.g., none knew, or had a score to settle with, either of the others). Arguably, their arbitrary placement furthers Sartre's point that it is others generally who are inescapable and insufferable (as well as essential), not just certain others.

37. Sartre, *No Exit,* 46.

38. For example, in Camus' *The Stranger,* Salamano and his mangy dog are tragic characters who nonetheless provide tremendous comic relief. Similarly, the cat spitter (an elderly man who spits at cats from his balcony) and the pea counter (an asthma patient who passes the time counting peas) introduce an element of comedy in Camus'

otherwise horrifying *The Plague*. Finally, in Samuel Beckett's "tragic-comedy" *Waiting for Godot,* Estragon and Vladamir are simultaneously pitiful and hysterical.

39. For further discussion, see my "The Function of Fiction: The Heuristic Value of Homer," in *The Simpsons and Philosophy: The D'Oh of Homer,* ed. William Irwin, Mark T. Conard, and Aeon J. Skoble (Chicago: Open Court, 2001), 215–32.

40. Though I do not agree with this assessment, one need only survey the titles of the more familiar works of existentialism to understand why people have come to assume that the movement is pessimistic. Indeed, given titles like *Fear and Trembling, Sickness unto Death, Nausea, The Plague,* and *The Anti-Christ,* it is hard to draw a different conclusion without reading the works themselves.

41. Camus, *The Plague,* 22.

42. See my "*Nausea, The Plague,* and *No Exit:* The Ability of Existential Dystopias to Promote Authenticity" (paper presented at the international conference Utopias and Dystopias in Literature and the Visual Arts, Atlanta, November 1999).

43. In *A Philosophical Enquiry into the Origin of Our Ideas of the Sublime and the Beautiful,* Edmund Burke states explicitly that horrific things and scenes of spectacular violence "at certain distances, and with certain modifications, . . . are delightful" (in *Aesthetics: The Big Questions,* ed. Carolyn Korsmeyer [Oxford: Blackwell, 1998], 257). Enumerating in "Realist Horror" the features of realist horror, Cynthia Freeland states that the genre relies "chiefly upon spectacle, . . . [namely,] that we are somehow attracted to . . . horrific spectacle itself" (in ibid., 287). Finally, in *The Philosophy of Horror,* Noel Carroll asserts that horror fictions attract their audiences "by means of trafficking in the very sorts of things that [normally] cause disgust, distress, and displeasure" (in ibid., 280). It is my contention that, in this respect, a number of existential fictions are stylistically similar to works of horror.

44. Burke, *Philosophical Enquiry,* 258.

45. Carroll, *Philosophy of Horror,* 280.

46. Sartre, *Nausea,* 159.

47. For a more thorough discussion of the effects of horror fiction, see Carroll, *Philosophy of Horror,* and Freeland, "Realist Horror." It is Carroll's position that our attraction to horror is fundamentally cognitive, rooted principally in the fact that horror piques our curiosity, particularly our desire to know the unknown. It is Freeland's view that our attraction to horror is more emotional than intellectual, i.e., that it is grounded in our fascination with violence and our enjoyment of the "thrill" (287) the genre produces. Aristotle, by contrast, maintains that humans have "a natural propensity . . . to engage in mimetic activity," take "pleasure . . . in mimetic objects," and "through mimesis [take their] first steps in understanding" (*Poetics,* in *Classics in Philosophy,* ed. Louis P. Pojman [Oxford: Oxford University Press, 1998], 231). Importantly, the pleasure that humans experience in witnessing mimesis serves to explain the long-standing attraction to various forms of fiction, not merely horror. Aristotle's comments also lend credence to the claim that fiction can facilitate understanding.

48. It is beyond the scope of this essay to examine this phenomenon in detail. For a

thorough analysis, see Martin Heidegger, *Being and Time,* ed. Joan Stambaugh (Albany: State University of New York Press, 1996). There, Heidegger argues that most people exist in a state of denial regarding the human condition, a state that he calls "inauthenticity" (40), and that they do so in an effort to avoid the feelings of anxiety that result from acknowledging the nature of the human condition, primarily their mortality. To the extent that most people are actively trying to suppress truths that pertain not merely to themselves but to all, anyone who brings these truths to light threatens the security of the collective lie. Thus, various means are used to discourage individuals from broaching certain subjects. For example, individuals might be made to feel strange or morbid if they think or talk too much about their mortality or the meaninglessness of existence. According to Heidegger, such strategies are successful at compelling silence because they play on both people's anxiety about being different from others and their fear that being different will result in their being permanently isolated from others (118).

49. It should be noted that I am not claiming that all dark comedies (or comedies generally) are instructive. Indeed, I am sympathetic to the concerns that philosophers like Aristotle have held with respect to genres that rely heavily on spectacle. While an attraction to spectacle may be natural in humans, it is not, therefore, a disposition that should be encouraged. Taking pleasure in witnessing the misfortune of others is not a laudable trait, and finding humor in misfortune is even less so. Indeed, the historical tendency to demean the heuristic value of comedy has everything to do with the problematic potential that comedic works have, not merely to heighten our interest in spectacle, but, more seriously, to distort our perception of reality and habituate us to finding humor in horror. Clearly, genres that rely heavily on spectacle often achieve their desired effect through exaggeration. This exaggeration can yield a distorted image of the subject matter. Freeland writes at some length about the "hyperbolic" ("Realist Horror," 290) excesses of realist horror and their undesirable consequences. One of those consequences is a certain "emotional flattening" (288) that results from repeated exposure to violence. Like Aristotle, she worries that works can skew our understanding and moral compass just as easily as they can foster understanding and moral growth. I share these concerns about realist horror. I have concerns about the effects of comedy to the extent that it shares certain features with realist horror. For these reasons I am restricting my claims to the specific works in question and would have to evaluate other works individually to determine whether I would designate them as instructive. To the extent that *After Hours* encourages viewer identification with its protagonist, it prompts viewers to laugh with, rather than at, Paul. Thus, it fosters empathy as opposed to a mean-spirited mocking of misfortune. Also, though misfortune is certainly a focal point, to the extent that the plot resolves positively and there is no gratuitous violence, the humor taken is not at the expense of another individual.

50. Sartre, *Nausea,* 127.

51. Camus, "An Absurd Reasoning," 31.

# The Pupkin Gambit

## Rationality and Irrationality in *The King of Comedy*

*Richard Greene*

In Martin Scorsese's 1983 film *The King of Comedy,* Rupert Pupkin (Robert De Niro) commits a crime in order to gain notoriety, serves a modest sentence, and then enjoys a life of wealth and fame. Even if the result of his actions exceeds his original, more modest goal of being "king for a night" as opposed to being "a schmuck for life," his plan works perfectly. I call this plan the *Pupkin gambit.* Michael Milken (the junk bond king) also employed a version of the Pupkin gambit (although it's not clear whether he intended to or merely foresaw it as an acceptable worst-case scenario). Milken bilked people out of hundreds of millions of dollars, paid some of that money back in fines, served a fairly modest sentence, and came out hundreds of millions ahead. While there is clearly something morally wrong with the Pupkin gambit (as it involves clear harm to innocent persons), it's not obvious that there is anything rationally wrong with it.

In this essay I consider the question of whether it is rational for one to employ the Pupkin gambit. In addressing this question I examine two broad theories of rationality. I argue that, paradoxically, in virtue of Rupert Pupkin's largely irrational nature—he is, at times, delusional and has difficulty distinguishing fantasy from reality—for him the Pupkin gambit is rational. A Pascal's wager–type argument will bear this out. On the other hand, for rational agents, such as Milken, the Pupkin gambit does not rise to the level of rational strategy.

## Some Cases

A little background information on the specific actions of Rupert Pupkin and Michael Milken will be useful. Pupkin is an aspiring stand-up comedian, working in the tradition of such Borscht Belt comedians as Shelley Berman, Mel Brooks, Shecky Greene, and Henny Youngman. Largely because he doesn't attempt to further his career in traditional ways (e.g., by performing at comedy clubs), he's having trouble breaking into the business. His initial attempts involve gaining face time with Jerry Landers (Jerry Lewis)—a Johnny Carson–type talk show host—by jumping into Landers's limousine and dropping off home recordings of his act at Landers's office. Predictably, Landers's producers give him the brush-off. A frustrated Pupkin ultimately resorts to kidnapping Landers. He then notifies the producers of the Jerry Landers Show that, unless he is allowed to perform his stand-up routine on the show that evening, Landers will be harmed. The producers eventually assent—reasoning that it's only a television program and it would not be worth the risk to Landers's well-being to prevent Pupkin from appearing. After the show airs, Pupkin is arrested, and he winds up spending a few years in jail. Of course, his appearance becomes a huge media event, and, by the time he is released from jail, he is a prominent celebrity, his life story is a best seller, and he is a hot ticket on the talk show circuit. It should be pointed out that the ending of the film is ambiguous. Throughout the film, Pupkin experiences delusions in which he actually believes that he is a friend and potential collaborator of Landers. Scorsese hints that Pupkin's acquired celebrity status may be a mere product of his imagination. So either Pupkin is a huge success, or he merely believes that he is. This is a point to which I return later.

Michael Milken was an executive vice president at the investment firm Drexel Burnham Lambert. During the 1980s, he amassed a fortune of approximately $1 billion while committing mail, wire, and securities fraud and was eventually arrested. He served two years in jail and paid $600 million in fines, leaving him with a net worth of approximately $400 million.

With these cases in mind, let's get clear on precisely what the Pupkin gambit entails. As a first approximation, consider PG, which can be understood as the most generalized statement of the Pupkin gambit:

> PG: Performing an act that has immediate, severe negative consequences for oneself or others, with an eye toward ultimately bringing about some overwhelmingly positive consequence.

As is often the case when principles are stated at their most general level, PG fails to capture subtle aspects of Pupkin's and Milken's actions, even though it can be truthfully asserted of both Pupkin and Milken. These aspects are highlighted by our intuitive reactions to their actions. Intuitively, we feel that both Milken and Pupkin engage in morally inappropriate behavior in employing the Pupkin gambit: Pupkin kidnaps a man and, essentially, steals time on a network television program, and Milken cheats investors out of hundreds of millions of dollars.

Contrast the cases of Pupkin and Milken with the case of the early-twentieth-century philosopher Bertrand Russell. Russell was jailed on two occasions for pacifist-related reasons: around the end of World War II he was imprisoned for his participation in antiwar protests, and in 1963 he spent a week in jail for his participation in an antinuclear protest. Both times he foresaw his likely incarceration and willingly accepted it as a means of publicizing his views.

Notice that Russell's actions are in accordance with PG; he performed actions that had severe negative consequences (namely, jail time) as a means of bringing about some good consequence (namely, increased public awareness of important social issues). Although these actions satisfy PG, it seems correct to state that Russell did not employ the Pupkin gambit. The missing component would appear to be the unethical nature of Pupkin's and Milken's actions. While there is a case to be made that anytime one breaks the law one is behaving unethically, it is not obvious that this is correct. Moreover, such a view lacks intuitive support in light of the actions of noted practitioners of civil disobedience, such as Martin Luther King Jr. Here, we will take it as given that Russell's actions are morally appropriate or, at minimum, not obviously morally inappropriate.

Perhaps the reason that the Russell case doesn't contain an unethical component is that, unlike Pupkin's and Milken's, Russell's ultimate goal is not self-serving. It's altruistic in nature. Russell accepts the negative consequences of his actions in order to bring about a positive consequence for others (as well as for himself, presumably). His goal is to bring about peace. In this light, his actions should be viewed as supererogatory in a moral sense; that is, they actually go above and beyond what is required by morality. A satisfactory account of the Pupkin gambit must reflect this. Hence, PG stands in need of modification. At present, it is too strong in that it fails to exclude cases that clearly do not involve Pupkin gambits.

Consider, then, PG*:

PG*: Performing an act that has immediate, severe negative consequences for oneself or others, with an eye toward ultimately bringing about some overwhelmingly positive consequence for oneself.

While this formulation is preferable to the first, there remains one worry:

there is good reason to think that it's often acceptable to perform acts that harm oneself in order to ultimately benefit oneself. Doing so is involved in making sacrifices, for example. Moreover, doing so is not obviously unethical. This point is illustrated by an episode of the HBO series *The Sopranos*.[1] In this particular episode, a hip-hop artist is the victim of a drive-by shooting. His "street cred" soars, and, as a consequence, his CD sales increase dramatically. On witnessing this, a second hip-hop artist hires a mobster to shoot him in the leg. He does so in hopes of achieving the same results as the first. Ultimately, it doesn't work out so well for the second artist, as the mobster accidentally shoots him in the ass, which leads to a huge decline in his street cred. At this point, it should be noted that the second artist did nothing wrong from a moral standpoint. A key difference between this case and the Pupkin and Milken cases is that both Pupkin and Milken harm others while making a sacrifice designed to ultimately benefit themselves. So PG* is also too strong as it fails to exclude legitimate and ethically permissible cases of self-sacrifice.

With this in mind, a small modification of PG* yields PG**:

PG**: Performing an act that has immediate, severe negative consequences for oneself *and* others, with an eye toward ultimately bringing about some overwhelmingly positive consequence for oneself.

This formulation captures each of the main features of the Pupkin and Milken cases—namely, that one harms others and accepts a negative consequence for doing so as a means of achieving some desirable benefit that either exceeds in value the sacrifice made or is at least something that one values more given one's own personal desires or goals. We can now turn to the question of whether the Pupkin gambit is rational—or, perhaps more precisely, the question of under which circumstances, if any, the Pupkin gambit is rational.

## Two Broad Accounts of Rationality

One question that emerges at this point in the dialectic is whether any action that is unethical could ever be rational. A number of prominent moral theorists have argued that it is always rational to do the ethical thing and never rational to do otherwise. This is a point worth addressing because, if it is correct, then any further analysis of the Pupkin gambit becomes unnecessary: to the extent that it involves unethical action, the Pupkin gambit would be irrational by definition. I touch briefly on this issue.

Plato argues (in bks. 2–4 of the *Republic*) that to be ethical is, ultimately, a matter of being psychologically healthy (i.e., having a well-ordered soul), which, in turn, gets defined as being rational (or, more precisely, having the rational or reasoning parts of the soul control the various other parts of the soul). Kant argues (in *Grounding for the Metaphysics of Morals,* esp. secs. 1–2) that rational actions are those that are in accordance with maxims that can be universalized and, hence, are not contingent on one's personal desires or sentiments. He further argues that, if an act is not contingent on one's desires yet one has a reason to perform that act, then one must be commanded by reason to perform that act. Thus, on Kant's view, moral acts are always, by definition, rational actions, and immoral actions are always, by definition, irrational. While both these views are controversial—and the problems of each are well documented—for our purposes it's enough to point out that the senses of *rationality* employed by Plato and Kant are fundamentally different from the way in which I employ the term here. Plato and Kant employ a notion of rationality that refers to the genesis of actions. They are essentially making claims about the origins of actions and asking whether certain actions are motivated by reason, as opposed to being motivated by desire, sentiment, or appetite. This can be understood as employing an *internalist* conception of rationality: one that references internal processes. The concern of this essay is an *externalist* conception of rationality, namely, one that makes reference to external states of affairs (such as achieving wealth or fame). Our question is whether it is rational to pursue certain external states of affairs via certain means. The question of what motivates such a pursuit is not strictly relevant.

To illustrate, one might wonder what motivated Pupkin to kidnap Landers. This question could be addressed in one of two ways: one could consider whether Pupkin was motivated by reason as opposed to desire (or vice versa), or one could consider Pupkin's ultimate purpose (explicated by some end or consequence) in performing his action. Both ways of addressing the question involve assessing Pupkin's action in terms of rationality. The former employs an internalist conception of rationality. Here, one might wonder whether Pupkin is a rational being (in the sense of being a sane or psychologically healthy being). The latter employs an externalist conception of rationality. Here, one might wonder whether Pupkin's strategy is rational with respect to his particular goal, regardless of his particular psychological makeup, that is, regardless of whether he is acting primarily on reason or desire.

There is at least one externalist (in the sense defined above) theory of rationality that links moral action to rational action—ethical egoism. Ethical egoists hold that actions are morally right if and only if they promote an agent's long-term interests. Given that rationality is typically tied to self-interest, it follows on this view that rationality is always linked to moral action. This, of course, does not pose a problem for our view because one must first determine whether an act is in one's long-term self-interest (and, a fortiori, a rational act) before one can determine whether that act is a moral act. Thus, further analysis of the rationality of an action is not rendered pointless in virtue of its connection to morality. Since, on the views under consideration, the connection between morality and rationality does not provide a prima facie reason for suspending consideration of the rationality of the Pupkin gambit, we can dispense with this worry.

In order to address the question of whether employing the Pupkin gambit is rational, we need to get clear on what constitutes rational behavior in the externalist sense described above. Theories of rationality tend to fall into one of two broad categories: instrumentality theories and maximizing theories. Instrumentality theories tend to focus on the means employed by agents as they attempt to meet various goals. Here, rationality (roughly) gets cashed out in terms of whether said means are effective or optimal for meeting said goals. Maximizing theories tend to focus on the goals of the agent themselves. Rationality (again, roughly) gets cashed out in terms of whether the goal itself is one that is rational to have, given the overall desire set of the particular agent.

I begin with a maximizing theory. Decision theory is a paradigmatic maximizing theory. According to decision theorists, rationality involves determining by means of a mathematical calculation which of all available actions will bring about the best state of affairs and then acting on the basis of that calculation. The mathematical calculation is a function of the relevant probabilities of a particular outcome resulting from a given action and the value of that outcome. The product of a decision-based calculus is the endorsement of the particular action or strategy that produces the optimal state of affairs, given the agent's overall set of desires. Such an action or strategy is considered to be the rational strategy or course of action.

For our purposes, decision theory alone cannot tell us whether the Pupkin gambit is a rational strategy simpliciter because whether it is rational depends on the entirety of the desire set of the agent in question. The very same strategy could be rational for one agent and irrational for another, just in case the two agents had sufficiently different desire sets.

Now consider an instrumentality theory. Jason Holt provides a typical account of instrumentality rationality. Holt argues that what he calls *medial rationality* involves having good reason for thinking that one's course of action is both a reliable and a feasible way of achieving one's goal. On this view, one considers one's means of achieving a particular goal and then determines whether said means are likely to bring about that goal.[2]

Notice that instrumentality rationality is not subject to the criticism raised for decision theory. One does not need to know facts about the entirety of an agent's desire set to determine whether a particular course of action is rational. That being said, there remains a problem: it seems that some knowledge beyond knowing the mere reliability and feasibility of a particular strategy or course of action is necessary to determine whether that strategy or course of action is rational. Consider the following case. Suppose that Pupkin desires to have a meal at an expensive restaurant, one well beyond his present means (Pupkin at one point tells Landers that he doesn't have much money but would like to take him out for a modest meal). It may well be medially rational for Pupkin to eat the meal and flee the restaurant without paying the bill, as a strategy of "dining and dashing" would appear to be both a reliable and a feasible means of satisfying his desire. Suppose further, however, that Pupkin has an even stronger desire not to run afoul of the law (of course, it turns out that Pupkin has no such desire). Given this, it seems correct to say that dining and dashing would not be rational for Pupkin. Committing a crime would be medially irrational with respect to this desire. Hence, medial rationality is a necessary condition for an act's being rational, but it is not a sufficient condition since it is possible that a medially rational action with respect to one desire may be medially irrational with respect to some other desire. Put another way, any act that is medially rational is only prima facie rational. For a medially rational action to be actually rational, an agent cannot have some other desire that simultaneously renders that action medially irrational.

My proposal, then, is a hybrid account of rationality—one that relies heavily on the notion of medial rationality but, following decision theory, takes other desires into consideration as well. An action or strategy is rational if and only if it is medially rational and the agent has no other desires (including potential future desires) that would render the action medially irrational.

## Pupkin and Pascal

We are now in a position to assess the rationality of the Pupkin gambit as employed by Pupkin and Milken. Let's begin with the case of Milken. Milken's strategy of gaining immense wealth by committing securities-related crimes fails to be medially rational. Specifically, it is not a reliable way of achieving his goal. While it worked in this instance, he certainly could not have anticipated acquiring the amount of wealth he obtained, nor could he have anticipated the minimal amount of jail time he served. In fact, things could have gone quite differently. He could have been fined an amount that exceeded the amount by which he profited. If we factor in other desires, then, as employed by Milken, the Pupkin gambit becomes even less rational. Certainly, there are close possible worlds in which Milken mourns the loss of his professional reputation and social status to the point where his residual $400 million ultimately provides little satisfaction.[3] (Economists would undoubtedly point out that the law of diminishing marginal utility offers support for this likelihood.)[4] Hence, for most people, the Pupkin gambit is not a rational strategy: the risk of extremely negative consequences, the strong likelihood of the gambit failing, and the potential for remorse serve to make it the case that both necessary conditions in our definition will go unsatisfied.

The case of Pupkin, however, is much different. Regarding the requirement that there be no other desires that would serve to render the strategy medially irrational, we don't have access to the entirety of Pupkin's other desires, but we do have some evidence for the claim that no stronger present desire exists. Pupkin ends his performance on the Jerry Landers Show by explaining to the audience what he has done and his reasons for doing it. He states that it's better to be "king for a night than a schmuck for life." This implies that he has weighed the expected negative consequences of employing his strategy against the positive benefits and determined the gambit to be worthwhile. An episode from earlier in the film also offers support for the claim that Pupkin is largely motivated by things such as fame and public perception (to the exclusion of all else). During one of his delusional episodes, he fantasizes about being on the Jerry Landers Show. In this particular fantasy, he is surprised by his old high school principal, who is also a justice of the peace. He is to marry a woman he is attracted to on national television. While the desire to marry this woman is strong (he's been pursuing her throughout the film), his desire to be perceived by those who know him and by the public as a success is considerably stronger. The ceremony gets interrupted as the high school principal goes off on a tangent about how everyone was wrong about Pupkin and about what a terrific success he is. It seems clear that Pupkin's strongest desires center on fame and public perception.

The more pressing worry about Pupkin's strategy is that it doesn't appear to be any more reliable than Milken's. It is pertinent that Pupkin is delusional. Recall that Scorsese leaves the ending of the film ambiguous.

It's not clear whether Pupkin really is a huge success or merely believes that he is. But, even if the latter is the case, his desire is, nevertheless, in an important respect satisfied. Although he is not rich, famous, and successful under this scenario, he is essentially having the experience of being rich, famous, and successful. So, either way, the Pupkin gambit turns out to be feasible and reliable.

In considering his gambit, Pupkin is in a position to recognize that he has a Pascal's wager–type argument in support of his strategy. Pascal argued that belief in God is rational as follows: If one believes in God and is right, there is a huge payoff—eternal salvation (or some such). If one believes in God and is wrong, then one has not sacrificed much. Conversely, if one doesn't believe in God and is wrong, there are severe consequences—eternal damnation. If one doesn't believe in God and is right, there is little gain. So the structure of a Pascal's wager–type argument is as follows: a course of action is rational if following it may pay huge dividends with no potential downside and not following it comes with great risk and no huge potential payoff.

In virtue of his delusional nature, Pupkin is in a position where employing the Pupkin gambit is virtually guaranteed to lead to good consequences, with no real downside from his perspective, and failing to employ the gambit comes with a likely great downside: schmuck for life. Thus, the Pupkin gambit is a special case of Pascal's wager: an instance that is rational only when the agent in question is *ir*rational at such a fundamental level that the wager's negative consequences do not carry the same weight they would for a rational agent and, in fact, are reconfigured by the agent's irrationality as positive. While not all irrational persons are demented, all demented persons are irrational (at least in the internalist sense detailed above). In other words, the Pupkin gambit is an instance of Pascal's wager that can be viewed as rational only through the lens of a certain irrational sensibility; for any rational agent, it would simply be a fool's wager. Ironically, for Rupert Pupkin, the Pupkin gambit is rational.

## Notes

Thanks to Nancy Balmert and Rachel Robison for helpful comments on earlier versions of this essay. Special thanks to Kasey Mohammad for suggestions pertaining to the final section of the essay and for providing helpful comments on the essay as a whole.

1. "The Fleshy Part of the Thigh," written by Diane Frolov and Andrew Schneider.

2. Jason Holt, "The Costanza Manuever: Is it Rational for George to 'Do the Opposite'?" in *Seinfeld and Philosophy,* ed. William Irwin (Chicago: Open Court, 2000), 121–38.

3. A possible world is a state of affairs that could (or could have) come about. A close possible world, then, is a possible world that, for the most part, resembles the actual world (just a small number of details are different). So, in this context, when we discuss close possible worlds (in which Milkin mourns the loss of his professional reputation etc.), we are simply asserting that it could very easily have turned out that way.

4. In its simplest form, the law of diminishing marginal utility holds that, the more you have of some good after some threshold is reached, the less value each unit of that good has. For example, if I am thirsty, a soda pop might have quite a bit of value for me (it will serve to quench my thirst). A second soda pop would likely have less value (it won't be quenching my thirst) but may still have positive value (I might be enjoying the flavor or getting a buzz from the caffeine and sugar). A third soda pop would likely have even less value (I may start to feel ill from so much sugar and caffeine). In Milkin's case, the fortune that he would have amassed through legitimate means (owing to his being an executive at a major investment firm) would have had great value for him—it would have allowed him to live a very comfortable life. It seems likely that the extra wealth attained via his criminal activities would not have had as much utility for him. In short, there aren't many experiences that someone with $400 million can have that a person with, say, $50 million can't have.

**Part 3**

# VISION, SALVATION, AND THE TRANSCENDENTAL

# The Last Temptation of Christ and *Bringing Out the Dead*

## Scorsese's Reluctant Saviors

*Karen D. Hoffman*

Directed by Martin Scorsese from screenplays written by Paul Schrader, *The Last Temptation of Christ* (1988) and *Bringing Out the Dead* (1999) chronicle the lives of individuals whose capacity to save others pushes them toward extreme self-sacrifice and renders them incapable of living ordinary, comfortable lives. Jesus Christ (Willem Dafoe) and Frank Pierce (Nicolas Cage), the films' central characters, are both tempted to relinquish their sacrificial roles and embrace the happy banalities of human existence. In what follows, I explore some of the similarities in the struggles that these characters face in their roles as saviors. Despite the fact that Jesus' temptation eschews his divinity while Frank's includes the possibility of embracing a false divinity, both men are tempted to live lives characterized, at least in part, by what Jean-Paul Sartre would call *la mauvaise foi* (bad faith). Both successfully resist the proffered temptations.

### Sartrean Immanence and Transcendence

In *Being and Nothingness,* Sartre explains that human beings have a dual nature inasmuch as each of us exists as both subject and object, as both *pour-soi* (for-itself) and *en-soi* (in-itself). The for-itself, "which is what it is not and which is not what it is," and the in-itself, "which is what it is," are both central to our humanity.[1] The for-itself constitutes the transcendent aspect of humanity—the aspect that represents an individual's potential to transcend who she currently is in order to become someone else in the future. When Sartre claims that the for-itself "is what it is not" and "is not what it is," he is insisting that an existing human being cannot be reduced to what she biologically is at any given moment. Given her freedom to choose what she will become and to actualize her potential, a person is always more than what she currently is.

One of the hallmarks of human consciousness is self-awareness. A human being not only acts in the world but is also aware of her self as making choices that influence the world and her place in it. She is aware of the fact that she is responsible for her choices and, Sartre argues, for creating her self as the product of all her choices. But the self is never a finished product as long as a person lives: choices must continue to be made, and new choices allow an individual to become a different person. As a result of the perpetual nature of this process, an individual human consciousness "is not what it is" but is always *more* than what it is. An individual could always become something other than what she is; she could choose to actualize her self as someone she is not (yet) but is in the process of becoming. Sartre claims that, while a human self is the product of human choices, it cannot be *reduced* to those choices. Human consciousness transcends what it *is* at any given moment and moves toward *becoming* what it will be as a result of future choices. This is what it means to say that human consciousness is transcendent.

The objects of the world are not capable of transcendence. Objects merely are what they are. They are pure immanence. They contain no interior potentiality and are incapable of becoming more than what they are. By contrast, human consciousness always transcends itself; it "is what it is not" (yet). As subjects, people cannot be reduced to the status of mere objects. Pure immanence is not possible for existing human beings.

Despite the impossibility of living a human life of pure immanence, people are tempted to try to do so anyway. The burden of acknowledging personal responsibility for their choices and of accepting moral culpability for their choices tempts individuals to disavow their freedom and to deny their transcendence. People who succumb to these temptations lead lives characterized by what Sartre calls *bad faith*. Scorsese's Jesus and Frank Pierce both struggle to avoid bad faith by resisting such temptations.[2]

## *The Last Temptation of Christ*

### THE STORY OF *THE LAST TEMPTATION*

Based on the Nikos Kazantzakis novel of the same name, *The Last Temptation of Christ* chronicles the life of Jesus of Nazareth from the time of his growing awareness of his divinity until the moment of his death on the cross at Golgotha—approximately the last three years of his life.[3] Scorsese's film follows the novel in emphasizing the humanity of Jesus, particularly as expressed in a dream sequence that occurs during the Crucifixion. In this controversial sequence, the Nazarene imagines living out his days as an ordinary man and is tempted by the devil to choose this path rather than the one God has ordained.

While a number of critics have voiced concerns about the content of Jesus' last temptation as well as about the film's emphasis on the humanity of Christ,[4] my purpose here is to analyze some of the philosophical implications of the film, not to assess its theological merits. My aim is to discuss Jesus as a character in a Scorsese film who exemplifies human striving and who is subject to human temptations; I leave aside the question of whether Jesus' human struggles are theologically consistent with his divinity.

Before delving into Scorsese's portrayal of the character of Jesus, there are a few aspects of the story of *The Last Temptation* that should be noted. The first is that, while many people appear in the film, there are only three central characters: Jesus, Judas, and Mary Magdalene. The screenwriter, Paul Schrader, explains that he decided to trim Kazantzakis's book by minimizing Jesus' relationships with the other disciples and by focusing instead on his relationship with Judas (Harvey Keitel), the man whom Jesus most loves, and with Magdalene (Barbara Hershey), the woman whom Jesus most adores.[5] Interestingly, although perhaps somewhat problematically, it is Jesus' preferential love for Judas and Mary Magdalene, rather than his universal love for humanity, that is emphasized in the film.

In a very real sense, Richard Corliss is right to identify *The Last Temptation* as "the ultimate buddy movie." Corliss notes that, for the fifteen years preceding the film, Scorsese directed secular drafts: "Two men, closer than brothers, with complementary abilities and obsessions, who must connive in each other's destiny."[6] On several occasions throughout the film, Jesus remarks that he will be unable to fulfill his mission without Judas's help; he even goes so far as to suggest that Judas's task is more difficult than his own: "That's why God gave me [Jesus] the easier job: to be crucified." At the beginning of the film, it is Judas who chastises Jesus for making the crosses used to execute Jews. In an early episode that prefigures the penultimate scene of the film, it is Judas who speaks as the voice of conscience for Jesus, issuing a moral command to stop being a traitor to his people—a command that Jesus ultimately obeys. The Judas of Scorsese's *Last Temptation* is, as Schrader puts it, the "backbone of Jesus."[7] Originally sent to kill Jesus, the Judas of the film becomes the savior's closest confidant and travels with him as he acquires an understanding of his divinity and of his divine mission.

Scorsese's film adopts the subjective perspective of Jesus and reveals Jesus' divinity to the viewer as it is revealed to Jesus himself. Moreover, the film unfolds in such a way that viewers make the journey with him. Visually

and aurally, the mise-en-scène of the film works to facilitate audience identification with Jesus' subjective state. In *The Last Temptation*, Scorsese trades
the urban landscapes of many of his earlier films for the barren landscape of
the desert, making the harsh physical world Jesus inhabits a reflection of the
character's inner turmoil.[8] At various points in the film, aural shifts signal
alterations in Jesus' subjective state, as in the silencing of the background
noise during his encounter with John the Baptist and during his crucifixion.
In several scenes, the speed of the film is altered to correspond with Jesus'
subjective perceptions. Notably in the brilliant scene portraying Jesus en
route to his crucifixion at Golgotha, Scorsese's film slows as time stretches
toward eternity for the heavily burdened savior. During the Crucifixion,
the sky darkens, and the camera shifts nearly a full ninety degrees as Jesus
experiences the destabilizing feeling that God has forsaken him. What was
true of the film's portrayal of Jesus' life is also true of its representation of the
afternoon of his death: viewers visually experience the disorientation and
confusion that Jesus feels. The way in which Scorsese tells the story of Jesus'
life makes it clear that it is Jesus' interior struggle to choose to become the
crucified Christ that is the true subject of *The Last Temptation*.

JESUS AS STRUGGLING SAVIOR

The internal conflicts that Jesus experiences are apparent from the first moments of Scorsese's film. *The Last Temptation* begins with the camera moving
rapidly past some trees—as if it is a bird in flight—and coming to rest on a man
lying on the ground in a fetal position with his eyes closed and his hand on the
earth. The camera momentarily hovers above him before cutting briefly to a
frontal shot of him from a lower angle. The final shot of this initial sequence
moves to a close-up of the man's face. Although viewers do not yet know that
this man lying alone under the trees is Jesus, Scorsese has introduced him
in a way that visually establishes much of what will be revealed in the film
that follows. The fact that Jesus is initially seen from above, coupled with the
fact that he is seen in a fetal position, might be intended to indicate that we
are viewing him from God's perspective, as the human Son of God. This, in
conjunction with the fact that Jesus is seen so close to the earth, makes the
image a dual reminder of his humanity and divinity.[9]

Already proximate to Jesus, the film transcends even the physical boundaries of his body to grant viewers access to the contents of his mind. The
first words of the film are Jesus' thoughts: "The feeling begins. Very tender,
very loving. Then the pain starts. Claws slip underneath the skin and tear
their way up. Just before they reach my eyes, they dig in. Then I remember."
Here the film shows what Jesus remembers: he makes the crosses used for

crucifixions. The narration continues as Jesus explains that, despite his acts of self-mortification, "the pain came back. And the voices. They called me by name: Jesus."

Early audiences might have been surprised at the revelation that the conflicted, guilt-ridden man they have been watching make crosses is actually the film's title character. Perhaps to help counter this initial shock and to bolster audiences' identification of the carpenter with the divine Christ, Scorsese immediately introduces a reminder of his coming death on the cross: in a gesture ostensibly aimed at measuring the length of the piece of wood he has been shaping, Jesus places his arms out to both sides in a posture that mimics the one he will assume during the Crucifixion.

After following Jesus to Lazarus's crucifixion, Scorsese's film shows us just how internally conflicted the Nazarene is. The camera focuses on a tormented Jesus writhing on the ground, screaming that he knows God loves him but that he wants God to stop; he can't take the pain: "I want him to hate me. I fight him and make crosses so he'll hate me. . . . I want him to find somebody else. I want to crucify every one of his messiahs." Admitting to his mother that he's not sure whether it is God or the devil talking to him, Jesus seems to lament that, if it is God, "you can't cast out God, can you?" The Jesus of *The Last Temptation* initially fights the internal God from whom he cannot escape.

To further highlight his internally conflicted, guilt-ridden nature, the film follows Jesus to Mary Magdalene's brothel, where he is forced to confront his sexual desire for her. In an interesting departure from the novel, Scorsese's film has only a few thin veils of sheer material separating Magdalene at work from her waiting customers. All day and into the evening, Jesus sits quietly and watches Mary have sex with men of various ages and ethnicities.[10] Once the sun has set and Jesus is the only one left in the room, he finally approaches the woman he loves and asks for her forgiveness, noting that he's "done too many bad things" and that the "worst things" have been done to her.[11]

This scene is significant both because it introduces the conflicted nature of Jesus' sexuality—he seems to have sexual desires that he refuses to indulge—and because it reinforces the fact that Jesus believes himself to be in need of forgiveness. While this need not imply that he has, in fact, committed any objective moral wrong, his request for forgiveness reveals that he at least feels subjectively guilty.

Jesus' feeling of guilt is emphasized again a few scenes later when he converses with a hermit (Barry Miller) atop a cliff in the desert. After lamenting that God wants to push him over the edge, Jesus exclaims: "Can't he see what's inside of me? All my sins? . . . I'm a liar, a hypocrite. I'm afraid of everything. I don't ever tell the truth. I don't have the courage. When I see a woman, I blush and look away. I want her, but I don't take her . . . for God. And that makes me proud. And then my pride ruins Magdalene. I don't steal, I don't fight, and I don't kill. Not because I don't want to, but because I'm afraid." When his interlocutor notes that "the more devils that we have inside of us, the more of a chance we have to repent," Jesus replies that he feels "Lucifer is inside" him, telling him: "You're not a man. You're the Son of man. And more. The Son of God. And more than that: God." Incredulous at the suggestion that he could be God, Jesus assumes that the internal voice proclaiming his divinity must be the devil's. Scorsese explains that this scene, which does not appear in Kazantzakis's novel, was added to *The Last Temptation* because it helps humanize Jesus:

> I was trying to make the association of Jesus as one of us, as a human being, and, therefore, he would have the same fears, the same concerns as we do. In this particular case, he confesses to things that he's ashamed of. . . . It makes him more accessible. . . . To an audience that's disposed to look at the film in an intelligent way, . . . he sounds like one of us. Therefore, if he could recognize these faults and these dangers in himself and then overcome them, then maybe we could; you see, that was the idea. . . . Just because he's dealing with these doubts and this self-loathing at times, it doesn't mean that, ultimately, he's not able to fulfill the role of the redeemer. It's part of the process of being fully human.[12]

Jesus' internal conflict continues until the final moments of the film, though its specific nature changes. As the film progresses, Jesus becomes increasingly aware of his divinity and comes to embrace this truth about himself. Accepting his role as a leader of men, he becomes conflicted about the direction in which to lead his people. Preaching first the doctrine of love, then briefly adopting the violence of the ax, he finally becomes cognizant of the fact that he must die on the cross. Uniting the two earlier approaches of love and violence, his crucifixion requires his blood to be violently but lovingly shed.

Once he becomes aware of the fact that he must be crucified, Jesus struggles to follow God's ordained path. Scorsese's Jesus is something of a reluctant savior: he is willing to die to redeem humanity, yet he wants to live the life of an ordinary man. His internal conflict sets the scene for his last temptation.

THE LAST TEMPTATION

Although Jesus is tempted on numerous occasions throughout the film, it is his last temptation that is the film's most important. Beginning as he hangs dying on the cross, the last temptation commences as the background noise disappears from Golgotha. A young girl (Juliette Caton) appears. Explaining that she is his guardian angel, she tells Jesus that God wants to give "mercy, not punishment," and that he doesn't want his blood. Instead, God has decreed: "Let him [Jesus] die in a dream, but let him live his life." Jesus breathes a sigh of relief as the girl helps him remove the bloody nails and come down from the cross.

Led away by the girl, Jesus notices an advancing wedding party. He soon learns that it is his own: he is to marry Mary Magdalene. Foregoing any representation of the wedding, the film moves directly into the marital bed. Magdalene cleans Jesus' wounds, and they proceed to make love. As if to emphasize that the real purpose of this coupling is procreation, Magdalene makes a point of uttering (twice), "We could have a child"—a point that Jesus echoes.

When the very pregnant Magdalene dies,[13] the young girl who led Jesus to Mary comforts him with the thought that "there's only one woman in the world. One woman with many faces." Although Mary Magdalene has died, Mary, Lazarus's sister, lives. "She's Magdalene with a different face. She's carrying your greatest joy inside her: your son."[14]

Jesus' path to Mary (Randy Danson) and Martha (Peggy Gormley), both of whom eventually bear his children, might have been surprising to early audiences not familiar with Kazantzakis's novel. But the Nazarene's life with Lazarus's sisters is anticipated by an earlier scene from Scorsese's film, one in which Jesus ends his desert fast by dining with Mary and Martha. During the meal, the two sisters pointedly ask Jesus if he misses having a home and a "real life." In response to his admission that he desires but will never have those things, the women argue that God is "in the home" and that God wants Jesus "to make children," not to spend his days fasting and praying. Furthermore, Mary and Martha seem to imply that Jesus is welcome to stay with them and start a family.[15]

Just as he was tempted in the desert by the snake who (speaking in Magdalene's voice) offered him the chance "to love and care for a woman and to have a family," Jesus has already been tempted to start a family with Lazarus's sisters. The last temptation, then, marks the third time in Scorsese's film that the same offer has been made to Jesus: live as a common husband and father. During the last temptation, however, the chance to have a family and to lead an ordinary life appears not as an abstract possibility but as a live option that plays out in Jesus' mind. Moreover, during the last temptation, it seems that Jesus *is*, in fact, tempted by what the devil masquerading as a young girl proffers. He desires to relinquish his divinity and to live instead the life of an ordinary man. The devil that appears to Jesus in the desert in the form of a lion appears to be mistaken in thinking that the Nazarene is "past the small temptations of a woman and a family."

Perhaps the devil is simply unaware of the depth and persistence of Jesus' desire to be a husband and father. Or perhaps the last temptation adds something that was importantly absent from the earlier offers, namely, the chance to not be crucified. In addition to the possibility of living as an average man, the last temptation offers Jesus the possibility of *not dying* as the Son of God. Scorsese's Jesus seems more drawn to a banal existence as a respite from his divine mission than he is drawn to such a life because of the pleasures it provides. During the last temptation, Scorsese's Jesus seems to be actively fleeing his divinity rather than actively pursuing ordinary human pleasures. His desire is primarily a negative one: to escape his sacrificial death on the cross, to not be the Son of God.

JESUS' FINAL TEMPTATION: A LIFE OF IMMANENCE

Paul Schrader notes that it is important to bear in mind that *The Last Temptation* is "an existentialist book written in an existentialist century."[16] As such, the primary focus is on Jesus' subjective struggle to come to terms with his own divinity and with his divine mission; the existential experience of being fully human and fully divine is paramount. Scorsese's Jesus faces an arduous task: the Nazarene must actively desire and choose his death on the cross; he cannot passively allow himself to be killed.

While individual choice is central to existentialism, it is precisely such choice that seems to be largely absent from Jesus' last temptation. From the first moments of the dream sequence until the final scene in which he finally chooses to die on the cross, Jesus is led through the various scenes of his temptation. He is merely the passive recipient of the devil's choices. Even though he loves Mary Magdalene, he does not *choose* to marry her so much as he is *told* that he is going to marry her. Even though he wants a child, he does not choose to have a sexual relationship with Lazarus's sister Mary; he is told that she is already pregnant with his child.

Indeed, until the final minutes of the film, Jesus seems to have almost no agency at all in Scorsese's version of the last temptation. Nor does he appear to experience much joy. In contrast to the Jesus of the wedding scene at Cana, who is shown dancing and laughing and generally full of passionate exuberance for life, the Jesus of the final dream sequence seems to be unable to feel much of anything. He is often shown sitting quietly by himself (or with only his young temptress by his side). The character he most resembles is the risen Lazarus, whom Scorsese portrays as something of a zombie, hovering between worlds, not fully alive, yet not entirely dead.

One way of interpreting why Jesus is so passive during the final sequence is to consider that, as part of the last temptation's rejection of his divinity, he is being tempted by the devil to reject the transcendent aspect of his humanity. Jesus is not so much being drawn *toward* the passions and joys of a fully human life as being drawn *away* from his divinity. Given his passivity and his seeming lack of passion, the Jesus of the last temptation almost seems to be attempting to live a life of complete immanence—a life of pure being, devoid of any becoming, eschewing transcendence of any kind. Yet, as existentialists note, such a life is impossible for any existing human being. As subjects, we cannot live as if we are objects. As free beings, we cannot live as if we are not free and responsible for our choices. Moreover, since transcendence is itself a part of the human condition, a Jesus who denies transcendence rejects his humanity.

The Jesus of *The Last Temptation* can be interpreted as making such an attempt to deny his transcendence. Jesus, the savior whose task includes helping humans cultivate their transcendence, is tempted by a life of immanence—a life in which he simply is what he is (an ordinary man) and in which the question of becoming something else (an extraordinary man, the Son of God, the savior of humanity) has been silenced.

Several passages from the end of Kazantzakis's novel bolster this interpretation. At the end of the last temptation, when the Jesus of the dream sequence is on his deathbed, Judas appears. Unlike the passive Jesus of the sequence, Judas has continued fighting; the blood (always deeply symbolic for Scorsese) is still fresh on his hands. In both the film and the novel, Judas calls his friend a traitor and a coward, admonishing Jesus for not fulfilling his divine mission: "Your place was on the cross. That's where God put you." The novel, however, goes beyond the dialogue of the film and adds something important to Jesus' reply: the Nazarene appeals to an image that rejects transcendence. Jesus argues: "Life on earth means shedding one's wings."[17]

The novel continues this discussion by having Judas reply that Jesus is mistaken: "Life on earth means: to eat bread and transform the bread into wings, to drink water and to transform the water into wings. Life on earth means: the sprouting of wings." Judas goes on to add that, during Jesus' ministry, the savior's disciples "all felt wings shoot out from [their] backs."[18] Transcendent in a way that is possible only for a god, Jesus has the ability to cultivate transcendence in others, helping them actualize their potential and advance toward becoming the individuals they would like to be. Yet the Jesus of the last temptation has rejected his ability to help others transcend and transform themselves. In being tempted to flee death on the cross and, instead, to live a life approximating pure immanence, he seems to have temporarily rejected even his own capacity for transcendence.

In tempting Jesus to reject his divinity, the devil has, during these final moments of Jesus' life, tempted the Nazarene to eschew nearly *all* transcendence, including the transcendence that is essential for full humanity. As a result, the Jesus of the last temptation has mistakenly rejected both his divinity *and his humanity.* He has been living in bad faith, retaining his human immanence, but rejecting his human transcendence. This prompts Kazantzakis's Judas to observe that Jesus is "dead and buried. He still stands up on his feet, he talks, he weeps, but he's dead: a carcass."[19] Jesus has, for all intents and purposes, been reduced to a body, a mere object.

Recognizing the truth of this statement, Kazantzakis's Jesus reclaims his transcendence, exclaiming that he should have been crucified and that he desires the chance to make this choice. Accepting both his divine mission and his human capacity for choice, Scorsese's Jesus begs God for forgiveness and loudly proclaims his desire to be the Messiah and to "pay the price." It is only then that he finds himself back on the cross, able to celebrate his choice to be crucified and to revel in the fact that "it is accomplished."

## Bringing Out the Dead

### THE STORY OF *BRINGING OUT THE DEAD*

Appearing a little over a decade after the release of *The Last Temptation of Christ, Bringing Out the Dead* reunites Martin Scorsese and Paul Schrader and addresses themes that are surprisingly similar to those developed in the earlier film.[20] While one might not expect a film that chronicles three days in the life of the paramedic Frank Pierce to have much in common with a film that portrays three years in the life of Jesus Christ, both films explore the difficulties of being a savior and the human struggle to avoid the temptation to relinquish this role.[21] Despite their vastly different external settings, both films traverse the internal landscapes of the angst-ridden male leads. Both employ voice-over narration that grants viewers direct access to the central character's inner thoughts, and both use a variety of techniques to project the subjective perspective of each savior onto the physical space he occupies. Where in *The Last Temptation* this physical space takes the form of barren, desert landscapes, in *Bringing Out the Dead* it takes the form of the frenzied atmosphere of Mercy Hospital and the turbulent streets of New York.

Set in New York City in the early 1990s, *Bringing Out the Dead* follows Frank Pierce as he works the night shift traveling the streets of Hell's Kitchen looking for people to save. Beginning on a Thursday night and ending on Sunday morning, the action of the film takes place on three consecutive nights, each one of which pairs Frank with a different partner.[22] Each partner seem to have found his own way of coping with the stress of the job: Thursday's Larry (John Goodman) focuses on food, Friday's Marcus (Ving Rhames) employs a strange combination of lustful leering (particularly at prostitutes) and Christian principles, and Saturday's Tom Wolls (Tom Sizemore) attempts to control himself and others through physical violence. Frank, however, lacks a strategy for coping with the violence and death he witnesses each night. He has "no walls." He absorbs rather than deflects the sorrows of others; he is a self-confessed "grief mop."

*Bringing Out the Dead* follows Frank as he absorbs the grief of Mary Burke (Patricia Arquette), the daughter of a man who suffers a debilitating heart attack early in the film, and as he bears witness to the loss of Rose (Cynthia Roman), a young woman whose memory haunts him. Frank seems to believe that he is at least partially to blame for both women's plights: Rose is dead because Frank could not properly intubate her in time; Mary's grief over her father's condition is exacerbated by the fact that Frank's resuscitation of the family patriarch occurred only after the man's brain had been deprived of oxygen for over ten minutes. As a result of Frank's actions, Rose is dead, and Mr. Burke (Cullen O. Johnson) hovers somewhere between life and death. The elderly man codes throughout the film, requiring that he be repeatedly (and brutally) shocked by the defibrillator. Throughout the film, Frank is, thus, doubly haunted: by a patient who has died and by one who has survived. The dead girl seems to Frank to be very much alive, while the living patient seems to him to be functionally dead. Moreover, Frank believes that the deceased Rose wants to live and that the living Burke wants to die. Ostensibly troubled simply by his inability to save people, Frank becomes increasingly troubled by his ability to "save" people, granting them a life approximating pure immanence in a persistent vegetative state.

By the film's end, Frank seems to conclude that saving people doesn't always require prolonging their physical existence: sometimes a person can be saved by being allowed to die. Realizing this, Frank takes matters into his own hands and, during some of the quietest moments of the otherwise raucous film, attaches Burke's heart-rate monitors to his own chest. In an attempt to fool the machines into thinking that Burke is still alive (so that the man can die in peace without having his heart forcefully shocked back into beating), Frank takes Burke's breathing tube into his own mouth, substituting his breath for Burke's own. Moments later, Burke is dead.[23] Frank saves Burke, the first patient of the film, by allowing him to die.

During the course of *Bringing Out the Dead,* Frank succeeds in saving several other people: Noel (Mark Anthony), a suicidal lunatic; Mary, a former addict whose inability to cope with her father's prognosis prompts her temporary return to drug use; and Mary's dealer, Cy Coates (Cliff Curtis).[24]

Frank's salvation of Mary is not the most dramatic rescue in Scorsese's film, but it is one of the most central to Frank's own redemption.[25] Where the other characters in the film are saved biologically, Frank saves Mary emotionally. While there is a physical aspect to the salvation—Frank carries Mary out of her dealer's apartment and saves her body from the impact of additional drugs—it is Frank's emotional support of her and his decision to end her father's suffering that, ultimately, help her achieve a kind of inner peace. Together, they find respite from their inner demons. The film ends with an image of Mary holding Frank as they recline on the bed at sunrise.[26] The long night of her father's death literally and figuratively behind them, they rest quietly together as the light shining in on them intensifies, encapsulating them. Although at this point the sound track is silent, viewers probably call to mind one of Frank's earlier reflections as they watch this final scene: when something good happens, "everything just glows."

FRANK PIERCE AS STRUGGLING SAVIOR

The action of *Bringing Out the Dead* begins when an ambulance en route to a call launches onto the screen, sirens whirling to the screeching music of the sound track. After only a few moments, the screen goes black. Scorsese then shows viewers a close-up of Frank's eyes lit by the ambulance's flashing red lights. After cutting to yet another black screen, the camera moves in rapid sequence to a series of shots: first of Frank's face, then of Frank and his partner Larry, then of Frank again. The effect produced is one of urgency. While the destination is unknown, the exigency is apparent.[27] In this respect, Frank might be considered the mirror image of Scorsese's Jesus: where the Nazarene moves very slowly along his path to redemption, Frank careens rapidly toward his. Where Jesus spends a great deal of time quietly meditating but experiences some difficulties in translating his reflections into a practical plan for action, Frank devotes his time to action but has difficulties finding enough quiet time to reflect on the events he witnesses.[28]

Narrating, Frank claims that he needs the quiet time that a few days off might provide. He then identifies the nascent source of his current mental anguish: "Things had turned bad. I hadn't saved anyone in months." Accustomed to relying on his skills to save people, Frank finds that his good fortune has left him; his job has become an exercise in futility. Instead of saving lives, he is forced to spend much of his time answering calls to rescue drunks, revive drug addicts, and interrupt suicide attempts. Indeed, many of the people with whom Frank interacts in the film are repeat visitors to the emergency room, such as the "chronic caller of the year . . . the duke of drunk, the king of stink, [the] most frequent flyer: Mr. Oh [John Heffernan]"—an alcoholic who is so named because of his incessant groaning.

Frank must come to terms with the fact that, even if he succeeds in saving the lives of the chronic callers, these people will just need to be saved again in a few days. Many of the patients with whom Frank interacts in the film repeatedly engage in self-destructive behaviors that work to undermine any attempts to save them.

Noel, the mentally unstable young man whom Frank uses mouth-to-mouth to save after Tom Wolls's violent attack, is one of the frequent occupants of the Mercy Hospital's emergency room who exhibits such self-destructive behavior. Prior to saving Noel's life, Frank interrupts a suicide attempt that Noel has started but appears to be unable to finish. As part of this encounter, Noel shakes his braids, splashing blood from them on Frank's face and torso. As in other Scorsese films, Frank is marked by the blood of another—blood that he makes no attempt to remove. Perhaps this is designed to prepare viewers for the larger responsibility Frank will have in saving Noel's life. By the film's end, Frank saves Noel from suicide and from being murdered.[29]

Throughout Scorsese's film, Frank struggles to feel compassion for Noel and for others like him.[30] To help call attention to the difficulties of harboring such compassion, the film presents viewers with pieces of two different but similar conversations between a nurse and her patient, one overheard as Frank enters the double doors of the emergency room, the other overheard on his way out. In the first, the nurse expresses her frustration with a man who has been snorting cocaine for three days and has come to the hospital because he feels like his heart is beating too fast. She exclaims that she doesn't see why the hospital should help him because the hospital "didn't sell him the cocaine" or "push it up his nose." Moments later, on Frank's way out, the same nurse is heard telling another man that she doesn't think she should help him with the fact that he gets drunk and falls down because he's just going to get drunk again. Like Frank, the other medical professionals struggle to feel compassion for all their patients and to overcome their reluctance to treat individuals who will continue to engage in self-destructive behavior.

Frank wrestles with other aspects of his job, too. Like Jesus, he is a reluctant savior who does not really want the job he has; he wants to be fired. His profession has wreaked havoc on his personal life; he seems to have lost almost everything of value, including his marriage. He cannot sleep. He fights to honor the memory of those who have died—to bear witness for them yet to not be haunted by them. He grapples with his human limitations, with his ability to save some people who would rather die, and with his inability to save other people who want to live. Finally, Frank struggles with the fact that the battle against death is, ultimately, a futile one: there are no lasting victories.

FRANK'S TEMPTATIONS

Like Jesus, Scorsese's other reluctant savior, Frank Pierce faces multiple temptations to relinquish his role. Frustrated by the demands of the job, he begs his boss (Arthur J. Nascarella) to fire him. Arriving late for work, he reminds his superior of his promise to fire him the next time he failed to arrive on time. Promising (first on Friday and then on Saturday) to fire Frank "tomorrow," Captain Barney apologizes for keeping him on the payroll and reminds him of his obligation to others: "Duty calls you, kid. The city needs you." Regardless of his own desires, and at great cost to his personal life, Frank must fulfill his duty to save others. Despite the fact that he does not particularly like his job, he avoids the temptation to simply quit.

Frank also avoids the temptation to escape reality through the use of mind-altering drugs, violence, or suicide. While most of the other characters in the film utilize these strategies for transcending their current situation, Frank seems to realize that these strategies are acts of bad faith. Although Frank momentarily yields to the temptation of drugs and violence, he quickly comes to recognize these as the untenable alternatives they are.[31]

Additionally, Frank overcomes the temptation to adopt the false transcendence of thinking of himself as God. He admits: "Saving someone's life is like falling in love. The best drug in the world. For days, sometimes weeks afterward, you walk the street making infinite whatever you see. Once, for a few weeks, I couldn't feel the earth. Everything I touched became lighter. Horns played in my shoes. Flowers fell from my pockets. You wonder if you've become immortal, as if you've saved your own life as well. God has passed through you. . . . For a moment there God was you." But Frank's way of phrasing his reflections here is telling: he says "God was you," not "you were God." While the difference between these two claims might seem to be negligible, it is not. His use of the former expression importantly reveals that Frank becomes an *instrument* of God in saving lives, not that he thereby acquires some kind of divinity. Additionally important is the fact that Frank acknowledges that it is only *for a moment* that God passes through him. While he acknowledges that his capacity to save people sometimes makes him *feel* divine, Frank also seems to recognize the danger of yielding to the temptation to think of himself as a god.

I think Frank avoids this temptation, even when, toward the end of the film, he allows Burke to die. Although some critics have interpreted Frank's interference with Burke's machines to be indicative of the enormity of Frank's God complex, I disagree.[32] Frank explicitly states: "'The God of Hellfire' is not a role that anyone wants to play." While Frank might be interested in playing another type of god, he recognizes that he would merely be *playing a role*. Moreover, given the humility that he demonstrates throughout the film as well as his use of ignoble images to represent himself, it does not appear that Frank thinks of himself as divine: "I realized that my training was useful in less than 10 percent of the calls, and saving someone's life was rarer than that. After a while, I grew to understand that my role was less about saving lives than about bearing witness. I was a grief mop. It was enough that I simply showed up."

Admitting that he has the face of a priest and that people frequently "spill their guts" to him, Frank considers himself to be a secular savior, an ordinary man. Even when he allows Burke to die, he does not actively kill him: he merely stops the machines from noticing his passing and alerting hospital staff. Motivated by his firm belief that Burke does not want to be indefinitely shocked back into existence, Frank puts aside his own desire to keep his patients alive in order to satisfy what he believes to be his patient's desire to die. This decision shows not that Frank has a "megalomaniac fantasy" or a "God complex"[33] but, rather, that his understanding of what it means to save people has changed by the film's end.

IMMANENCE AND TRANSCENDENCE IN *BRINGING OUT THE DEAD*

In avoiding the temptation to consider himself divine, Frank eschews a false transcendence—one that would deny important elements of his humanity. Where Jesus is tempted to think of himself as something other than the divine savior, Frank is tempted to think of himself as something other than an ordinary man. Where Jesus is tempted by a life of false immanence, Frank is tempted by a life of false transcendence.

In addition to avoiding the temptation to think of himself as a god, Frank also successfully avoids the temptation to pursue the false transcendence of an addict's drug-induced high. Scorsese's film seems to be calling particular attention to Frank's rejection of this possibility, both in its depiction of so many despairing addicts and in its illustration of Frank's explosive physical rejection of the one pill he takes at Cy's apartment. Interestingly, as Frank's observation of Cy's sleeping customers makes clear, the attempt to transcend the givens of one's present life through drugs actually diminishes one's capacity for transcendence and, instead, produces greater immanence: agency is lost as the mind's subjectivity gives way to the body's objectivity. This is part of what makes drug use a kind of false transcendence and an addict's life one of bad faith.

The fact that it attempts to transcend the difficulties of life by eliminating transcendence is also what makes suicide an act of bad faith. In a film where so many of the characters problematically attempt to escape their lives by committing suicide—where so many people ostensibly seek transcendence through an alternative that, if successful, can result only in pure immanence—Frank reveals that he is an exemplary man by refusing to contemplate suicide as a way of relinquishing his role as a savior.

As Sartre explains, a full human existence is one of immanence and transcendence; the attempt to eliminate either results in a loss of humanity. Burke's persistent vegetative state in *Bringing Out the Dead* is troubling precisely because it is a state in which he approximates pure immanence. Unable to display—and probably unable to experience—self-consciousness, Burke is functionally reduced to the status of an object. It is from this state of false immanence that Frank liberates him, allowing him to die in peace.

## Finding Redemption

*The Last Temptation of Christ* and *Bringing Out the Dead* highlight the difficulties of the human struggle to live a life of immanence and of transcendence while avoiding the various temptations to exaggerate or deny either aspect of human existence. With screenplays by Schrader, both Scorsese films explore the difficulties of being a man and finding oneself cast in the role of savior. The characters of Jesus and Frank both accept their given roles at the same time that they struggle with what it means to save others and with the personal costs of being a savior. While Jesus and Frank are differently tempted to relinquish their roles, both successfully resist the proffered temptation. Saving themselves by saving others, both come to embrace a humanity that recognizes the significance of immanence and transcendence. Both ultimately make choices that lead them to grace and redemption.[34]

# Notes

I am grateful to Alan Hoffman for his comments on earlier drafts of this essay. I am especially indebted to Mark Conard for being such a careful reader and for offering thoughtful remarks on earlier versions of the essay.

1. Jean-Paul Sartre, *Being and Nothingness: An Essay on Phenomenological Ontology,* trans. Hazel E. Barnes (New York: Washington Square, 1969), 785.

2. The kind of Sartrean transcendence being discussed here is understood primarily in terms of potentiality. Humans are transcendent inasmuch as we are in the process of actualizing our potential in a particular way. We are, therefore, always more than what we are at any given moment: we are also who we are in the process of becoming.

Scorsese's Jesus is in the process of becoming the risen Christ. As I argue in this essay, the existentialist elements of *The Last Temptation of Christ* suggest that, inasmuch as he is human, Jesus struggles to become the person God wants him to be. Jesus seems to possess potentiality that he attempts to actualize. Thus, he seems to possess human transcendence. Moreover, Jesus' struggle to accept his human transcendence is the focus of Scorsese's film.

Complicating matters is the fact that Jesus also possesses divine transcendence. Divine transcendence, however, is importantly different from—and in tension with—Sartrean human transcendence. Where Sartrean human transcendence concerns potential to be actualized through free human choices, divine transcendence concerns the fact that, as a fully actualized being, God transcends all other existing things. According to many traditional theologians, the Christian God is a fully actualized being. God's nature is complete. God contains no potential. God is not in the process of becoming. God simply is. To say that the Christian God is transcendent in a divine sense is to say that, as a fully actualized being, God is more than all the other actual things in the universe.

3. Although the film opens with a disclaimer noting that the character of Jesus is a fictional creation, not the historical figure of the Gospels, the Jesus of *The Last Temptation* is shown recounting a number of the parables, performing several of the miracles, and otherwise participating in many of the events of the life of the biblical Christ. The fact that the fictional Jesus of Schrader's screenplay and Scorsese's film so closely resembles the biblical Christ yet is supposed to represent only a fictionalized version of the savior has been the source of much of the controversy surrounding the film. Carol Iannone argues that Scorsese's film contains "more than enough dialogue and connection with the gospels to bring the thrill, or shock, of recognition" ("*The Last Temptation* Reconsidered," *First Things* 60 [February 1996]: 51). Similarly, W. Barnes Tatum maintains that the film "disclaim[s] too much": "As with the Kazantzakis novel, the film is based in some sense on the story of Jesus as narrated in the four gospels" (*Jesus at the Movies: A Guide to the First Hundred Years* [Santa Rosa, CA: Polebridge, 1997], 165).

4. Some critics have gone so far as to accuse the film of being, as Michael Morris puts it, "theologically wacko" for having Jesus lament that his God is fear and that Lucifer is inside him as well as for portraying the Nazarene as attempting to flee from God ("Of God and Man," in *Scorsese: A Journey through the American Psyche,* ed. Paul A. Woods [London: Plexus, 2005], 172).

Other critics have questioned the sexuality of Jesus as revealed through his imagined encounters with Mary Magdalene, Mary, and Martha. Still others have challenged the film's extensive use of violence and blood, which, in Lloyd Baugh's words, shifts "the 'low' Christology of Kazantzakis to the even 'lower' Christology of Scorsese's film." As a result, Baugh argues: "Scorsese represents Jesus the Christ with an anthropology so diminished that he ceases to be a normal human being" ("Martin Scorsese's *The Last Temptation of Christ:* A Critical Reassessment of Its Sources, Its Theological Problems, and Its Impact on the Public," in *Scandalizing Jesus: Kazantzakis's "The Last Temptation of Christ" Fifty Years On,* ed. Darren J. N. Middleton [New York: Continuum, 2005], 175).

Baugh goes on to note that the Greek Orthodox Church "chastised Kazantzakis because his image of Jesus was judged heretical" and that "the Roman Catholic Church condemned Scorsese's film because its image of Jesus was deemed unbalanced, unacceptable," particularly since his "deeply troubled human dimension—in eternal conflict within itself—overshadows in an exaggerated way the divine." Baugh calls attention to the fact that the narrative of Scorsese's film fails to mention some of the purported signs of Christ's divine nature, such as the circumstances surrounding his conception and birth. He adds: "Scorsese removes most of the indications given in Kazantzakis that point to Jesus as the Messiah, as the Son of God, indications recognized by others and by Jesus himself" (183). By way of example, he mentions the visit of the magi, the meeting with a Samaritan woman at the well, and Jesus' transfiguration.

Moreover, the film adds details that might seem to counterindicate the divinity of Jesus: he is not merely a carpenter but one who fashions the crosses used in executions; he not only helps carry these crosses to Golgotha but actually participates in the crucifixion of Jews. In a small but important shift from the novel, the Jesus of the film is seen helping nail an individual to a cross instead of merely witnessing this action. Notably, in the process, Jesus' face is splashed with blood—blood that acts as a leitmotif and that plays a significant symbolic role in this, as in any other, Scorsese film. As a result of the blood that he has shed and that he literally wears, one is tempted to wonder whether the carpenter Jesus at the beginning of the film is himself in need of redemption.

Despite Scorsese's claims to be somewhat surprised by the strength and tenacity of the opposition to *The Last Temptation,* particularly in light of his belief that the film's humanized Jesus in no way questions or diminishes the full divinity of Christ, Paul Schrader admits that using Jesus as a metaphoric representation of humanity's struggles might be blasphemous. He notes: "To use Jesus Christ as a character, as a metaphor for the human condition, is technically a form of blasphemy since, as God, how can he be a metaphor for man?" But, he goes on to add: "That's also the conundrum of Christianity: it contends that Christ was both fully human and fully divine." Schrader continues: "If Jesus is a metaphor for our struggle to become divine, then he has to incorporate all those human elements of temptation, and that makes a lot of people uncomfortable." He elaborates: "The film could be faulted for overemphasizing the humanity of Jesus as opposed to the divinity of Christ, but maybe it's a healthy sort of counterbalance to a lot of Christianity that tends to push aside the more uncomfortable human elements and just focus on the more glorious and miracle-working and redemptive spiritual elements" (Paul Schrader's commentary is included on the 2000 Criterion DVD of *The Last Temptation of Christ*).

5. Schrader, DVD commentary.

6. Richard Corliss, "Body . . . and Blood," *Film Comment* 24, no. 5 (September–October 1988): 43.

7. Schrader, DVD commentary. Schrader concedes that he had expected this aspect of the story to scandalize people but that this "took a back seat" to some of the other protests.

8. Conversely, when Jesus walks the verdant earth during the dream sequence at the end of the film, he finds the landscape to be much altered. Commenting that he finds it beautiful and inquiring what has changed, he is told that *he* has changed.

9. Additionally, the fact that this opening sequence includes three shots of Jesus, one from above, one from the front, and one close up, might be interpreted as representing the Holy Trinity of Father, Holy Spirit, and Son. If so, this would serve as another indicator of Christ's divinity.

10. Scorsese explains: "The point of the scene was to show the proximity of sexuality to Jesus, the occasion of sin. . . . And I wanted to show the barbarism of the time, the degradation to Mary. It's better that the door is open. Better there is no door. The scene isn't done for titillation; it's to show the pain on her face, the compassion Jesus has for her as he fights his sexual desire for her. He's always wanted her" ("Richard Corliss 1988," in *Martin Scorsese: Interviews,* ed. Peter Brunette [Jackson: University Press of Mississippi, 1999], 121).

11. In a move that will be echoed in Jesus' last temptation on the cross, Magdalene indicates that her body is her soul and pulls back the covers on her bed to reveal her naked body. Placing Jesus' hand on her body, she tells him: "Here's my body. Save it."

In a later scene in the film, Judas also argues for the significance of the body. Questioning Jesus' desire to save souls and to center his ministry on love, Judas argues for the importance of first freeing the body (from the Romans): "You don't build a house from the roof down; you build it from the foundation up." Jesus answers that "the foundation is the soul" and that you have to change what is inside first or else you'll just "replace the Romans with somebody else."

12. Martin Scorsese's commentary is included on the 2000 Criterion DVD of *The Last Temptation of Christ.*

13. It is rather surprising that Magdalene dies so soon after the last temptation has begun. One might expect that, since this sequence is itself a fantasy, it would not include the death of the object of Jesus' desire. The devil leading Jesus through the last temptation follows the novel in belaboring God's agency in Magdalene's death: "God killed her." Interestingly, this fact might indicate that God is trying to prompt Jesus to awaken from the dream he is momentarily living. The death of Magdalene might serve as a reminder from God that all finite things, including the body, cannot properly be the subjects of infinite love and attachment. Mortal beings will perish; God is the only proper object of infinite attachment and eternal love.

Interpreting Magdalene's death in such a way might help explain the appearance of

Paul in the last temptation. Perhaps he too represents another attempt by God to awaken Jesus from the temptation and remind him of his mission. Judas might then be sent as part of God's third attempt to awaken Jesus—an attempt that is finally successful.

One final aspect of Magdalene's death is worth noting: Scorsese's film trades the novel's extremely violent portrayal of Mary's death by stoning for her peaceful passing (in a flash of light). What makes this particularly interesting is that the film is often chastised for *adding* unnecessary violence and blood to the novel. Yet here is one instance where Scorsese inexplicably—and, perhaps, mistakenly—chooses to *eliminate* bloodshed. The novel's violent rendering of Magdalene's death seems to serve as an indication that the Jesus of the last temptation—a Jesus who is not a savior—is unable to save sinners like Magdalene from a bloody demise.

14. Much has been made of Scorsese's decision to import Kazantzakis's puzzling equation of all women, particularly since this equation seems to contradict Jesus' persistent preferential love for Magdalene. Perhaps seeing individual women as mere instantiations of the universal woman is done to minimize the lustful nature of the physical union and to emphasize the procreative possibilities: the women of the last temptation are all equally capable of bearing Jesus' children. Moreover, the way in which the girl leading Jesus through the last temptation presents the case for going to Lazarus's sisters suggests that the aim is paternity rather than sexual pleasure. En route to the home of Lazarus's sisters, the "angel" explains: "This is way the savior comes: gradually, from embrace to embrace, from son to son."

15. It is worth noting that Kazantzakis's novel makes it quite clear that the coupling between Jesus and Martha is motivated by Jesus' desire to give Martha the children she wants: "Of what importance was her name, where she came from, or the shape, color, beauty or ugliness of her face? It was the feminine face of the earth. Her womb was smothering her: many sons and daughters were within, suffocating and unable to emerge. She had come to the man so that he might open a way for them. Jesus's heart overflowed with compassion" (Nikos Kazantzakis, *The Last Temptation of Christ,* trans. P. A. Bien [New York: Simon & Schuster, 1960], 466).

16. Schrader, DVD commentary.

17. Kazantzakis, *The Last Temptation of Christ,* 493.

18. Ibid.

19. Ibid.

20. Schrader adapted the screenplay from Joe Connelly's novel *Bringing Out the Dead* (New York: Vintage, 1999).

21. Noting that Scorsese's films generally emphasize the questions and problems of human existence more than they attempt to provide explanations and solutions, Robert Kolker claims that Scorsese's "often-commented-on Catholicism" appears "in the form of a purgatorial sense of his characters' serving in the world, not looking for grace but attempting survival and barely making it" (*A Cinema of Loneliness,* 3rd ed. [New York: Oxford University Press, 2000], 190).

Scorsese's saviors appear as struggling individuals who are reluctant to play their assigned roles. Yet, despite their reluctance to be saviors and their focus on mere survival, Jesus and Frank do, importantly, find grace. Even Kolker admits that Frank "finds some Bressonian grace" in Mary's affection (219).

22. Critics have noted that *Bringing Out the Dead,* Scorsese's twenty-second film, is "literally his darkest" since "the two-hour production clocks in with a total of four-and-a-half minutes of daylight" (Mark Jolly, "A Terrible Beauty," in Woods, *Scorsese,* 241).

Despite the literal darkness of the film, the figurative darkness of *Bringing Out the Dead* is mitigated by the fact that the film ends with Frank and Mary bathed in the bright sunlight of a Sunday morning. Like Jesus, Frank appears to have found new life by the time of Sunday's sunrise.

In light of his admission that he has been criticized for including "too much Good Friday and not enough Easter Sunday" in his films (Scorsese, DVD commentary), perhaps Scorsese intends *Bringing Out the Dead,* with its redemptive ending (on a Sunday morning), to function as a partial corrective of his tendency to emphasize violence and suffering.

23. This act of breathing for another in order to allow him to die extends the instances earlier in the film in which Frank breathes for others as part of his attempt to save them, first in the case of a premature baby Frank is unable to resuscitate, then in the case of Noel, a lunatic whom Frank is able to save.

Schrader's screenplay calls particular attention to the significance of breathing for another person as part of a discussion that occurs among several paramedics. The general consensus of the group seems to be that giving mouth-to-mouth is entirely too risky and that to perform it would take one well beyond the requirements of the job. When Frank offers that he has performed this procedure on an infant—something that we then see him do in the film—the others claim that, because of its innocence, a baby is an exception to the general rule of avoiding mouth-to-mouth. In the scenes that follow, Frank breathes first for a bloody premature baby, then for a bloody suicidal lunatic, and finally for Mr. Burke. Given the paramedics' conversation, it seems reasonable to conclude that Frank's willingness to perform mouth-to-mouth is supposed to be indicative of his willingness to go beyond the requirements of duty and to place himself at risk in order to save others.

24. Frank saves Cy when the dealer finds himself impaled on the railing of a balcony as result of a botched attempt to elude a rival dealer. Frank holds Cy's head as workers cut through the metal railing that pierces his torso and saves him from plunging to his death once the cutting is complete.

25. Perhaps to help ensure that viewers realize that Frank saves himself by saving Mary, Scorsese shows him washing his face in Mary's bathroom while contemplating the fact that "it felt good to be in a woman's room again, especially a woman who wasn't comatose or severely disabled." Frank explains: "I felt like perhaps I had turned a corner—like I saved someone—though I didn't know who." Since Frank is staring at himself in Mary's mirror as he speaks these lines, viewers are encouraged to assume that, while he may not know it, the person whom he has saved by helping Mary is himself.

26. Interestingly, Mary and Frank recline in the same pose that Judas and Jesus assume as they sleep in the desert. Mary holds Frank the same way Judas holds Jesus.

27. "We swirl through an emergency room filtered in harsh, ultra-realistic greens and creams; we see fragmented images of Nicolas Cage and Tim Sizemore speeding past a stream of lurid neon that winks like a battered old whore still glamming it up for the boys; we close in tight on Cage's face, the colour and life drained almost entirely, just a pallid wash of death. . . . Never has Scorsese used music so effectively, so poetically, mixing punk and soul—the perfect anthems for the film's twin themes: chaos and redemption" (Jolly, "A Terrible Beauty," 250).

28. The speed at which the ambulance travels is directly proportional to the deterioration of Frank's mental stability, the escalation of his despair. As if to ensure that viewers make this connection, Scorsese increases the speed of the film and shows Frank rapidly shifting gears and canvassing the streets as he explains that he is "driving out of myself."

29. Interestingly, Frank saves Noel from suicide by promising to kill him. In one of the many humorous exchanges of the film, Frank agrees to kill Noel in order to get the man to ride in the ambulance back to the emergency room: seeing him lie down on a busy city street, Frank explains that he can't kill Noel there because "we have rules against killing people on the street, OK? It looks bad."

It should be noted that one of the strengths of *Bringing Out the Dead* is its extensive humor. The calls that come over the dispatch, announced by Scorsese himself, include such oddities as a man who has set his pants on fire and an elderly woman who claims to have been "abducted by her cat." Numerous exchanges in the film introduce levity to the literal and figurative darkness of the subject matter. For example, when Frank and Larry arrive at Mercy with Mr. Burke and confer with Dr. Hazmat (Nestor Serrano), viewers are treated to the following humorous exchange, delivered with impeccable comic timing:

DR. HAZMAT: What's wrong with him?
LARRY: You should know. You pronounced him.
DR. HAZMAT: You told me he was dead. Flatline.
FRANK: He got better.
DR. HAZMAT: I hate pronouncing people dead over the phone.

30. Frank occasionally loses this battle. For example, at one point in the middle of the film, on encountering yet another botched suicide attempt, Frank pulls out his pocketknife, gives the man some helpful tips on the proper way to cut one's wrists, and encourages him to just kill himself and be done with it.

31. While Frank does admit to drinking every day, he does not appear to be under the influence of alcohol on the job. In fact, at one point he makes a point of saying, with respect to his job: "Sobriety's killing me."

32. Maria T. Miliora argues, I think mistakenly: "Like Travis [Bickle], Frank believes,

grandiosely, that he has the personal power and the responsibility to change things as well as the omniscience to know how things should be changed." She goes on to add that Frank's act of enabling Burke's death "is indicative of his unconscious fantasies of omnipotence and omniscience." According to Miliora's problematic interpretation of the film: "Rather than having gotten past his own ego or childlike narcissism, it appears that Frank has simply reformulated his megalomaniac fantasy to include allowing some of his patients to die" (*The Scorsese Psyche on Screen: Roots of Themes and Characters in the Films* [Jefferson, NC: McFarland, 2004], 119–20).

33. Ibid.

34. In his review of *Bringing Out the Dead,* Glenn Kenny rightly notes: "The film-making is as exhilarated, and as exhilarating, as that of *Taxi Driver.* But *Bringing Out the Dead* chronicles alienation, insanity, and ultimate redemption; *Taxi Driver* doesn't get to that last bit—which really makes all the difference" ("*Bringing Out the Dead,*" in Woods, ed., *Scorsese,* 250).

# Flying Solo

## *The Aviator* and Libertarian Philosophy

*Paul A. Cantor*

> The first thing a genius needs is to breathe free air.
> —Ludwig von Mises

### The Billionaire Underdog

Martin Scorsese is the cinematic champion of the underdog, even if he happens to be the richest man in the world. That explains how *The Aviator* (2004) fits into the impressive body of work Scorsese has created in his long and distinguished career as a director. At first glance, the billionaire aviation tycoon Howard Hughes does not appear to be the sort of subject that would attract Scorsese. As a rich and powerful businessman, a handsome playboy, and a media celebrity, Hughes seems to be the archetypal top dog. He is exactly the kind of person a typical Scorsese protagonist can only dream of being. A Travis Bickle (*Taxi Driver,* 1976) or a Rupert Pupkin (*The King of Comedy,* 1983) stares at public figures like Hughes and is driven to commit crimes in the hope of entering the charmed circle of their publicity. Scorsese is the great poet of the American underclass, focusing on the loners, the losers, the misfits, and the malcontents, those on the outside of society desperately struggling to get in. As an Italian American, he has often dwelled in particular on the plight of immigrant subcultures as they try to fit into the mainstream of American society, culminating in his dark tribute to the immigrant experience in *Gangs of New York* (2002). Howard Hughes would seem to be the opposite of all this. Stepping right out of the American heartland, he was born in Texas and inherited a fortune and, hence, social respectability. As a record-setting aviator, he seems cut out of the mold of the quintessential all-American hero Charles Lindbergh—and, hence, worlds removed from a typical Scorsese psychotic criminal like Max Cady (*Cape Fear,* 1991).

Yet *The Aviator* manages to turn Howard Hughes into a trademark Scorsese underdog, the Jake La Motta of the aviation industry. Scorsese's Hughes is a street fighter, sometimes a bully, and always a scrapper. He is portrayed as continually at odds with the establishment, whether in Hollywood or the aviation industry, and, ultimately, he runs afoul of the law and finds himself pitted against the U.S. government itself.[1] Despite the fact that he is surrounded by beautiful women and, at times, an adoring public, the film reveals him to be at heart a loner and a misfit, even a freak. To be sure, Hughes is far more successful than the typical Scorsese protagonist in pursuing his ambitions, and he does accomplish what they can only dream of doing. Yet, in the end, Hughes is just as tormented as Travis Bickle, Rupert Pupkin, or Jake La Motta. Like these earlier Scorsese figures, he pursues his dreams obsessively, compulsively, monomaniacally, and, therefore, cannot remain content even when he achieves his goals. Driven by a perpetual dissatisfaction with himself and the world around him, he seems destined to unhappiness.

Still, Scorsese finds something triumphal, and, perhaps, even redemptive, in Hughes's tortured psyche because it is, after all, the source of his creativity. Precisely because the world does not satisfy him, Hughes is always out to change it and improve it. His obsessive perfectionism continually drives him to new heights of achievement. He wants the perfect motion picture, the perfect airplane, and, one might add, the perfect woman, and, in each case, he keeps on molding and remolding reality to make it fit his visionary expectations. Scorsese uses Hughes's story to explore the thin line between madness and genius and, ultimately, shows that the line cannot be drawn. Hughes's psychological obsessions make his achievements possible, but in the end poison them and incapacitate him. The artist as madman, the madman as artist—here is Scorsese's deepest point of identification with Hughes and the reason why he is able to give such a sympathetic portrait of a figure who could easily be presented in a very negative light.

Scorsese obviously saw a great deal of himself in Hughes—and with good reason. As an independent filmmaker who bucked the Hollywood studio system, as a perfectionist who kept reshooting scenes and reediting film footage, thereby continually going over budget, Howard Hughes was the Martin Scorsese of his day. As Scorsese himself describes Hughes: "When he made *Hell's Angels* (a picture I've always loved), he was a truly independent filmmaker, and he literally spent years and a small fortune trying to get it right."[2] Many of Scorsese's films have drawn on autobiographical material, most obviously whenever he dealt with Little Italy, the New York neighborhood in which he himself grew up. But it is remarkable how, in turning to what at first seems to be subject matter utterly alien to his own immigrant background, Scorsese nevertheless found in Hughes a mirror of his own struggles as a creative artist. The Hollywood scenes of *The Aviator* are probably as close as we will ever come to seeing *Raging Director: The Martin Scorsese Story.*

## The Businessman as Visionary

As a result of Scorsese's identification with Hughes as a filmmaker, *The Aviator* offers something rare in a Hollywood movie—a positive portrait of a businessman, precisely in his role as a businessman. In the typical Hollywood production, whether in motion pictures or television, the businessman often appears as a villain.[3] Businessmen are generally presented as greedy, corrupt, uncaring, and willing to do anything for the sake of profit. They typically cheat customers, employees, colleagues, and investors, despoil the environment, subvert the due process of averaging law, and commit all kinds of crimes. In one mystery after another, the murderer turns out to be a businessman, trying to eliminate a rival, cover up an earlier misdeed, or just make a buck at the expense of his fellow human beings. Over against the capitalist villain, Hollywood offers a variety of altruistic, public-spirited heroes who, by contrast, put the common good above their narrow economic interests. Public prosecutors, the police, government officials of all kinds, together with an army of social workers, investigative journalists, environmentalists, and other do-gooders, are presented as necessary to rein in the antisocial impulses of private enterprise. Oliver Stone's *Wall Street* (1987)—which ironically immortalized Gordon Gekko's phrase "greed is good"—is only an extreme example of the negative image of businessmen that Hollywood usually projects.[4]

Scorsese himself has participated in this antibusiness trend in American popular culture. In movies such as *The Color of Money* (1986) and *Goodfellas* (1990), he portrays the corrupting effects of the profit motive and works to link the world of business with the world of crime. As part of his sympathy for the underdog or little guy, he has generally adopted a left-wing attitude toward big business/corporate America, namely, that it is evil and corrupt and leads to the big fish preying on the little fish. But, in *The Aviator,* Scorsese seems to strike off in a new direction and look at the positive side of business for a change, perhaps because he is dealing in part with his own business, filmmaking. The story of Howard Hughes allows him to portray the businessman as visionary and creative, even heroic. Hughes was, of course, heroic in a conventional Hollywood sense. As a pioneer in aviation and, specifically, a daring aviator himself, often serving as the test pilot for his own innovative planes and setting speed and distance records, he was obviously courageous in the way in which the traditional Hollywood hero normally is. With the title of *The Aviator,* one could imagine Scorsese's film assimilating Hughes to conventional Hollywood models of the heroic aviation pioneer, from Charles Lindbergh to Amelia Earhart to John Glenn. Hughes did have the right stuff. But, although the heroic aviator archetype is integral to Scorsese's portrayal of Hughes, the movie reveals much more than his raw courage in an airplane.

Scorsese's Hughes is heroic as a businessman, displaying a different kind of courage in his willingness to take economic risks, above all with his own money. *The Aviator* is unusual among movies in capturing what it is specifically to be an entrepreneur, a genuine innovator in business. Scorsese's Hughes is creative in all his activities, not just in his work as a filmmaker. What unites his activities in the film and aviation industries is his ability to predict the future. He is always alert to emerging technological possibilities and the new demands of consumers, and he is willing to bet his own money on what he thinks the wave of the future will be. In most movie portrayals, the businessman has nothing to contribute to the common good and, in fact, makes his money only by cheating, defrauding, or otherwise exploiting the public. By contrast, *The Aviator* presents Hughes as a progressive force in two industries, someone who gives the public what it wants (e.g., talkies rather than silent movies) and, more remarkably, correctly anticipates what the public would want if it were made available (e.g., transcontinental and transatlantic flights in reliable, fast, and comfortable aircraft).

Thus, even though Scorsese may share the left-wing political opinions typical of Hollywood, *The Aviator* in many respects celebrates the spirit of free enterprise and, more generally, embodies a kind of libertarian philosophy. One may profitably interpret the film in terms of concepts derived from classic defenders of the free market such as Adam Smith and also draw on the work of the so-called Austrian school of economics, one of whose chief representatives is Ludwig von Mises. The emphasis in Austrian economics on the special role of the entrepreneur and his ability to deal with the risk and uncertainty endemic to economic life makes it particularly relevant to understanding *The Aviator.* Although Smith and Mises are conventionally categorized as economists, their work has a large philosophical component. Smith was, in fact, a professor of moral philosophy at the University of Glasgow and wrote on many philosophical subjects. Mises devoted a significant portion of his writing to epistemological issues, and he always approached economic questions from a larger philosophical perspective. Both Smith and Mises can properly be regarded as social philosophers, and, indeed, they rank high among the developers of a philosophy of freedom. Their support for liberty is grounded in an economic understanding of the virtues of free markets, but it encompasses a larger philosophical vision of freedom as the proper condition of humanity.

It is unlikely that Scorsese was influenced by Smith, Mises, or any other libertarian thinker; nevertheless, he may share the broad outlines of their philosophy of freedom. There has always been a rebellious and antiauthority streak in his movies that suggests an affinity with libertarianism. In *Gangs of New York* and *The Aviator,* Scorsese seems to be focusing on the government—and specifically the federal government—as a prime enemy of liberty. In many ways, the most distinctive—and libertarian—component of *The Aviator* is the way in which it ends up championing the lonely figure of the private businessman against the vast oppressive apparatus of the federal government brought to bear on him. Normally in Hollywood movies, the private businessman is the villain, and a noble representative of the government—often a congressman or a senator—is necessary to bring him to justice.[5] *The Aviator* reverses this Hollywood stereotype, casting the crusading senator as the corrupt villain and the businessman as the victim of government injustice. Usually in American popular culture, the government is presented as the solution to all our problems ("there ought to be a law"), and we almost never see the idea that free market forces might be the real answer. By contrast, *The Aviator* seems to suggest that the government itself is the problem, and the entrepreneurial spirit is presented as the key to improving the world. I do not wish to associate Martin Scorsese with Ayn Rand, but I will say that not since the courtroom scene in *The Fountainhead* (King Vidor, 1949) has a Hollywood movie vindicated the philosophy of rugged individualism as forcefully as *The Aviator* does in the Senate hearing scene.

## Some Issues of Interpretation

Before turning to a detailed analysis of the film, I want to take up briefly two preliminary but important issues of interpretation, one involving Martin Scorsese, the other Howard Hughes. I have been talking about *The Aviator* as if it were simply a Martin Scorsese creation and he were solely and completely responsible for its content. In fact, *The Aviator* is a rare example of Scorsese becoming involved in a film project that he did not initiate himself. The actor who plays Hughes, Leonardo DiCaprio, was the driving force behind doing a film on the subject and worked closely in developing the screenplay with John Logan—a talented and successful writer whose screen credits include *Gladiator* (Ridley Scott, 2000), *The Last Samurai* (Edward Zwick, 2003), *Any Given Sunday* (Oliver Stone, 1999), and *Star Trek: Nemesis* (Stuart Baird, 2002). Scorsese was not even the first choice to direct the film, but, when Michael Mann backed out (he stayed on as coproducer), DiCaprio wisely approached the director he was working with on *Gangs of New York*. Thus, the story of *The Aviator* had largely taken shape before Scorsese started to work on the film, as we can see from his own description of Logan's screenplay: "He had written a character who was both tragic and triumphant, whose brilliance was inseparable from his mania, whose vulnerability was inseparable from his callousness, whose private vision of perfection drove him forward and stopped him dead in his tracks, and then drove him forward once more. Which is to say that *The Aviator* was a portrait of the artist, writ large across the landscape of 20th century America."[6]

Clearly, many of the ideas I have been attributing to Scorsese he found already embodied in the script that was handed to him. Thus, any full account of *The Aviator* must acknowledge Logan's contribution to the creative process, and DiCaprio also played an important role. Film is a collaborative medium, and, despite the attractions of French auteur theory, one cannot regard any movie as the product of a single creator. Nevertheless, it is still reasonable to talk about *The Aviator* as a Martin Scorsese film. As I have shown, it fits quite neatly into his body of work as a whole and, in fact, reflects many of his characteristic preoccupations as a filmmaker. And, of course, the finished motion picture bears the unmistakable stamp of his unique cinematic genius. The genesis of *The Aviator* is an excellent example of the creative serendipity that is more typical of popular culture than we like to think. We might wish that *The Aviator* were a project that Martin Scorsese had carefully planned out himself from start to finish. But, in fact, he was handed a script that was tailor-made for his distinctive vision of the world and, what is more, gave him a chance to develop that vision in new directions. The happy result was one of Scorsese's most successful movies—artistically, critically, and commercially—and, if he was not single-handedly responsible for it, one may still say that the film carries his full endorsement and embodies his view of the world.

The other issue I must deal with briefly is the question of the accuracy of the movie's portrayal of Hughes. It appears that we will never know the truth, the whole truth, and nothing but the truth about the real Howard Hughes. His life has become surrounded by so many myths, mysteries, mystifications, fabrications, and lies that we will probably never be able confidently to separate fact from fiction in his case. *The Aviator* is grounded in a great deal of research into Hughes's life and draws on Charles Higham's biography (the movie offers, however, a much more positive interpretation of Hughes than the book does).[7] DiCaprio studied newsreel footage of Hughes in preparing for the role, as is particularly evident in the Senate hearing scene. Substantial newsreel clips from the actual hearing survive, allowing DiCaprio to imitate Hughes's behavior on this occasion quite closely (much of the dialogue in this scene is transcribed verbatim from the recorded testimony). At the same time, *The Aviator* takes some artistic liberties with the historical truth. The hearings were not, in fact, televised, and Hughes's persecutor, Senator Owen Brewster, was only a member of the Senate committee, not, as the film claims, its chairman. With exceptions such as this, *The Aviator* is, in general, true to the facts about Hughes that can be determined, but, like any work of art, it selects and interprets those facts and, thus, ends up emphasizing certain aspects of Hughes's life at the expense of others.

Insofar as I have been able to sort out the historical facts, I would say that the Howard Hughes we see in *The Aviator* is generally a more admirable and attractive figure than the real Howard Hughes. The mere fact that the film deals with only the first half of Hughes's career—before he completely withdrew from public life and became a bizarre recluse—means that we view him in a more favorable light. *The Aviator* does acknowledge the dark sides to Hughes's character and presents some of his more questionable deeds, but it does so in the larger context of treating him as a hero rather than a villain. Thus, I want to make it clear that, in this essay, I am discussing a fictionalized portrait of Hughes, the Howard Hughes of Scorsese's film, not the real Howard Hughes. The historical Hughes would be a much more dubious choice as a poster child for free enterprise. Particularly in the second half of his career, when he earned most of his money from secret defense contracts, he became a part of the military-industrial complex and, hence, largely a partner of the federal government, even its creature, not someone who heroically stood up to it. It is, of course, interesting to point out the ways in which the historical Hughes differed from the fictionalized portrait given in *The Aviator,* but it would not be a refutation of the idea that the film embodies a libertarian philosophy to say that the real Howard Hughes was not truly a good model of a free market entrepreneur. For the purpose of analyzing *The Aviator* as a Scorsese film, what matters is how it portrays Hughes, not what Hughes was really like. In fact, by comparing the historical Hughes with the film's significantly idealized portrait of him, one gets a sense of what the director was trying to emphasize, namely, the heroic side of the entrepreneur.

In sum, when I use the phrase *Scorsese's Hughes* or just plain *Hughes* in this essay, it should be read as shorthand for the more cumbersome phrase *the fictionalized image of Howard Hughes shaped by Martin Scorsese, John Logan, Leonardo DiCaprio, and other contributors to* The Aviator, *an image based in a mass of historical facts about the real Hughes but departing significantly in artistic ways from the full truth about Hughes insofar as it can be determined.* In short, in this essay I am writing about a character in a movie, not a historical figure, and it is that character, I am claiming, who is a celebration of the entrepreneur in the spirit of libertarian philosophy.

## Risking One's Own Money

*The Aviator* begins with a brief prologue, a scene of Hughes's childhood, that attempts to locate in his relation to his overprotective mother the source of his lifelong obsessions with cleanliness and with his health. The film then jumps ahead to Hughes as a young man, soon after the death of his parents left him extremely wealthy as the owner of Hughes Tool Company. Hughes is in Southern California making *Hell's Angels* (1930), a film about World War I flying aces and their aerial combat. We get our first glimpse of Hughes the perfectionist as he does everything he can to make the movie on a truly epic scale. He has assembled "the largest private air force in the world" for the picture,[8] and, as the story begins, he has decided that an unprecedented total of twenty-four cameras is still not enough to shoot the aerial combat scenes the way he wants them—he needs two more. In his quest for the elusive additional cameras, he approaches one of the grandest of movie moguls, Louis B. Mayer, and the film introduces the motif of Hughes's ongoing battle with the establishment. Mayer treats him with contempt as an outsider in Hollywood and dismisses him with the curt comment: "MGM isn't usually in the practice of helping out the competition" (8).

In the opening sequence of the film, we are, thus, immediately confronted with images of Hughes's visionary power and his iron will in making his dreams come true. His first words in the film, as he deals with technical problems with the aircraft, are appropriately: "Don't tell me I can't do it! . . . Don't tell me it can't be done!" (3). These words could serve as the defining motto of the Howard Hughes of *The Aviator*. At every step of the way, he refuses to compromise and accept the seemingly practical solution that, according to conventional wisdom, the situation demands. For example, after he concludes that he needs clouds in the background to make the excite-ment of aerial combat visible to movie audiences, he waits months—despite mounting costs—for the proper weather conditions to materialize. After finally finishing the film—well behind schedule and over budget—he is on the verge of releasing it in theaters when he discovers the first talking picture, *The Jazz Singer* (Alan Crosland, 1927) with Al Jolson. Without hesitation, he announces to his weary business manager, Noah Dietrich (John C. Reilly): "You see, this is what people want. Silent pictures are yesterday's news, so I figure I have to reshoot *Hell's Angels* for sound" (22–23).

Hughes's perfectionism is vindicated when *Hell's Angels* turns out to be a critical and a commercial success. But, as we see throughout *The Aviator,* Hughes pays a price for perfection, literally in terms of how much money it costs him to keep reworking *Hell's Angels* to meet his high standards. Fortunately for Hughes, his inheritance ensures that he has enough money to pursue his dreams, as he tells Dietrich: "My folks are gone now *so it's my money*" (4). *The Aviator* keeps emphasizing this point—that Hughes's own money is at stake in his artistic and business ventures. It is not just that he is a visionary—"Leave the *big ideas* to me" (10)—it is even more important that he has the courage of his convictions and is willing to put his money where his mouth is. Even when he borrows the money to finance his enter-prises, he puts up all his personal assets as collateral. To raise the money to finish *Hell's Angels,* he instructs Dietrich: "Mortgage Toolco. Every asset." The results could, of course, be disastrous, as his second in command tells him: "If you do that you could lose everything" (26). But, as a businessman, Hughes is a gambler, and he plays for high stakes. He does not simply risk his money; again and again he risks it all. *The Aviator* distinguishes itself from most movies about business by constantly reminding us why entrepreneurs are rewarded. It is for taking risks, and the biggest winners are often those who take the biggest chances.

The motif of "one's own money" runs throughout *The Aviator* and devel-ops a moral dimension. Hughes makes many daring decisions, and he often makes them on the spur of the moment and by himself, against the advice of others. At times, he appears to be erratic, eccentric, or irresponsible. But, the film implies, as long as it is his own money that he is risking and he is willing to bear the consequences himself, he has the right to do so. In the last main plot sequence in the film, when Hughes is building the giant flying boat that he called the Hercules and that a skeptical public came to know as the Spruce Goose, the moral basis of his business conduct alters precisely when, as a defense contractor, he starts risking taxpayers' money. *The Aviator* would truly be a libertarian film if it were suggesting that Hughes's eagerness for government contracts was what, in the end, corrupted him as a businessman, but I am not sure that the film goes that far. But it does at least begin to raise doubts about his morality as a businessman only when he enters the world of big-government spending and factors like bribery become more important in winning contracts than genuine economic competitiveness. Hughes is able to vindicate himself at the Senate hearings only when he returns to the motif of one's own money, telling the committee: "You see the thing is I care very much about aviation. It's been the great joy of my life. So I put my own money into these planes. . . . I've lost millions, Mr. Chairman" (179).

## The Nature of the Entrepreneur

Beyond the moral dimension of risking one's own money as a business principle, *The Aviator* suggests that doing so makes one a better business-man. In his struggle to get *Hell's Angels* right, Hughes reveals what is driving him to perfection: "My *name* depends on this picture. If it doesn't work, I'm back to Houston with my tail between my legs, making goddamn drill bits for the rest of my life" (10). Hughes's personal pride is bound up with his personal fortune, and we see that the fact that he has such a personal stake in his business enterprises makes him a much better steward of the money he has at his disposal. If he were spending other people's money, as government bureaucrats do, he would have less incentive to be careful with it. In such circumstances, if he made a mistake, he would not suffer the financial consequences himself, and, if he made the right decision, he would not reap the financial reward. But, as *The Aviator* shows, Hughes is a true entrepreneur because he plays a high-stakes game in which he stands to lose or gain millions personally.

The film thus displays a solid grasp of the libertarian understanding of the entrepreneurial function in the free market, a point made cogently by Mises when he distinguishes the true entrepreneur (who invests his own money) from the mere manager (who handles other people's money):

> Society can freely leave the care for the best possible employment of capital goods to their owners. In embarking upon definite projects these owners expose their own property, wealth, and social position. They are even more interested in the success of their entrepreneur-ial activities than is society as a whole. For society as a whole the squandering of capital invested in a definite project means only the loss of a small part of its total funds; for the owner it means much more, for the most part the loss of his total fortune. But if a

manager is given a completely free hand, things are different. He speculates in risking other people's money. He sees the prospects of an uncertain enterprise from another angle than that of the man who is answerable for the losses. It is precisely when he is rewarded by a share of the profits that he becomes foolhardy because he does not share in the losses too.[9]

When people complain about the "obscene" profits entrepreneurs make, they conveniently forget about the appalling losses they risk at the same time. Entrepreneurs are fundamentally rewarded for taking risks, indeed, for living with a level of risk that most people would find utterly unacceptable. *The Aviator* shows clearly that Hughes's great financial successes were constantly haunted by the prospect of financial disaster. The movie grasps the difference between a true entrepreneur and a mere manager, and, indeed, it shows Hughes always concentrating on the big investment picture while leaving the details to his managers. In portraying Hughes as willing to make a big business decision, stick to it, and accept the consequences, *The Aviator* celebrates the authentic courage of the entrepreneur.

One would think that more Hollywood filmmakers would appreciate the role of the entrepreneur, given the fact that filmmaking is one of the most entrepreneurial of businesses.[10] Huge amounts of money are made and lost in Hollywood as producers try to anticipate what entertainment the fickle public wishes to see. The entrepreneurial character of *The Aviator* itself is stressed in an article appropriately subtitled "This Year, the Safe Bets Are Off" by Patrick Goldstein. Goldstein discusses what distinguished the five Oscar nominees for best picture in 2004: "They were largely financed by outside investors. . . . Most of the nominees aren't even classic outside-the-system indie movies. They're artistic gambles financed by entrepreneurs. . . . *The Aviator*, though released by Miramax, was financed largely by Graham King, who was responsible for roughly $80 million of the film's $116-million budget (the rest coming from Miramax and Warner Bros. Films)." Ironically, the chief reason it proved difficult to raise the money to make *The Aviator* was Scorsese's reputation as a difficult director, one who has trouble respecting schedules and budgets. Goldstein cites King: "He says *The Aviator* met with rejection everywhere, even with DiCaprio attached to star. Everyone was scared that Scorsese would be uncontrollable." As it turned out, despite wildfires on location in California that interrupted shooting, Scorsese managed to finish the film on schedule in November 2003 and without large cost overruns. Still, everyone involved in the film had reason to feel grateful to King for his $80 million gamble on the project. Goldstein writes of the way

DiCaprio showed his gratitude: "Hanging in King's office in Santa Monica is a framed picture of the star kneeling in front of one of the film's biplanes, with the hand-scrawled inscription: 'To Graham, thank you for being the only one to have the [guts] to make my dream a reality.'"[11] Goldstein adds his own tribute to King: "It's no wonder why King alone has produced three best picture nominees in the last five years: *The Aviator, Gangs of New York* and *Traffic*. Unlike the studios, King, who bankrolls his films by selling off the rights in foreign territories, is in the risk-taking business."[12] The story of the making of *The Aviator* neatly parallels the story the film itself tells. Indeed, it is the same story of the courage of the entrepreneur in risking large sums of his own money on what he believes will sell in the marketplace.

## The Way of the Future

In this business of anticipating consumer demand, *The Aviator* also celebrates the intellectual qualities of the entrepreneur. As we have seen, the key to Hughes's success is his orientation toward the future. He immediately sees that the arrival of talkies has made the silent movie obsolete, and he acts accordingly, without hesitation. He is a great pioneer in aviation because he is always asking himself what the public wants and how airline service could be improved. He builds TWA into a major airline by following his vision of the future: "We build a plane that flies *above* the weather and we could get every man, woman and child in this country to feel *safe* up there. . . . An airplane with the ability to fly into the substratosphere—across the country—across the world. . . . Now that is the future" (37). At the end of *The Aviator*, right after Hughes has finally gotten the Spruce Goose to fly, he is still thinking about the future of aviation as he turns his mind to the potential of jet aircraft for commercial use. This is one of the points where the film departs from historical accuracy. The real Howard Hughes was, in fact, slower than his competitors in equipping his airline with jet aircraft.[13] But, to strengthen its presentation of the entrepreneur as visionary, *The Aviator* shows Hughes one step ahead of his competition even in this area: "I've been thinking about something. Something new—*jet airplanes*. . . . Whoever can start utilizing jet technology on commercial airlines is gonna win all the marbles. . . . We gotta get into it. Jets are gonna be the way of the future. The way of the future. The way of the future. The way of the future . . ." (189–90). *The Aviator* emphasizes Hughes's role as a forward-looking entrepreneur by choosing these as his last words in the film. The film ends with him repeating this phrase over and over again while his aides hustle him off so that no one can see him finally plunging into madness. In the film's view, Hughes was a victim of what is now called obsessive-compulsive disorder, and the perfectionism that made him succeed as a businessman was linked to a pathological condition that eventually drove him crazy.[14]

The film links Hughes's madness to his genius by suggesting that it is what makes him think outside the box. He does not behave the way ordinary people do, and he does not think the way they do either. When he orders a meal, it must be "New York cut steak, twelve peas, bottle of milk with the cap on" (42)—twelve peas, no more, no fewer, arranged symmetrically. We see here his childhood obsession with order and cleanliness at work, and it makes him appear weird. But the same obsessiveness is at work when he sets out to produce the world's fastest plane: "The rivets have to be completely flush, every screw and joint countersunk. No wind resistance on the fuselage. She's gotta be clean" (36). In short, it is precisely because Hughes is a misfit that he stands out from the crowd. He is always doing what is least expected of him and proves the value of a contrarian stance in economic matters. Once again, *The Aviator* develops a portrait of the entrepreneur that is familiar in libertarian philosophy in general and Austrian economics in particular. Here is Mises's classic description of the entrepreneur:

> The real entrepreneur is a *speculator*, a man eager to utilize his opinion about the future structure of the market for business operations promising profits. This specific anticipative understanding of the conditions of the uncertain future defies any rules and systematization. It can be neither taught nor learned. If it were different, everybody could embark upon entrepreneurship with the same prospect of success. What distinguishes the successful entrepreneur and promoter from other people is precisely the fact that he does not let himself be guided by what was and is, but arranges his affairs on the ground of his opinion about the future. He sees the past and present as other people do; but he judges the future in a different way. In his actions he is directed by an opinion about the future which deviates from those held by the crowd.[15]

*The Aviator* is fully in accord with Mises's conception of the entrepreneur. By acknowledging that there may be an element of madness in entrepreneurial genius, it emphasizes the individuality of the great businessman, the uniqueness of his vision, the fact that he simply does not see the world the way ordinary people do.

## A Socialist Dinner Party

While celebrating the visionary power of the entrepreneur, *The Aviator* also does a remarkable job of identifying the sources of opposition to this creativity and originality. As the representative of the future, the entrepreneur is constantly running afoul of all the representatives of the past, members of the establishment who have a vested interest in seeing the status quo remain undisturbed. In *The Aviator,* the establishment consists of three principal forces: old money, big business, and big government. Hughes ends up in conflict with old money as a result of his affair with Katharine Hepburn, who, according to the screenplay, comes from a "patrician Yankee clan." When the actress brings Hughes home to her "ancestral Connecticut manor" (66) to meet her family, he cannot fit into this upper-class environment and is rejected by the Hepburns as a nouveau riche upstart. Here is another point where the film departs from historical accuracy. To emphasize the contrast between Hughes and the Hepburns, it downplays the fact that Hughes was not exactly nouveau riche, having inherited a great deal of money himself. And his family did send him to an exclusive New England boarding school in the Boston area (Fessenden).[16] But the film may be allowed some poetic license here for the sake of creating a dramatic contrast and making an important point about old money. Moreover, with his roots in Texas and California and his stake in the motion picture and aviation industries, Hughes does represent the brash new economic forces from the West Coast and the Southwest that challenged the supremacy of the East Coast establishment in twentieth-century America.

*The Aviator* presents this struggle as a culture war. Hughes represents the new popular culture of Hollywood, while the Hepburns represent the old high culture of New England, with its ties to Europe. Even though Katharine Hepburn is a movie actress, from her first appearance she makes it clear that she prefers traditional drama to film: "I adore the theater. Only alive on stage" (33). The Hepburn family looks down on Hughes as crass, uncultivated, and uncouth, as a kind of mechanic who has no appreciation for art and all the other finer things in life. He reads "flying magazines" (actually aviation journals); they "read books" (71–72). In the arts, the Hepburns keep current with all the fashionable contemporary trends. The painter in their little artist colony is "abstract of course" (68), and they sit around debating the merits of Goya versus Picasso while quoting Jean Cocteau about Edith Piaf (72–73). The film presents the Hepburns as affected snobs of the worst kind. The screenplay reads: "Welcome to Fenwick where all the blood is blue and all the jaws are clenched" (68). Clearly, we are meant to sympathize with Hughes in this scene. For once, he seems to stand for normality in the midst of all this aristocratic pretension and pseudointellectualism.

What is most interesting about the presentation of the Hepburns in *The Aviator* is their politics. Although they are wealthy and upper-class, they are left-wing in their political opinions. In fact, almost the first thing Mrs. Hepburn says to Hughes at the dinner table is: "We're all socialists here!" (68). In practical political terms, the Hepburns are Democrats and fans of Franklin Delano Roosevelt and his New Deal, with all its antibusiness policies. Mrs. Hepburn announces to Hughes with all her aristocratic hauteur: "I will not have sniggering at Mr. Roosevelt at my table" (69). Roosevelt was, of course, from an old, established, socially prominent East Coast family himself. The idea that aristocrats might be socialists and favor antibusiness policies may, at first, appear strange. But, as several libertarian thinkers have argued, the extreme Left and the extreme Right often meet in their distrust and hatred of the free market.[17] Like socialists with their commitment to central planning, aristocrats believe in a static social order and reject the supposed messiness and chaos of the free market. *The Aviator* explores the socioeconomic dynamic of "aristocratic socialism" by the contrast it draws between Hughes and the Hepburns.

We tend to lump the wealthy together into a single class, but *The Aviator* suggests that how one acquires one's wealth makes a great difference. The Hepburn family scene culminates in a pointed exchange between Hughes and his hosts:

> LUDLOW: Then how did you make all that money?
> MRS. HEPBURN: We don't care about money here, Mr. Hughes.
> HOWARD: That's because you have it.
> MRS. HEPBURN: Would you repeat that?
> HOWARD: You don't care about money because you have it. And you've always had it. My father was dirt poor when I was born. . . . I care about money, because I know what it takes out of a man to make it. (74)

*The Aviator* suggests that those who are comfortably born into money take it for granted. The wealthy entrepreneur, by contrast, has made his money by his own efforts and appreciates both the money itself and the struggle it takes to accumulate it. Understanding how markets work, the entrepreneur favors economic freedom and opposes government policies that limit the

flexibility entrepreneurs need to respond to ever-changing market conditions. The representatives of old money are hostile to economic change
because they worry that it can only undermine their upper-class status.
Hence, old money may, paradoxically, support socialist or antibusiness
policies because they hamstring the entrepreneurial activities that lead to
the formation of new money. To preserve its privileged position, old money
may favor government intervention in the market that hinders the accumulation of new wealth by the next generation. The sociological analysis
implicit in the Hepburn family scene in *The Aviator* is subtle and accords
with libertarian thinking on the subject. In exploring the conflict between
old money and new, the film complicates our understanding of social class
and reminds us that, just because people are wealthy, they do not necessarily share a common interest or the same opinions about economic policy.
Hughes is, in many respects, at his most sympathetic in this scene, which
shows how Scorsese can treat even a wealthy man as an underdog. And
where else has Hollywood ever portrayed supporters of Franklin Delano
Roosevelt so unsympathetically?[18]

## The Senator from Pan Am

The other source of opposition to Hughes in *The Aviator* is the sinister alliance between big business and big government. The film builds up to and
climaxes with Hughes's struggle against the efforts of Pan Am, in collusion
with a U.S. senator, to keep TWA out of the international airline business.
*The Aviator* thus ends on a distinctively libertarian note, dwelling on the
confrontation between the heroic individual and the leviathan state.[19] As
Hughes himself puts it when being cross-examined by Owen Brewster: "I am
only a private citizen, while you are a Senator with all sorts of powers" (170).
In the contrast it draws between Hughes and Juan Trippe, the president of
Pan Am, *The Aviator* again differentiates what many analysts, Marxist and
otherwise, mistakenly lump together. Not all businessmen are alike; some
are genuine entrepreneurs and serve the public, while others use the power
of the government to stifle free competition and, hence, innovation. Tripp
represents the business establishment, which is comfortable working with
the government and its regulations, especially when the regulatory powers
of the government can be exploited to entrench a company's market position. In contrasting Hughes with Trippe and TWA with Pan Am, *The Aviator*
suggests that there are two ways that a business can come to dominate an
industry. TWA under Hughes's leadership gains its market share the legiti-

mate way, by providing the public with what it wants in an economically efficient manner. Pan Am under Tripp's leadership exemplifies the dark side of business. Using its influence with the government to restrict access to its markets, it does not have to worry about being competitive in the services it offers.[20] *The Aviator* clearly distinguishes between genuinely competitive business practices in a free market environment and monopolistic practices in an environment of government regulation.

*The Aviator* presents Hughes as fighting explicitly against the principle of monopoly: "No one airline should have a *monopoly* on flying the Atlantic. That's just not fair! . . . [Juan Trippe] owns Pan Am. He owns Congress. He owns the Civil Aeronautics Board. *But he does not own the sky. . . .* I have been fighting high hat, Ivy League pricks like him my whole life" (105). *The Aviator* adopts the concept of monopoly familiar in libertarian thinking. Unlike Marxists, libertarians do not view monopoly as the inevitable outcome of economic competition and, indeed, the ultimate stage of capitalism. On the contrary, they view it as the opposite of capitalism, a holdover from the precapitalist system known as *mercantilism,* in which governments granted special privileges to businesses, often chartering them as the exclusive proprietors in a given field. The script of *The Aviator* makes it clear that Senator Brewster's Community Airline Bill has nothing to do with capitalism; it is, instead, based on a European socialist model of nationalized industries: "Senator Brewster is saying that domestic competition will kill expansion into the global market—because the nationalized foreign carriers, like Air France and Lufthansa, can offer lower fares 'cause they don't have to *compete,* right? So, hey, let's get rid of all that messy competition and have a *nationalized* airline of our own. And, hey, why don't we make it Pan Am?" (116).

In his private meeting with Hughes before the hearings, Brewster tries to present himself in typical big-government fashion as the friend of the consumer:

> HOWARD: You think it's fair for one airline to have a monopoly on international travel?
> BREWSTER: I think one airline can do it better without competition. All I'm thinking about is the needs of the American passenger. (145)

At the actual hearing, Hughes is able to cut through Brewster's rhetoric and focus on the real reason behind his legislation: "This entire bill was written by *Pan Am executives* and designed to give that airline a *monopoly* on international travel!" (175). *The Aviator* supports the claims of many opponents of government intervention in the market—the agencies created to regulate the market become clients of the very businesses they are supposed to be regulating.

At its heart, *The Aviator* thus champions the American principle of free market competition against European socialism and the model of nationalized industries. At the hearing, Hughes demolishes the pretense of big government to represent the public interest and shows that corrupt senators like Brewster are simply serving one private interest (Pan Am) at the expense of another (TWA). The film clearly suggests that the public interest is, in fact, better served by an economic system in which genuine entrepreneurs are free to compete with each other to introduce innovations in the marketplace. In the Senate hearing scene, *The Aviator* brilliantly plays with a Hollywood stereotype.[21] When one sees anyone hauled before a Senate committee on charges of corruption, one normally expects to find the public-spiritedness of the government triumph over the greed of the private individual. But Scorsese uses all his cinematic powers to craft a scene that shows just the opposite, revealing what often turns out to be the reality behind the illusion of big-government benevolence. One company is simply using its influence with the government to gain an unfair advantage over a legitimate competitor.

## The Invisible Hand

In the way in which *The Aviator* differentiates the good businessman from the bad, it provides a useful reminder that free market thinkers are not lackeys of big business, as Marxists often try to portray them. Libertarians do not uncritically support businessmen; they defend a system that forces businessmen, often against their will, to compete with each other in serving the interests of consumers. Libertarian thinkers are acutely aware that many businessmen resent the sharp discipline of the marketplace and turn to governments to relieve them from competitive pressures by granting them economic privileges. Libertarians champion only the true entrepreneur, the one who accepts the challenge of competing in an open market. For that very reason, libertarians are very suspicious of big business, which, as *The Aviator* shows, is often all too eager to collude with big government to eliminate competition. That is one of the central claims of Adam Smith's *The Wealth of Nations*. Smith defends free trade and other free market principles, but he often speaks of businessmen in extremely negative terms. In fact, he is no friend of businessmen because he is a friend of free markets. He believes that businessmen must be forced into free competition. In his view, their natural inclination is to seek out economic privileges from governments.

Smith sees the baleful influence of businessmen behind the protectionist policies of the European regimes of his day as well as the mercantilist doctrine that stood in the way of free trade:

> That it was the spirit of monopoly which originally both invented and propagated this doctrine, cannot be doubted. . . . In every country it always is and must be the interest of the great body of the people to buy whatever they want of those who sell it cheapest. The proposition is so very manifest, that it seems ridiculous to take any pains to prove it; nor could it ever have been called in question, had not the interested sophistry of merchants and manufacturers confounded the common sense of mankind. Their interest is, in this respect, directly opposite to that of the great body of the people. . . . It is the interest of the merchants and manufacturers of every country to secure to themselves the monopoly of the home market.

Most people do not realize that Smith traces the lack of freedom in the marketplace to what he calls "the monopolizing spirit of merchants and manufacturers."[22] In the way in which it portrays the battle between Hughes and Trippe, *The Aviator* offers a concrete illustration of this basic libertarian principle. People have a hard time grasping the fact that free market thinkers support capitalism but not necessarily individual capitalists—especially when they turn out to be working against the very principles of the free market. Libertarians argue that free market principles are needed precisely to discipline individual businessmen, to prevent them from seeking out unfair advantages at the expense of their fellow entrepreneurs.

This disciplinary power of the market is one way of formulating the famous principle of "the invisible hand," as articulated by Smith. Smith argued that the best social order is not one that attempts to pursue the public good directly. Far preferable is an order in which human beings are free to pursue their private good as they themselves understand it. The larger good of the public will, in fact, emerge out of this free competition in pursuing private goods. As Smith writes in one of the best-known passages in *The Wealth of Nations:*

> As every individual, therefore, endeavours as much as he can both to employ his capital in the support of domestick industry, and so

to direct that industry that its produce may be of the greatest value; every individual necessarily labours to render the annual revenue of the society as great as he can. He generally, indeed, neither intends to promote the publick interest, nor knows how much he is promoting it. By preferring the support of domestick to that of foreign industry, he intends only his own security; and by directing that industry in such a manner as its produce may be of the greatest value, he intends only his own gain, and he is in this, as in many other cases, led by an invisible hand to promote an end which was no part of his intention. Nor is it always the worse for the society that it was no part of it. By pursuing his own interest he frequently promotes that of the society more effectually than when he really intends to promote it. I have never known much good done by those who affected to trade for the publick good.[23]

This famous passage might serve as a gloss on *The Aviator*. The film shows that those who claim to be pursuing the public good are often hypocrites, secretly pursuing their own private good behind a facade of respectability and, in fact, stifling the entrepreneurial activity that is the only real source of progress. And, in its complicated and ambivalent portrait of Howard Hughes, the film makes a fundamental libertarian point—one does not have to be a morally good man in order to serve the public good. Scorsese's Hughes has many faults. He is ambitious and vain, with a compelling need to be the center of attention. He is a fierce competitor who is often willing to resort to unscrupulous means to achieve his ends. He is not public-spirited in any conventional sense. On the contrary, he is always looking out for himself, interested primarily in his own fame and fortune. Yet *The Aviator* suggests that, in pursuing his private obsessions, he ends up benefiting the public. He advances two of the great arts of modernity—aviation and the motion picture—and, thereby, helps build the world of the twentieth century. One is reminded of another famous passage in Smith: "It is not from the benevolence of the butcher, the brewer, or the baker, that we expect our dinner, but from their regard to their own interest. We address ourselves, not to their humanity but to their self-love."[24] This may sound like a very cynical doctrine, but it is also a realistic one. There are many fantasy elements in *The Aviator*—it is, after all, in part about the dream factory of Hollywood—but, as we have seen, it is rooted in an unusually solid grasp of economic reality. It offers one of the fullest, most complex, and most insightful portraits of the nature of the entrepreneur ever to appear in a film. And, in celebrating the visionary career of Howard Hughes, *The Aviator* becomes one of the great American motion pictures because it celebrates the entrepreneurial spirit that made America great.

## Notes

1. In an interview, Scorsese says of Hughes: "He became the outlaw of Hollywood in a way" ("Martin Scorsese Interview—'The Aviator,'" http://movies.about.com/od/theaviator/a/aviatorms121004.htm).

2. Martin Scorsese, introduction to *The Aviator: A Screenplay by John Logan* (New York: Miramax, 2004), vii. Elsewhere, in response to the question: "Do you see any parallel between Howard Hughes' obsessions and yours?" Scorsese replied: "I have [had] over the years, some close friends and acquaintances who have said, who have described me at one point, 'Don't go in the room. He's got the tissue boxes on his feet.' . . . But basically I couldn't presume to say I've been like Howard Hughes. Howard Hughes was this visionary. . . . I usually like to lock myself in the screening room and just screen. That's maybe the only similarity I see" ("Scorsese Interview"). Leonardo DiCaprio was more candid when asked whether he could relate to Hughes: "The *Hell's Angels* sequence, being a part of films that have gone on for many, many months and you're sitting there with the director trying to get things perfect and do things over and over and over again, that was something that I think Scorsese and I immediately identified with" ("Leonardo DiCaprio Talks about 'The Aviator,'" http://movies.about .com/od/theaviator/a/aviatorld121004.htm).

3. A perfect example of Hollywood's negative portrayal of the businessman is the cruel banker Mr. Potter in the classic *It's a Wonderful Life* (Frank Capra, 1946). For a comprehensive survey of the portrayal of businessmen in American popular culture, see Don Lavoie and Emily Chamlee-Wright, "The Culture Industry's Representation of Business," in *Culture and Enterprise: The Development, Representation, and Morality of Business* (London: Routledge, 2000), 80–103. Here are some representative figures from media studies: "Of all the antagonists studied in over 30 years of programming, businessmen were twice as likely to play the role of antagonist than any other identifiable occupation. Business characters are nearly three times as likely to be criminals, relative to other occupations on television. They represent 12 percent of all characters in identifiable occupations, but account for 32 percent of crimes. Forty-four percent of all vice crimes such as prostitution and drug trafficking committed on television, and 40 percent of TV murders, are perpetrated by business people" (ibid., 84).

4. On the hostility to business in culture in general, see F. A. Hayek, *The Fatal Conceit: The Errors of Socialism* (Chicago: University of Chicago Press, 1988), 89–105, and Ludwig von Mises, *The Anti-Capitalistic Mentality* (Princeton, NJ: Van Nostrand, 1956). For an interesting analysis of the psychology of detective stories, see Mises, *Anti-Capitalistic Mentality*, 52–55.

5. The Hollywood archetype of the idealistic senator who takes on the business

interests in his state and fights corruption, even in the Senate itself, is, of course, Jimmy Stewart's Mr. Smith in Frank Capra's *Mr. Smith Goes to Washington* (1939).

6. Scorsese, introduction, viii. Elsewhere, Scorsese says of the movie: "The approach on this material really, really comes from John Logan, the writer" ("Scorsese Interview").

7. See Charles Higham, *Howard Hughes: The Secret Life* (New York: Putnam's, 1993).

8. *The Aviator: A Screenplay*, 6. For the sake of convenience, I have quoted from the published version of the screenplay, even though the spoken dialogue occasionally departs in minor ways from the text. Page numbers for subsequent citations are given in the text.

9. Ludwig von Mises, *Human Action: A Treatise on Economics* (New Haven, CT: Yale University Press, 1949), 303. On this point, see also Adam Smith, *An Inquiry into the Nature and Causes of the Wealth of Nations* (1776; reprint, Indianapolis: Liberty, 1981), 1:454, 456.

10. For speculation on why people in Hollywood generally condemn capitalism, see Mises, *Anti-Capitalistic Mentality*, 30–33.

11. The bowdlerization in brackets is courtesy of the *Los Angeles Times*. My guess is that what DiCaprio really wrote was *balls*.

12. Patrick Goldstein, "The Big Picture: This Year, the Safe Bets Are Off," *Los Angeles Times*, January 26, 2005.

13. See Higham, *Howard Hughes*, 179.

14. See Leonardo DiCaprio, foreword to *The Aviator: A Screenplay*, vi. Elsewhere, in response to the question: "Do you think Howard Hughes would have been the genius that he was without the OCD [obsessive-compulsive disorder]?" DiCaprio replied: "I think they're a direct result of one another. It's like he would have not been as obsessed about making the largest plane ever built. He wouldn't have been obsessed about breaking every speed record. He wouldn't have been obsessed about flying around the world faster than anyone else. He wouldn't have been obsessed about reshooting *Hell's Angels* for sound, having that movie go on for four years. . . . It was all completely a part of his obsessive nature and his OCD that made him have such an amazing, astounding life" ("DiCaprio Talks").

15. Mises, *Human Action*, 582.

16. See Higham, *Howard Hughes*, 24.

17. See, e.g., Mises, *Anti-Capitalistic Mentality*, 44–45. Joseph Conrad's novel *The Secret Agent* (1907) provides a brilliant analysis of aristocratic socialism and also traces the convergence of the extreme Left and the extreme Right in a hatred of capitalism.

18. For a parallel in Scorsese's work, one might look to the treatment of Abraham Lincoln in *Gangs of New York*. With its suspicion of federal war policies—and especially the draft—the film seems to sympathize with the hostile response of New Yorkers to a stage representation of Lincoln. American presidents who vastly expanded the power of the federal government do not appear to be faring well in Scorsese's latest movies.

19. Scorsese and DiCaprio agree on this point. Scorsese says: "Ultimately, what I

really liked was the way the story developed into a struggle between [Hughes] and the government and Pan Am. I thought that was interesting. I think it has a lot of resonance for today, particularly the investigation committee smearing people" ("Scorsese Interview"). DiCaprio says: "How the hell do you make this situation with Juan Trippe and Pan American Airways and this Senator become a sympathetic situation towards Howard Hughes? . . . I realized . . . it has to do with corporate takeover and the involvement of huge corporations with our government, and they're in cahoots and it's going on today with the Enron scandals and numerous other things. That's what really made me say, 'Okay, here's this one man, he's his own boss, he is rich but he is a stand-up individual and here he is with all these horrible things going on with himself mentally, standing up in front of the Senate and battling the Senate to stop the monopoly on international travel.' I think, ultimately, people kind of got behind that. . . . They really loved this one individual taking on the entire system, taking on the government, taking on huge monopolies and corporations" ("DiCaprio Talks").

20. Let me reiterate here that I am not talking about the historical facts of this case, only about the way *The Aviator* presents them.

21. Specifically, Scorsese seems to have in mind the great Senate hearing scene in Francis Ford Coppola's *The Godfather: Part II* (1974). Although we are sympathetic to Michael Corleone even in this scene, there can be no question that he is, in fact, guilty of the crimes that the Senate committee is investigating. Given Scorsese's lifelong rivalry with Coppola, it is difficult to believe that he was not trying to show that he could create a Senate hearing scene as powerful as the one by his fellow Italian American director. A number of the details in Scorsese's scene—Hughes's consultation with his "consigliere," Noah Dietrich, his reading of a prepared statement, his appeal to his patriotism, the confusion and consternation among the senators when the hearing fails to go the way they planned—all point to Coppola's corresponding scene. Note that both scenes take place just after World War II; even the cinematography of Scorsese's scene echoes Coppola's. Read against Coppola's scene, Scorsese's takes on added meaning—Scorsese is showing that the senators are the gangsters. (Coppola's film already hints in this direction; one of the senators on the investigating committee, Pat Geary, is shown to have ties to the Corleone family.)

22. Smith, *Wealth of Nations,* 1:493–94, 493.

23. Ibid., 456.

24. Ibid., 26–27.

# Art, Sex, and Time in Scorsese's *After Hours*

*Richard Gilmore*

> Sex and art are the same thing.
>
> —Pablo Picasso

*After Hours* (1985) was an important film for Scorsese. He had completed *The King of Comedy* in 1983, and it was a commercial flop. He then made his first attempt at what had long been a dream film of his to make, *The Last Temptation of Christ* from the novel by Nikos Kazantzakis, but, when the project spiraled over budget and a major theater line said that it would not show the film, the producers withdrew all funding, and filming had to be abandoned. People, the money people, were losing confidence in Scorsese, and he was losing confidence in himself. He needed an inexpensive, successful movie to regain the lost ground. He made *After Hours,* and it won the best director award at the Cannes Film Festival in 1986.

The movie begins in an open office area full of desks topped with computers, phones, papers, and general office clutter. We hear the click of typewriters, the hum of computers, and see people moving around, busy at their work. The camera tracks its way through this busy space until it comes to rest on the scene of two men, Paul Hackett (Griffin Dunne) and Lloyd (Bronson Pinchot, whose character is not given a last name), sitting before a computer. Paul is teaching Lloyd, who is obviously a new recruit to the office, some things about computer programming. When they get through the particular maneuver they are working on, Lloyd confesses to Paul that he does not really care about this work, that for him it is only temporary, and that his real interest is in literature and starting his own publishing house. As soon as Lloyd starts his confession, Paul seems to be sent into a kind of fugue state that is marked by the nondiegetic music of the Air from J. S. Bach's Orchestral Suite no. 3 in D Major (BWV 1068), popularly known as the *Air for the G String.* In this fugue state, Paul's gaze moves apparently randomly around the office space, lighting on particular details that do not seem to have any connecting meaning or pattern: a phone, a person's fingers typing on an electric typewriter, a calendar, a photograph of someone's child. Lloyd's mention of art seems to send Paul into a kind of interstitial space and time, a kind of secret realm of mind within the regimented space-time of the office, a realm that has always been available to Paul but, one senses, is not often accessed by him. This realm is dominated by a counterlogic to the institutional logic of the office space, and it seems to be a primarily aesthetic logic. His fugued gaze isolates particular tableaux for no particular reason other than the beauty of their composition. This fugue state continues, if the music is to be believed, even after his workday is over. He seems to be still in it as he leaves the office building, which he barely escapes, its huge golden gates just closing as he slides his way out between them.

## The Logic of the Same

In *Totality and Infinity,* Emmanuel Levinas talks about the "*way* of the same."[1] The logic of the same is the logic of totality. It is the logic that one uses to make sense of the world. The logic of the same is very useful. Many can share the same logic of the same and work together to impose it on a given social space. An office space will have a logic to it, and it will be a logic of the same. Let's give a name to a logic of the same; let's call it, after Lyotard, the *logic of maximum efficiency.*[2] A person who employs this logic will evaluate all things in the world around him according to the criterion of efficiency. The criterion of efficiency is, ultimately, that which produces the most excess money, which is the logic of the same of capitalism, in general, and of corporate businesses like the one Lloyd and Paul work at, in particular. With this criterion of efficiency, speedy, accurate typing may be considered very good; even though it is quite removed from the actual production of excess money, its goodness nevertheless derives from the idea that, eventually, such efficient, proficient typing will translate into the production of excess money.

What has happened in the beginning of *After Hours* is that Lloyd has defied the logic of the same of the office space. He speaks in appropriately hushed, conspiratorial, confessional tones, but because he is saying things that he knows are inappropriate in that space. He says the thing that should not be said: "I do not intend to be stuck doing this for the rest of my life." This statement debases the essential logic of the space. Paul Hackett can't hack it, cannot hear it; he immediately becomes unavailable to Lloyd, who, rejected, looks at Paul with a look that reveals his hurt and humiliation. He has been rebuked by Paul; his gesture of intimacy has been rejected. He opened himself up to Paul, which means that he made himself vulnerable to rebuke. Presumably, there is something about Paul that elicits his trust, that makes him think that Paul will be receptive to his confession, but he was proved wrong.

Of course, Lloyd is not really wrong about Paul. Paul longs for intimacy, longs to be true to the possibilities of the aesthetic, to a counternarrative to the logic of the office space, that surrounds him. As Lloyd speaks, Paul glances at his watch, the ultimate gesture of enforcement of office space logic, then turns away as though he could not care less about what Lloyd is saying. But, even as he seems to uphold the logic of the office space, Paul himself slips out of it as his fugued gaze moves around that space, resting first on one and then on another detail in the space around him. His gaze focuses on specific tableaux with the kind of decontextualizing concentration with which an artist sees. Lloyd's words have, like a virus—perhaps a benign virus—wormed their way into Paul's thinking, into his consciousness, creating a crack in his logic of the same, destabilizing his totality, hinting at the possibility of an infinity that is present, available, accessible. The opposite attitudinal stance from that of being locked in the bubble of the same is that of being open to the possibility of infinity, the openness to unlimited possibilities of meaning in the other.

Paul goes home after work, still immersed in the mood indicated by the Bach. We see the fruits of Paul's "totality": an empty, spare apartment and a phone message machine with ten message buttons but no messages. Haunted by his fugue, Paul goes out into the night for some dinner at a local diner. He is reading Henry Miller's *Tropic of Cancer*. It is a novel about a life that is everything Paul's is not—disorderly, bohemian, full of spontaneous sex, and completely devoted to art. Paul seems to be oblivious to the presence of Marcy (Rosanna Arquette), just a table away, but she starts speaking to him. She says she loves Henry Miller and then quotes from memory a wonderful passage from *Tropic of Cancer*: "This is not a book. This is a prolonged insult, a gob of spit in the face of Art; a kick in the pants to truth, beauty, God . . . something like that." It is a gesture of intimacy. She has made herself vulnerable in several ways: she has spoken first to a complete stranger, a strange man, in a strange public place; she has confessed a love of art and of a particular artist, a risky business in the United States; she attempts to quote from memory, which is always a little scary. And, in the end, she does seem to be a little flustered by her own brazenness. But this time Paul responds. He returns the intimacy. He is charming and works hard to see her, to respond to her, to act as though everything she says matters. Then, in a kind of mythic gesture, she leaves him, but she leaves him with a clue as to how to find her. It is indirect, as clues are, and the pathway is opened up by an artwork. The explicit offer is a plaster of paris bagel and cream cheese. The implicit offer—if he can figure it out and has the courage to pursue it—is, of course, her.

He does figure it out, and he does pursue it, and he calls her. She invites him down to where she lives, down to SoHo. It is already late, he presumably has work the next day, he seems to calculate for just a moment (the power of the logic of the office space), but then he accepts the invitation with enthusiasm (the power of desire) and heads out once again into the night. At this point, the theme of the movie is pretty explicitly on the model of the *katabasis*, the descent into the underworld. There is a violent taxi ride "down" to SoHo; the accompanying music is flamenco, a music that is meant to emerge from and to evoke the dark, passionate spirit that the Spanish call *duende*. The cabdriver has the glowing red-rimmed eyes of Charon, the boatman to hell. In the chaos of speed, wind, and swervings of the ride down, Paul loses his one piece of folding money, a twenty-dollar bill, and, thus, has nothing with which to pay the cabdriver. Technically, according to the myth, if you can't pay, you can't cross, but, in Paul's case, he can't pay, so he won't be able to leave.

What follows is a scene that Scorsese himself refers to as "the signature scene" of the film.[3] Paul rings the doorbell for a third-floor apartment. He tries the door to the foyer, but it is locked. An interesting detail is a small poster on which we see, outlined in white, the figure of a man. The figure is abstract, but it appears to be simultaneously running and responding to something with horror. It is, no doubt, a warning. Kiki Bridges (Linda Fiorentino) calls out from a window above: "Are you Paul? . . . Here, catch." She then throws down a huge ring of keys. The key ring is heading right at Paul, and he has to move out of the way to keep from getting what could be a deadly blow given how many keys are on it. As the keys strike the pavement, there is a crack of thunder, signifying the momentousness of this event. As Scorsese says: "If he accepts the keys, the game is on."[4] He accepts the keys.

Once he gets up to the apartment, he comes on Kiki busy at work on a papier-mâché sculpture of a man. Paul says: "I like that . . . very much." He recognizes that it is a kind of three-dimensional version of Edvard Munch's *The Scream,* but he misidentifies the work, calling it *The Shriek*. Kiki corrects him and then sets him to work on it as well. I take his recognition and appreciation of the artwork as an identification with it and his misidentification of the title as a further personalization of that identification.

So far, art has made several appearances in *After Hours*. Mozart's Symphony in D Major accompanies the opening and closing credits. Lloyd's description of his desire for a life connected with the art world seems to set up a mood in Paul that will make him receptive to some new things. This mood is itself identified by means of the Bach air. Marcy quotes from a novel a passage explicitly about art and then leaves Paul a clue about how to find her via an artwork. On entering her apartment, Paul is confronted with an artwork that he seems to identify with, a papier-mâché man in the pose of someone who seems to be being exposed to some terrible horror. What is the role of art here?

## Art

There are two primary philosophical theories of art and beauty that I want to appeal to here, those of Immanuel Kant and John Dewey. In *Critique of Pure Reason*, Kant famously gives a metaphysical description of reality that is based on two worlds. The first world is the world of our experience, the world of things as we encounter them, the world that is most accurately described by science. There is, however, and must be, according to Kant, another world, the world of things-in-themselves. This is the world of how things are independent of our experience of them. About this world science can say nothing. In the first of these worlds, the world of things as we experience them, our experience is dominated by what Kant calls *interest*. That is, we evaluate everything we encounter in terms of what things can do for us, how they can augment our happiness. The dominant theoretical activity in this world might be said to be economics, how to do cost-benefit analyses, how to maximize our long-term satisfaction. The second world, however, gives rise to the possibilities of human experiences that transcend mere interest, to the possibility of morality, of art, of philosophy.[5]

For Kant, we inhabit both these worlds simultaneously at all times, but we can experience only one of them at a time. It is a situation a little bit like the duck/rabbit example to which Ludwig Wittgenstein refers in *Philosophical Investigations* (see the figure on page 194). As Wittgenstein points out, you can see the figure either as a duck or as a rabbit, but not as both at the same time.[6]

Similarly, we can experience the world either from the perspective of interest, in which case everything will have a price,[7] or from the perspective

To illustrate the effect of perspective on human experience, Ludwig Wittgenstein uses the example of a picture that can be seen as either a duck or a rabbit.

that transcends all interest, from a disinterested perspective. It is from this latter perspective that we experience art (as well as morality).

Capitalism encourages us to experience the world in terms of interest. It encourages us to evaluate everything we encounter in terms of a price. Capitalism is an ideology, a system of values that we inhabit; we are surrounded by it. We are in it, as Theodor Adorno says, "like a fish in water."[8] Presumably, if one were to ask a fish about water, it would say: "Water as opposed to what?" That is, from within an ideological system, the alternatives are not apparent. It is as though we were taught from a very early age to see only the rabbit. If someone were to suggest that there was a duck there, we would say: "What duck?" From a very early age we are taught about capitalism, about costs, interests, exchange values, good shopping. Art is about the duck. Art is about a different narrative from the narrative of interest. Art is about things that are, in some sense, priceless. (That is why, when people try to price art, they seem to go crazy—either wildly overvaluing it, spending millions for some paint on a canvas, or wildly undervaluing it, considering it worthless because it is only some paint on a canvas.) In the United States, and in capitalistic societies in general, the vast majority of people tend to dismiss art as useless and, hence, worthless. Kant would agree that it is useless, but he also thinks that it and morality are the only things that are really humanly important, that really have any worth besides human beings themselves.

## Art as Experience, Experience as Art

In *Art as Experience,* John Dewey holds that there are laws of nature, like the law of gravity or the laws of motion, and that there is a kind of law of experience. Dewey distinguishes *an* experience from experiences in general. *An* experience is something that happens that is memorable, that is meaningful, that has its own narrative with a beginning, a middle, and an end. Not everything, not most things, that happen to us become for us *an* experience. As Dewey says: "An experience has a unity that gives it its name, *that* meal, that storm, that rupture of friendship. The existence of this unity is constituted by a single *quality* that pervades the entire experience in spite of the variation of its constituent parts." An experience is characterized by "flow": "In such experiences, every successive part flows freely, without seam and without unfilled blanks, into what ensues. . . . In an experience, flow is from something to something. As one part leads into another and as one part carries on what went before, each gains distinctness in itself." The quality of an experience, this sense of flow, is essentially aesthetic in nature. As Dewey says: "The experience itself has a satisfying emotional quality because it possesses internal integration and fulfillment reached through ordered and organized movement. This artistic structure may be immediately felt. In so far, it is esthetic."[9]

"An experience has pattern and structure, because it is not just doing and undergoing in alternation, but consists of them in relationship."[10] So what is the basic pattern or structure, the law, of an experience? The basic pattern involves a certain retroactive component. That is, an experience begins when something unusual happens to us (or when we experience something usual in an unusual way), something that puts us out of our sphere of comfort and familiarity, out of our logic of the same. We negotiate it with the tools we have, the knowledge that we have gained from all the experiences we have had in the past. For an experience to become *an* experience, however, there must be a period of what Dewey calls *consummation,* a period of detachment and reflection in which we make the connections between the various events that we have undergone so that they become unified. So every experience will have this pattern: an event, a process of negotiating the event, a period of consummation in which we detach and compose our negotiations into a single narrative having a particular quality. This is, for Dewey, fundamentally an aesthetic process, and it is most purely experienced in the experience of art.

What are the enemies of the aesthetic? "The enemies of the esthetic are neither the practical nor the intellectual. They are the humdrum; slackness of loose ends; submission to convention in practice and intellectual procedure. Rigid abstinence, coerced submission, tightness on one side and dissipation, incoherence and aimless indulgence on the other, are deviations in opposite directions from the unity of experience."[11] Another way to say this is to say that the enemy of the aesthetic is our uncritical acceptance and imposition of the logic of the same. To have an experience, then, requires a certain amount of discipline and courage as well as imagination and understanding. One must be willing to think in new ways in order to successfully negotiate new situations. What one needs to understand, what requires a certain amount of faith, is that, if one is courageous and imaginative, meanings will emerge; you *will* have an experience.

## The Plaster of Paris Bagel and Cream Cheese and the Papier-Mâché Man

Kiki Bridges is the holder of the keys, she is the one who seems to know, and she is an artist. Her first appearance is as a voice *acousmétre,* a disembodied voice, from above, like the voice of God.[12] The two recurring artworks in the film, the plaster of paris bagel and cream cheese and the papier-mâché man, are both her creations. There is, I want to say, a kind of dialectic between them. The plaster of paris bagel and cream cheese is what Paul came for, and he is the papier-mâché man. The papier-mâché man is terrified and hollow. Paul's immediate response is, basically: "I get that!" What is the papier-mâché man terrified of? He is terrified of the plaster of paris bagel and cream cheese.

What is the significance of the plaster of paris bagel and cream cheese? It plays a recurring role in the movie, which suggests that it is not just arbitrary but meaningful. It serves as both the initial point of connection between Marcy and Paul—it's how he finds her after she leaves him in the diner—and the ostensible subject of their parting. After a series of mutual failures at connecting with one another, in a not incomprehensible but still weird outburst of impatience Paul demands to actually see a plaster of paris bagel and cream cheese since that, ostensibly, is what he came down to SoHo to do:

> PAUL: Where are those plaster of paris paperweights, anyway? I mean, that's what I came down here to see in the first place. Well, that's not entirely true, I came to see you, but where are the paperweights? That's what I wanna see now!

MARCY: What's the matter?

PAUL: I said I wanna see a plaster of paris bagel and cream cheese paperweight, now cough it up.

MARCY: Right now?

PAUL: Yes, right now!

MARCY: They're in Kiki's bedroom.

PAUL: Then get 'em, cause as we sit here chatting, there are important papers flying rampant around my apartment cause I don't have *anything* to hold them down with.

In response to Paul's outburst, Marcy runs sobbing into Kiki's room, and Paul picks up his coat and slips out of the apartment. When he returns, Marcy is dead.

What is the source of Paul's sudden impatience? Why the sudden demand to see the plaster of paris bagel and cream cheese? What is going on here? What does the plaster of paris bagel and cream cheese signify? How to be delicate, but to the point? There is something decidedly pudendal about a bagel and cream cheese. Consider what a bagel and cream cheese is: it is a viscous substance around a hole. A plaster of paris bagel and cream cheese is a reified, inedible, but artistic version of that. Is this not what Marcy seems to be offering Paul? Is it not, at least from Paul's perspective, an offer to come down and see her bagel and cream cheese? There is some ambiguity here about what is being offered as well as about what Paul wants. Which is being offered, and which does Paul really want: the art version or the real, edible thing? When he makes his demand to see an actual plaster of paris bagel and cream cheese, he is frustrated to the point of anger with what seems to him a perpetual postponement of what he has come down for, although, I would say, he himself is not altogether sure what that is.

There are some ironies here. One irony is that Paul explodes at just the moment that Marcy seems to be genuinely offering herself to him sexually. That suggests a certain ambivalence on Paul's part. It suggests that he does not really want what he thinks he wants and that his unconscious knows that and is working for his real desire. What he thinks he wants is an impersonal, low-cost sexual experience. This is a kind of infantile, solipsistic approach to sex.

Several times *After Hours* nicely invokes Alfred Hitchcock's *Rear Window* (1954), a movie that also involves a contretemps between a man suffering from some sexual ambivalence and a very blonde woman. First, as Paul goes up the steps to Kiki's apartment, we hear piano music reminiscent of the piano music that is being played in one of the apartments being watched by

Jeff (James Stewart) in *Rear Window*. Later, Paul looks out Marcy's bedroom window and sees two people having sex, which is the pure expression of his own fantasy and desire at that moment. Still later, fleeing a crowd after his head, he climbs a fire-escape ladder and sees in the opposite building a woman shooting a man several times. This too is, presumably, an objective correlative of the dramas of his internal fantasy space, where he feels both fear and deserving of this fate himself. Films, in general, create a sense of the oneiric, the dream state, where our fantasies, our desires and fears, are projected and played out. As Jean Douchet says of the film spectator and of the character of Jeff in *Rear Window*: "What he [the spectator] sees on the screen (and so what Stewart watches in the apartment on the other side of the courtyard) is the projection of his own self."[13] Like Jeff, Paul feels some ambivalence about his own desires and retreats from them and their object. The Lacanian formula is that enthusiasm increases with distance and anxiety with proximity to the object of our desire, a fitting equation for both Paul and Jeff.

So another irony is that what Paul really wants is precisely the plaster of paris bagel and cream cheese, not the real version. When Marcy finally seems to be ready to offer, as it were, the real thing, it is just then that Paul seems to flip out and then flees the scene. He makes a dramatic shift from not having enough of what he wants to having way too much, the equation of enthusiasm and an anxiety á la Lacan. In support of this line of interpretation that the papier-mâché man and the plaster of paris bagel and cream cheese are invoking issues that have to do with male anxiety about female genitals, let me just refer to a truly horrific scene in *Taxi Driver* (1976). The scene I have in mind is that in which a cab passenger, played by Martin Scorsese himself, rants to Travis Bickle (Robert De Niro) about what he would like to do to his girlfriend with a .44 magnum. That scene portrays this particular male anxiety magnified to a terrifying degree, so Scorsese does have these things in mind. The question, then, is how does one appropriately negotiate a plaster of paris bagel and cream cheese?

## Sex

How are sex and art the same thing, as Picasso says? Both sex and art demand of us an experience. That is, both sex and art represent an encounter with an other, an encounter with a logic that will inevitably challenge our logic of the same. Both demand from us a transformation, an adaptation to something completely new. Both present us with a challenge that threatens to undo us as we are. Both demand that we leave behind the world of interest and the simple calculus of exchange values. Both challenge us to engage in the much more difficult logic of dealing with subjectivities, with nonfungible, hence priceless, autonomous people and artworks. The authentic encounter with an other is always a challenge to who we are, and we may not survive it. As Nietzsche says, what does not kill you makes you stronger, but that suggests that sometimes things just kill you. Hence the terror we may feel at the possibility of having to have an authentic encounter with an other.

One strategy is to try to avoid an authentic encounter with an other. One does that by trying to impose on the other one's own logic of the same, by insisting that the other conform to what one expects and wants the other to be. This happens in both sex and art. We reduce the other to, essentially, a figure in our fantasy space, to an object (a denial of his or her autonomous subjectivity). This is an encounter with another that does not include authentic intercourse and, thus, is, ultimately, fundamentally, solitary. We do this with people by refusing to acknowledge anything about them other than what we want them to be, say, available to us sexually in a compliant way. We do this with art in the same way; we reduce the paralogical newness and oddness of an artwork to the comfortable logic of our predetermined expectations. From this perspective, we may like or dislike the artwork, but in neither case are we really challenging ourselves to encounter the real artwork itself in all its autonomous uniqueness.

This is the strategy that Paul employs throughout *After Hours*. He is repeatedly confronted with the paralogical, with people and artworks that challenge his logic of the same, and, except for one brief moment of open responsiveness when he first gets down to SoHo and first encounters the papier-mâché man, he becomes increasingly resistant to the appeals made on him by people who want to be encountered, who want to be seen by him, in all their strange difference. This persistent denial of their autonomous subjectivity will rouse the people of SoHo to rise up against him, and he will stand, as a symbol, for all society's logic of the same that denies acknowledgment of difference. Nor can he really be blamed. He is the product of an ideology. One strongly feels that he does not particularly want to be cruel but that somehow he cannot help himself. This, I believe, is something with which many of us can identify.

How does one have a successful sexual encounter? Given that everything I have been saying indicates that an authentic encounter demands a responsiveness to the new and, hence, makes any formulaic prescription anathema, let me present one philosophical account of how a successful sexual encounter goes, an account that is especially appropriate to a repeated theme in *After Hours*. In his essay "Sexual Perversion," Thomas Nagel picks up and extends a model of the sexual encounter from Jean-Paul Sartre's *Being and Nothingness,* what Sartre refers to as "a double reciprocal incarnation." Nagel says: "Sexual desire involves a kind of perception, but not merely a single perception of its object, for in the paradigm case of mutual desire there is a complex system of superimposed mutual perceptions—not only perceptions of the sexual object, but perceptions of oneself. Moreover, sexual awareness involves considerable self-awareness to begin with—more than is involved in ordinary sensory perception. The experience is felt as an assault on oneself by the view (or touch, or whatever) of the sexual object."[14] This description brings in a lot of what I have been talking about with respect to authentic encounters with people (and art) in general. Self-awareness requires a certain detachment from one's immediate interests. An authentic encounter is, above all, about perception, about being able to see the other in his or her otherness (as opposed to imposing one's own expectations onto the other and seeing only those). A sexual encounter, then, will really be only a specialized form of what any authentic encounter with another will be like. And, as in any authentic encounter, in the sexual encounter one experiences a certain element of danger, of risk.

Nagel constructs a situation to illustrate Sartre's idea of a double reciprocal incarnation. This situation involves a series of mirrors in which two people in a cocktail lounge begin to notice one another. The idea that he is illustrating is that people's (sexual) responses develop and change, first, as they become aware of the other person becoming aware of them and, second, as they see the other person's responses begin to change and develop in response to their own developing responses. One's initial response to someone one finds attractive Nagel calls a *solitary* response. That is, the response is just about you and your own pleasure, but that response becomes reciprocal and authentic intercourse, that is, nonsolitary, when you start responding to the other person's responses.[15]

Nagel traces this development through several iterations of mutual visual awareness via the mirrors and increasing mutual reciprocal embodiment until some further intercourse (presumably, a conversation and then later maybe even sex) ensues. The point I want to take from this, however, is that the authentic encounter will always involve some kind of mutual reciprocal perception and responsiveness and that, in the authentic sexual encounter, this will include a kind of mutual reciprocal embodiment (which would be a difference between sex and art, Picasso's claim notwithstanding). In *After Hours,* Paul is repeatedly shown looking in mirrors at his own reflection. It is a perfect visual trope for showing his entrapment in his own logic of the same, his essential solipsism, his inability to see and respond to the other and, thus, have his sexual arousal be anything but solitary. My sense is that his final self-examination in a mirror, just before he goes out to dance with June (Verna Bloom) in the Club Berlin, is different. In that scene, he is looking at himself to see how he will look to June. This is a change; this involves some detachment from himself. It is an attempt at some self-awareness. It is the potential beginning of an authentic encounter with another.

## "Lies"

The original title of Joseph Minion's script for *After Hours* was *Lies*. That title raises certain questions, poses certain conundrums, like who is lying to whom, and when? Certainly, Paul is lying when he calls Kiki Bridges about his interest in a plaster of paris bagel and cream cheese, but it is so transparent a lie, and Kiki is so not fooled by it, that it hardly seems to count. Marcy seems to be enacting some kind of psychodrama about being burned, but she never *says* that she has burns, and Paul has his own issues with burns, which lead him to misrecognize a tattoo on her inner thigh as a burn, so the whole thing about Marcy's burns seems way beyond any kind of simple lie. Paul explicitly accuses Marcy of lying about the pot they are smoking, but that is just a bizarre accusation and is immediately followed by Paul's meltdown about the plaster of paris bagel and cream cheese. So to what is the original title referring? On the other hand, neither Paul nor Marcy is really being straight with the other. Marcy really is burned in the sense of having just been dumped by her boyfriend, but she never tells Paul about that, and that is pretty important information for him to have in order to understand what she is thinking. He is pretending to be nicer and more interested in something other than sex than he is. This mutual dishonesty makes all their conversations pretty painful for all involved, including the audience.

For Levinas, the way in which totality opens itself up to infinity is through authentic conversation.[16] *Conversation,* from the Latin for a "turning with," suggests a mutual reciprocal responsiveness and transformation. Authentic conversation (so, clearly, there is inauthentic conversation, faux conversation, ersatz conversation) requires, therefore, a lowering of one's guard at the totalizing borders of one's logic of the same. Authentic conversation requires a certain vulnerability; it requires that one allow the penetration of and subsequent influence on one's logic of the same by alterity, by the other. Alterity itself is just the logic of the same of the other, and the other must simultaneously allow its own logic of the same to be influenced by your logic of the same. This is the situation of totality opening itself up to infinity. This is what authentic conversation is really about.

The experience of infinity, of another person in all his or her otherness, is the experience of a general paralogism. The old logics no longer apply. Space will not quite be space, time not time. Things will seem to happen by chance. Having a conversation, then, can be a dangerous business. It can also be a transcendent experience. Alterity gets transformed into, in Mark Taylor's phrase, *altarity* (altar-ity), something spiritual.[17] A great conversation can be as though two minds become one. (And this can even lead to a physical union, physical intercourse.) This sense of the unification of pluralities is characteristic of the sense of the spiritual. This, presumably, is what both Paul and Marcy are really after, but both will fail to make such an experience possible for the other and, thus, will fail to achieve it for themselves.

## The Club Berlin

The Club Berlin functions as a kind of allegory within the story. Do not Paul's experiences with the Club Berlin recapitulate, in a different narrative form, his experiences with Marcy? He wants to get in, he tries to get in, but entrance is refused. Suddenly, he gets what he wants, he gets in, but it is crazy in there, it is too much for him, and he flees, as if for his life. It recapitulates the story of *The Wizard of Oz* as well. That too is a story of someone who wanted something, a more exciting life, but then, finding the reality pretty terrifying, tries to get home. *The Wizard of Oz* (Victor Fleming, 1939) makes its explicit appearance in *After Hours* in the story that Marcy tells Paul about her first husband, who had a thing for the movie. Apparently, at the moment of climax during sex he would yell out: "Surrender Dorothy!" This was too much for Marcy, and she left him. And this is just what Paul wants to yell: "Surrender Marcy!" That makes him, in this context, both like Marcy's ex-husband and something like the Wicked Witch of the West. Of course, he is also Dorothy, someone who wished for a more exciting life, got his wish, and then only wanted to get back home again.

The first Club Berlin sequence is a re-creation of Franz Kafka's short story "Before the Law."[18] In the story, there is a gatekeeper who guards the gate of the law. A man from the country comes to the gate and wants to enter, but the gatekeeper refuses him entrance. The dialogue of the bouncer at the Club Berlin is right from the translation of Kafka's story. In the story, the man waits at the gate for years, always trying to gain access, until his death. At the point of his death, the man asks the gatekeeper why no one else has come to this gate, and the gatekeeper tells the man that the gate was for him alone and then closes the gate. What is the law to which this gate is the entranceway? Inside the Club Berlin, illuminating the scene of chaos below from the rafters above, is the figure of Martin Scorsese, another allegory within the allegory of the story.

## The Gatekeeper and the Law and the Anamorphic Spot

What is the law, and who is the gatekeeper? One interpretation might be that the law is simply the law of experience that Dewey describes, the law that says that, in order to have an experience, one must abandon one's logic of the same. In order to gain access to the realm where the meanings are, in order to actually encounter, enter into an authentic relationship with, another person, one must open oneself up to the infinity of possible meanings of his or her being. This requires making oneself vulnerable to that person's influence. It requires thoughtful perceptions of the signals he or she is sending and thoughtful responses to those signals in one's own behavior. The thoughtfulness requires some detachment from one's immediate responses since those come out of one's logic of the same. What one is looking for is what Slavoj Žižek refers to as the *anamorphic spot,* the things that do not fit or seem to make sense (because they point to a realm of meaning, a logic that obtains, outside your own logic of the same).[19] The claim is that there is always an anamorphic spot, a distortion in the scene, that generates, if one pays attention to it, a counternarrative to the apparent narrative of the scene. A certain kind of attention, a certain kind of being open to the possibility that there might be more going on than first appearances suggest, can help one identify that spot. To identify the spot and to be responsive to its indications is to begin to see the deeper patterns of meaning in a situation. To see, or to understand, the deeper patterns of meaning is to be empowered, to achieve another level of freedom, and it is what it means to do philosophy.

The sheer multiplicity of invisible but operative narratives is something that has been brought much more to the forefront of the general consciousness by postmodern and multiculturalist social critiques. Feminist issues, ethnic issues, gender issues, all have become much more visible to the general population but were once almost completely invisible to, especially, the dominant social groups (men, Protestants, northern Europeans, and the upper middle class). Certainly, Paul's adventures in SoHo immerse him in a kind of 1980s WASP nightmare of multicultural empowerment where women and homosexual men seem to dominate the social spaces.

Reading signs to figure out what is really going on is something that we tend not to do when we are comfortable and feel in control, but it is something that we are forced to do when we are confronted with things that are threatening or that make no sense to us. Good movies frequently confront us with things that do not make sense to us right away, and, thus, we are compelled to start trying to read the signs, to try to figure out the larger narrative behind the apparent facts that are being portrayed. And what we are looking for is, of course, the anamorphic spots, the things that do not quite fit that suggest something else that might be going on. This is what philosophers are doing all the time, trying to put together some larger truth from all the anamorphic signs that do not fit into the dominant social narratives. The narratives that we are told, that we are given, cannot be right if there are all these counterindications, but what, then, is the true narrative? Good movies, like life itself, confront us with this deep question.

Marcy, to Paul, is like a jumble of anamorphic spots. Practically every other sentence she utters is an anamorphic spot in their conversation. That is, she is constantly giving Paul mixed signals, signals that suggest two very different narratives of what she wants from him. On the one hand, she is sending signals that suggest that she is interested in having sex with him that very night. On the other hand, she is sending signals that she is deeply troubled about something, and that she wants to talk to him about it, and that she really does not want to have sex with him right then at all.

In a sense, the same pattern pertains to each of the women (except Kiki Bridges, the holder of the keys) Paul meets in SoHo. Julie (Teri Garr) sends him what is both a cry of her own anguish and also an echo of his own inner voice, a note saying: "I hate my job." They go to her apartment, and she suggests, among other things, that he touch her hair. The signals seem to be that she would like to have sex with him; the not so subtle anamorphic spots, however, are all the mousetraps around her bed. Once again Paul feels overwhelmed by these contradictory signals. Once again he wants to flee. Once again a plaster of paris bagel and cream cheese artwork is an object of potential intercourse, an object presented as a gift, a gift that he does not know how to receive or what to do with. I take it as further evidence of the pudendal significance of the plaster of paris bagel and cream cheese that, when Julie offers it to him as a reward for his return, she holds it right in front of her pelvis.

A similar encounter ensues with Gail (Catherine O'Hara). Like Julie, Gail seems to be strangely, inordinately attracted to Paul. Like Julie (like Circe and Calypso with Odysseus), she tries to keep him within the island sanctuary of her apartment for herself.[20] Gail is, ostensibly, trying to help him with his bleeding arm and with a phone so that he can call someone to come get him out of SoHo. Her ingenious method of undoing this help is to recite arbitrary numbers as he tries to dial the number he gets from directory assistance. Again, there are clearly mixed signals being sent by Gail, and Paul receives them in sheer disbelief. He responds badly, which makes Gail a little edgy, not a thing one wants Gail to be once one gets to know her better. She discovers and reads an oracular piece of newspaper stuck to Paul's shoulder from his work helping Kiki with her papier-mâché statue. The news story recounts a terrible mob attack on a man in which they collectively beat him to death, in the process, according to the story, pummeling his face beyond recognition. Gail says: "Whoa! What does a guy have to do to get his face pummeled?" Paul and we, the audience, have the distinct sense that this story may be about him somehow, but what the answer to Gail's question is, that is, what exactly it is that he has done to deserve such treatment, remains unclear. Interestingly, within moments, Gail will be at the head of a mob that seems intent on doing to Paul just what was recounted in the story. Whatever it is that Paul is guilty of, Gail seems to feel herself a victim of it.

Each of the people Paul encounters in SoHo offers him the possibility of intimacy, the possibility of an experience. It is almost as though Paul himself were a kind of walking, talking anamorphic spot. Each person he encounters seems to see in him the possibility of a genuine encounter, the possibility of a genuine conversation. This is exactly what Paul is looking for as well; it is why he is in SoHo, although it is not clear that he knows this about himself. It seems like he may think that he is there for something like easy sex. That is not what he really wants or really needs, and, in this case, others seem to understand this about him better than he understands this about himself. He is trying to keep his attention, first, on sex, then, later, on escape, but these are misinterpretations of his own desires. What he really wants is intercourse, intercourse that may include sex but is not limited to or is not, ultimately, only about sex.

## Time

A question is raised in *After Hours* about time. The title itself raises the question: What is "after hours" time? Time is a very tricky subject. As Augustine says in his *Confessions:* "What then is time? Provided no one asks me, I know. If I want to explain it to an inquirer, I do not know."[21] Time seems to have a dual metaphysical aspect, much like Kant's description of the world in general. The classic expression of this contrast occurs in the different conceptions of ancient Greek time, the *kronos/kairos* distinction. *Kronos* time is the ticktock time of everyday busyness. Capitalism is all about *kronos* time. As Michel Foucault describes in *Discipline and Punish,* capitalism gives rise to what he calls *disciplinary space* and *disciplinary time.*[22] *Kronos* is a form of disciplinary time, a discipline enforced in our Western world by means of a proliferation of clocks and watches. *Kairos* time is associated with heroic time, time that feels fluid, infinite, outside time. In *kairos* time, a minute can seem like an hour, and an hour can pass by as if it were a minute.[23] When Mihaly Csikszentmihalyi talks about *flow,* he is talking about what I understand *kairos* time to be and nicely connects Dewey's idea about having an experience, his idea of the aesthetics of experience, with *kairotic* time.[24]

Flow occurs when the activity we are doing is so matched in difficulty to our abilities that it takes all our skill and concentration to perform it—but, in devoting all that energy, we successfully perform it. Flow is a kind of hyperdrive during which time is completely relativized. The absence of flow ontologizes time, makes it a veritable physical presence, heavy and obdurate. Maximum satisfaction is experienced during flow conditions. To achieve flow is an art. It transcends mere efficiency; there are no rules for how to get there. It takes training, skill, practice, knowledge, and a complete, honest immersion in the activity itself. When flow is achieved, the activity is not just satisfying; it feels meaningful. Of course, flow can be experienced in seduction as well. If the seduction is not going well, time slows and oppresses. Paul is no expert at seduction, so the clock keeps ticking.

There is an additional component to *kairos* time that does not belong to *kronos* time, an ethical dimension to it. In *kairos* time, one is doing what Aristotle is advocating in the *Nicomachean Ethics;* that is, one is in the groove of doing the right thing at the right time for the right reason. *Kairos* time, for example, makes an appearance in Plato's *Phaedrus.* The first speech that Socrates gives he will later describe as *akairotic.*[25] It is a speech that is a bad speech given at the wrong time for the wrong reasons. Socrates tries to correct this perversion of time and speech by presenting a *kairotic* speech, one that is true, heartfelt, appropriate, and timely.

Paul is not really a bad person, but he does not really know himself, and he does not really know what he is doing, so he does things badly. This *badly* has both a practical component (he is not very good at getting what he wants) and an ethical component (everyone he encounters seems to suffer from the encounter with him). The question, then, is: How can he become better? How can he be a better person?

## The End

The ending of the movie is even more surreal, if that is possible, than the surreality that has come before it. There is one theological moment in the film, perhaps a reference to what was then the aborted *Last Temptation of Christ*, when Paul falls to his knees, looks up into the night sky, and cries: "What do you want from me?" It is a moment in which Paul explicitly acknowledges the limits of his own powers, the uselessness of his own logic, and his sense of larger patterns at work. It is a moment that will make possible the beginnings of his redemption. Chased by the maenads (which makes him a kind of proto-Orpheus), who really do seem to want to simply tear him to pieces, he flees to the Club Berlin, a club to which he failed to gain free access earlier in the movie. He had gone there earlier looking for Kiki Bridges, and, presumably, that is why he is returning there now, but this time he has an invitation flier to get him in, an invitation to a conceptual art party at the club.

When Paul gets to the Club Berlin this time, everything is different. Where he could not gain access previously, this time he is let in immediately, as though the door were just for him (as it is in Kafka's story). When he gets inside, the place is virtually empty, just the bartender and an older woman sitting by herself at a table, drinking from a silver cup. Paul is not the same person he was at the beginning of the movie.[26] His confident arrogance, along with his easy boredom, has been stripped from him. He is on the run for his very life, and, in the process of running, he seems to have discovered that he wants to live. He goes to the older woman, June, and offers himself to her. It is a desperate, vulnerable, sincere offering. She receives it as a gift, but it will be she who has the gift to give to him, the gift of life, the gift of art. His trials have finally rendered him able to give a gift, made him able to really see another person in her loneliness and pain and, thus, to be seen by another person in his loneliness and pain. He will need her help when the maenads come beating at the door, looking for his head, and she will help him. She will turn him into a work of art, an artwork of a tormented man cringing at his fate. He will become externally what he has for a long time been internally. That is not what the maenads are looking for, and they will be deceived.

Each form of reality contains the anamorphic spots that, if attended to, open up to that reality's contrary. What is needed is a way of mapping the landscapes of these various realities. Art will provide the doorways to alternate realities, but it will take philosophy to get a perspicuous overview of the landscapes, to map the interrelations of the various realities. The meanings emerge only in the transitions. Without the transitions, we are locked in our logics of the same. We *see* new relations, new meanings, when we make the transitions, when the reality we inhabit gets transformed. This seeing is an ethics, an ethics in Aristotle's sense of something that empowers and emancipates while simultaneously connecting us to others and to the larger social whole. This is the way in which life itself becomes meaningful.

Apparently, Scorsese was uncertain about how to end *After Hours,* but the ending he settled on seems right. The Paul Hackett sculpture falls out of the back of a careening van and breaks open before the golden gates of his very own office building. This certainly seems to be a kind of rebirth from the womb of art. Paul dusts himself off, enters the building, goes to his desk, and sits before his computer, which greets him with: "Good morning, Paul." The camera tracks around the office space as it did at the beginning of the movie. People are coming in, ready to start a new business day. Weirdly, as the camera tracks back and passes by Paul's desk, he is no longer there. Gone to another plane of reality, perhaps, a lesson, perhaps, for us all.

## Notes

1. Emmanuel Levinas, *Totality and Infinity: An Essay on Exteriority,* trans. Alphonso Lingis (Pittsburgh: Duquesne University Press, 1969), 38.

2. Jean-François Lyotard, *The Postmodern Condition: A Report on Knowledge,* trans. Geoff Bennington and Brian Massumi (Minneapolis: University of Minnesota Press, 1984), xxiv.

3. Martin Scorsese, commentary included on the DVD of *After Hours* (released by Warner Home Video in 2004).

4. Ibid. The scene of the keys falling, which includes a shot from the perspective of the keys, was complicated to set up, especially with the budget that Scorsese had. His first attempt to get it was by tying a bungee cord to a camera and throwing it off the roof with Griffin Dunne standing patiently below. It was so crazily dangerous that he ended up splurging on a crane for the shot.

5. Immanuel Kant, *The Critique of Pure Reason,* trans. Norman Kemp Smith (New York: St. Martin's, 1965). Kant's theory of aesthetics is contained in what is known as the *third critique, The Critique of Judgment,* trans. J. H. Bernard (Amherst, NY: Prometheus, 2000).

6. See Ludwig Wittgenstein, *Philosophical Investigations,* trans. G. E. M. Anscombe (New York: Macmillan, 1968), pt. 2, sec. 11.

7. See Immanuel Kant, *Foundations of the Metaphysics of Morals,* trans. Lewis White Beck (New York: Macmillan, 1989), 53 (Akademie ed., 435).

8. Theodor Adorno, *Minima Moralia: Reflections on a Damaged Life,* trans. E. F. N. Jephcott (New York: Verso, 2005), 23.

9. John Dewey, *Art as Experience* (New York: Perigee, 1980), 37, 36, 38.

10. Ibid., 44.

11. Ibid., 40.

12. On *acousmétre,* see Michel Chion, *The Voice in Cinema,* trans. Claudia Gorbman (New York: Columbia University Press, 1999), esp. 17–31.

13. Jean Douchet, "Hitch and His Audience" (1960), trans. David Wilson, in *Cahiers du Cinéma, 1960–1968: New Wave, New Cinema, Reevaluating Hollywood,* ed. Jim Hillier (Cambridge, MA: Harvard University Press, 1986), 150–51.

14. Thomas Nagel, "Sexual Perversion," in *Mortal Questions* (New York: Cambridge University Press, 1979), 44–45.

15. Ibid., 45. This is the way in which Nagel constructs the situation:

> Suppose a man and a woman we may call Romeo and Juliet, are at op-posite ends of a cocktail lounge, with many mirrors on the walls which permit unobserved observation, and even mutual unobserved observation. Each of them is sipping a martini and studying other people in the mirrors. At some point Romeo notices Juliet. He is moved, somehow, by the softness of her hair and the diffidence with which she sips her martini, and this arouses him sexually. . . . At this stage he is aroused by an unaroused object, so he is more in the sexual grip of his body than of hers.
>
> Let us suppose, however, that Juliet now senses Romeo in another mirror on the opposite wall, though neither of them yet knows that he is seen by the other (the mirror angles provide three-quarter views). Romeo then begins to notice in Juliet the subtle signs of sexual arousal, heavy-lidded stare, dilating pupils, faint flush, etc. This of course intensifies her bodily presence. . . . His arousal is nevertheless still solitary. But now, cleverly calculating the line of her stare without actually looking her in the eyes, he realizes that it is directed at him through the mirror on the opposite wall. . . . This is definitely a new development, for it gives him a sense of embodiment not only through his own reactions but through the eyes and reactions of another. (45)

16. Levinas, *Totality and Infinity,* 39.

17. Mark Taylor, *Altarity* (Chicago: University of Chicago Press, 1987).

18. This story can be found complete at http://www.mala.bc.ca/~johnstoi/kafka/beforethelaw.htm.

19. Slavoj Žižek, *Looking Awry: An Introduction to Jacques Lacan through Popular Culture* (Cambridge, MA: MIT Press, 1997), 88–91.

20. There are many suggestions in *After Hours* of parallels with Homer's *Odyssey.* Like Odysseus, Paul just wants to get home. Like Odysseus, he encounters a series of very powerful, sometimes dangerous, always challenging women. For Odysseus, these include not just Circe and Calypso but also the Sirens (who lure men to their death for food), Nausicaa, and even the wily Penelope. Odysseus, however, is much better at handling difficult situations than Paul is.

21. Saint Augustine, *Confessions,* trans. Henry Chadwick (New York: Oxford University Press, 1992), 230 (chap. 11, sec. 14 [par. 17]).

22. See Michel Foucault, *Discipline and Punish: The Birth of the Prison,* trans. Alan Sheridan (New York: Vantage, 1997), 141–62.

23. For an extended discussion of the *kronos/kairos* distinction, see Frank Kermode,

*The Sense of an Ending: Studies in the Theory of Fiction* (New York: Oxford University Press, 1968), 46ff.

24. Mihaly Csikszentmihalyi has written several books, including *Flow: The Psychology of Optimal Experience* (New York: Harper & Row, 1990), *The Evolving Self: A Psychology for the Third Millennium* (New York: HarperCollins, 1993), and *Creativity: Flow and the Psychology of Discovery and Invention* (New York: HarperCollins, 1996).

25. Plato, *Phaedrus,* trans. R. Hackworth, in *The Collected Dialogues of Plato,* ed. Edith Hamilton and Huntington Cairns (Princeton, NJ: Princeton University Press, 1961), esp. 517ff. (Stephanus pagination: 272ff.).

26. In her very interesting essay "Baudrillard, *After Hours,* and the Postmodern Suppression of Socio-Sexual Conflict," *Cultural Critique,* no. 34 (Autumn 1996): 143–61, Cynthia Willett offers a very different reading of the ending of *After Hours* from the one I give here. Her reading is that Paul remains the same at the end, that the movie portrays a kind of postmodern failure of character development.

# The Ethical Underpinnings of *Kundun*

*Judith Barad*

## A Film Rife with Questions

Martin Scorsese's *Kundun* (1997) tells the true story of the Dalai Lama's childhood and youth. The film begins with the recognition in 1937 of the two-year-old Lhamo Dhondrub as the reincarnation of the thirteenth Dalai Lama, who had died in 1935, and, thus, an incarnation of Chenrizi, the Buddha of Compassion, and follows him through his training and enthronement as the fourteenth Dalai Lama, Tibet's spiritual and secular leader. Tibetan Buddhism, or Vayrayana, is distinguished from other forms of Buddhism by its monastic order of lamas, or monks. Much of the Dalai Lama's childhood and early adolescence was spent in rigorous study in the philosophy of Vayrayana. The story of *Kundun* follows his development until his exile from Tibet in 1959, when China invaded and enforced its rule on this peaceful country. Scorsese uses the perspective of the Dalai Lama (a title of respect meaning "Ocean of Compassion") throughout the film. The title of the film comes from another title of respect used of the Dalai Lama, one that means "the Presence."

In telling the story of the Dalai Lama, Scorsese portrays a man of peace whose life is devoted to the Buddhist virtue of compassion. Yet viewers may wonder how the Dalai Lama can maintain a compassionate attitude in the face of the violent assaults on his people and their culture. They may question whether it's appropriate for him to maintain his belief in nonviolence while knowing that the Chinese army has killed and incarcerated hundreds of thousands of Tibetans. Isn't his continued belief in nonviolence a sign of weakness or cowardice? One problem with *Kundun* is that Scorsese never makes Buddhist teachings on nonviolence understandable to an audience that is all too familiar with violent images on television as well as in video games and enjoys violent sports.

Other aspects of the film may be even more puzzling to viewers. The exquisite sand mandala, shown at the beginning and end of the film, is never explained. We see this geometric diagram being painstakingly created by the Tibetan monks, and we marvel at their patience and artistry. Yet, after this work of art is completed, the monks sweep it away like so much garbage. Since works of art are valued in the West, an audience may not understand the seemingly cavalier attitude of the monks expressed by their action. An even more disturbing scene occurs when the Dalai Lama's dead father is chopped up and fed to the gathering vultures. A Western audience may wonder how anyone can allow his father to be treated as meat. The Four Noble Truths are mentioned, but viewers may have no idea what the Dalai Lama is discussing. Further, how can any parents accept having their young son taken away from them to be raised by strangers? How can anyone condone making a young child bear the heavy responsibilities that come with being the spiritual and secular leader of a country that had off and on for years been under threat of invasion?

## Ethics from East to West

These questions about the film center on Tibetan Buddhism's beliefs, particularly its ethical beliefs. If we come to understand its ethics, most of the questions that the film raises dissipate. More importantly, we then see the film in a more appreciative light, a light that may even motivate us to reflect on and apply some of its insights to our lives. Since Tibet is situated far away from the West, some may think that its Buddhist ethics is just as far removed from Western thought, Western philosophy. Yet this isn't the case. In fact, Tibetan philosophy shares much with Western ethics.

Tibetan Buddhist ethics bears the most similarity to the virtue ethics that Western society inherited from the ancient Greeks.[1] The kind of virtue ethics most closely allied with it is the philosophical school known as Stoicism, which began in Greece and flourished in Rome. Comparing some tenets of Stoicism with Tibetan Buddhist ethics may help Western viewers understand *Kundun* because many of Stoicism's teachings have a very Christian tone. In fact, the early church fathers were quite influenced by Stoicism's spiritual quality. As a result of this influence, Stoic philosophy was transmitted via Christianity to the Western world. In this way, it has served as a transition between Western philosophy and spiritual values.

Since Tibetan Buddhist ethics also connects philosophy and spiritual values, Stoicism can facilitate our understanding of this Eastern blend of philosophy and spirituality.

Buddhist ethics in general stresses the importance of practicing the virtue of compassion. We see this in the ethical development of the Dalai Lama as he grows from age two (a role played by Tenzin Yeshi Paichang) into a compassionate young man (Tenzin Thuthob Tsarong). Soon after he is announced to his people as the Buddha of Compassion, his regent tells him: "We name you Tenzin Gyatso. Your job is simple. You are to love all living things. Just love them. Care for them. Have compassion for them. As long as any living thing draws breath, wherever he shall be, there, in compassion, shall the Buddha appear, incarnate." It takes about ten years for this teaching to sink into the mind of the young Tenzin. While he is interiorizing these beliefs, his learning is replaced by experience. As a youth in Lhasa, the Dalai Lama was deeply moved while teaching love and compassion. He writes: "I began [at the age of fifteen] to think less of myself and more of others and became aware of the concept of compassion."[2]

Compassion isn't only a Buddhist virtue; it's also found in Western teachings. Discussing *Kundun* in an interview, Scorsese explained his attraction to the "Catholic Church, which preached compassion, love and literally loving one's neighbor and enemy." Adding that he still strongly adhered to the "basic idea of Catholicism," Scorsese admitted: "I don't know if I'm capable of the compassion that Christianity expresses or wants one to be like, or even capable of the compassion of Tibetan Buddhism, but that's one of the reasons I was attracted to making the film about it."[3]

Many parents, not necessarily Catholic ones, teach their children the seeds of compassion when they ask their children: "How would you feel if you were in so-and-so's shoes?" The question asks children to imaginatively feel what someone else feels. If a child imagines this, he or she is experiencing empathy. In *Kundun*, we see the young Tenzin gazing fondly at the mice that eat the offerings placed before the Buddha statues. Is he imagining himself in their place? The film even more clearly shows the young Tenzin experiencing empathy when, while visiting his parents' house on the palace grounds, he asks his father (Tsewang Migyur Khangsar, in real life a Tibetan American scholar): "Can I save the sheep from going to the market? So they don't die." The little boy is clearly sharing in the suffering of the sheep as he imagines them being killed. The Dalai Lama explains: "Compassion is understood mainly in terms of empathy—our ability to enter into and, to some extent, share others' suffering."[4]

## The Conundrum of Compassion

Yet empathy is just the beginning of compassion. As this feeling of connection with others develops in the growing child, it eventually incorporates reason. At this point, it is no longer just a feeling; it's a virtue. Tibetan Buddhists maintain that this virtue reaches its fullness when it both is unconditional and extends to all sentient beings, including those who harm us.

Now, viewers may wonder how Tibetan Buddhism can claim to extol compassion when it is so uncompassionate as to take a young child away from his parents. Even the Dalai Lama admits that his separation from his parents (which occurred when he was three years old) was an unhappy period in his life.[5] Doubtless, his parents must also have suffered from the separation. Many Westerners may insist that, since compassion is so important to Buddhism, the family should have been left intact. In fact, doesn't compassion begin in the feelings we have toward our family?

Buddhism doesn't deny that compassion can originate within the family. But, it then asks, should compassion, once learned, be restricted to the family? After all, compassion is the kind of virtue that can be extended limitlessly. Unlike material goods, compassion can't be exhausted. If we grant this, a further question emerges: Shouldn't the compassion extended to the family have a privileged status over the compassion extended to other beings? In response to such an question, Tibetan Buddhism observes that, as compassion increases in scope or breadth, it also increases in depth. The person who practices compassion can feel the same depth of love, the same intimacy, toward all sentient beings that he or she feels toward family and close friends.

## Reincarnation and Interconnection

The monks who separated Lhamo from his parents believed the boy to be the reincarnated Buddha of Compassion. Commenting on his film, Scorsese has said: "With Buddhism, the idea is that it's the same boy who was here the last time, and the one before that, and the one before that. At one point, when he's 16 years old, [the Dalai Lama] asks this fellow who sweeps the kitchen and played with him when he was little, 'Do you ever wonder if the regent found the right boy?' And the man says back, 'No. Of course he did. Who else would be here?'"[6] The monks who found the toddler were confident that he would naturally grow into the role of putting others before himself. Compassion involves acting out of concern for others. It acknowledges that we are connected to a wider community of beings than just our family. This connection is so close that our own interests and the interests of others are barely distinguishable.

Perhaps Stoic thought can help us understand the Tibetan viewpoint here. Stoic philosophers would say that, as the Dalai Lama and not as Lhamo, the young boy has obligations that stem from the nature of his position, regardless of how he or his parents feel about it. According to the Stoics, duties aren't based on the feelings or preferences of the individuals involved. Instead of focusing on personal attachments, we should focus on duty and cultivate a sense of a broader community. The Stoic philosopher Epictetus, who, like the Dalai Lama, was forced to live in exile, maintains that all people are equal members of one large community. As a part of this larger community, the individual has a duty to sacrifice his own interests for the sake of the larger whole of which he is a member. Epictetus argues that we can't fulfill our own interests unless we perceive ourselves as integral parts of our society and the world. If we separate our personal interests from the larger community, we are like detached limbs; we can't function as people with truly human concerns.

Like Stoicism, Tibetan Buddhism doesn't think of any one person's interest as isolated from the interests of everyone else. The Dalai Lama writes: "Due to the fundamental interconnectedness which lies at the heart of reality, your interest is also my interest."[7] In this more expansive view of self, an individual's interest is part of the broader community's interest. So, when the monks took Lhamo from his parents, they were acting for the good of the child, his parents, and all of Tibet. The connection between all of them is so close that it's difficult to distinguish among their interests.

Moreover, the Buddhist view of life incorporates long-term consequences, valuing them over short-term gratification. While our society often emphasizes instant gratification, we also acknowledge that we may have to pass up short-term pleasures to attain more fulfilling goals. The Dalai Lama illustrates this point in a way most of us can understand: "Usually we do not allow our children to do whatever they want. We realize that if given their freedom, they would probably spend their time playing rather than studying. So instead we make them sacrifice the immediate pleasure of play and compel them to study."[8] If we combine the monks' belief in reincarnation with their expanded notion of self and add the value of taking a long-term perspective, we can understand that they didn't fail to be compassionate when they separated the three-year-old from his parents. From this perspective, little Lhamo was the reincarnation of the Buddha of Compassion, who should know that his interests were connected to those of his people. Moreover, even if he wasn't aware of his compassionate nature at a very young age, the monks knew that his study would help him grow into this awareness. They took a long-term view.

## Inner Peace

Few of us practice this kind of extended compassion on a daily basis. Social pressure encourages us to think: "What's in it for me?" We can see what's in it for us when it comes to our family and friends, whom we see as part of our own identity. But compassion for others doesn't seem to fit in with the self-interested attitude that our culture promotes. In response to the issue of self-interest, the Dalai Lama observes that all sentient beings have an innate desire for happiness and dislike suffering just as much as we do. Because others want the same thing we do, if we treat others with love and respect, they will treat us the same way. When we approach others with compassion, we create an atmosphere congenial to "receiving affection or a positive response from the other person."[9] The more we treat others affectionately, the more affection we receive. In other words, compassion is contagious. The Dalai Lama urges us to "experiment" with compassion, to give it a try. Those who do, he writes, "will discover that when we reach beyond the confines of narrow self-interest, our hearts become filled with strength. Peace and joy become our constant companion."[10]

Stoic philosophy echoes this teaching. For the Stoics, the affection of parents for their children and of friends for each other and feelings of compassion for humanity are natural. But excessive emotions like fear, envy, and grief should be eliminated because they detract from the good life. When the virtuous life is combined with detachment from excessive emotions, the result is tranquillity and peace. Stoicism, like most ancient Greek ethics, recognizes that all people want happiness. But the type of happiness the Stoics were thinking of wasn't a life of continual pleasure or excitement. Rather, they saw happiness as a life of serenity, tranquillity, and inner peace. Likewise, the Dalai Lama writes: "The principal characteristic of genuine happiness is inner peace." The inner peace he discusses, like the tranquillity and peace the Stoics aim at, allows for feelings, affection, and compassion. This peace, he says, "is rooted in concern for others and involves a high degree of sensitivity and feeling. . . . I attribute my sense of peace to the effort to develop concern for others."[11]

In making *Kundun,* Scorsese was aware that people yearn for the kind of inner peace the Dalai Lama exhibits. During one interview, the director said: "There's kind of a hunger for peace of mind. On the downside, it may signal a lack of faith in our traditional religions in the West. That doesn't mean everybody's going to become Buddhist, but I think you could learn certain things from Buddhism."[12] Imagine the change in Western societies if inner peace were prevalent in people! In fact, imagine the change in your own life if you strove for this as your goal! The sincere and persistent attempt to achieve inner peace would bring you closer to achieving it than would be the case if you made no attempt. The benefits of inner peace are well worth the effort.

## Other Virtues

Inner peace leads us to another issue of *Kundun*. The Dalai Lama writes: "If there is no peace in one's mind, there can be no peace in one's approach to others, and thus no peaceful relations between individuals or between nations."[13] Compassion is not only the root of inner peace; it's also the foundation of outer peace. Outer peace is manifested in *Kundun* in the Dalai Lama's insistence on nonviolence. But His Holiness could not have been so sure of the nonviolence he advocates without the inner peace that is generated by compassion. As we develop compassion, other virtues begin to arise within us, such as hope, courage, determination, forbearance, generosity, humility, patience, tolerance, and forgiveness.[14]

If we explore a couple of these virtues from a Tibetan Buddhist perspective, we can begin to understand all of them. One virtue that seems clearly related to compassion is generosity. This is a virtue that seems very other directed, and it is. Yet, beyond its other-directed nature, the generosity that comes from compassion is the kind that gives selflessly without any condition. For Tibetan Buddhists, giving becomes a virtue only when the giver is pleased with the joy that the gift brings to the receiver. The person who gives to a charity in order to receive a tax credit doesn't have this virtue. Generosity does not just consist in giving material goods to others; it includes giving of our time and energy to help others. Generosity should not be extended with any thought of return. Expecting a reward or recognition is also incompatible with this virtue. Instead, generosity is a virtue because it entails an authentic caring for others; it is rooted in compassion. The good feeling that results from generosity is simply the gravy, the side effect of this virtue.

We see the Dalai Lama's courage, patience, and forbearance as he deals with the Chinese. Recall the scene, for instance, where he is given a copy of the Seventeen Point Agreement by General Chian Chin-Wu (Ben Wang). Maintaining a dignified silence, he doesn't display an attitude that stems from fear or weakness. Rather, he displays what the Tibetans call *sö pa*, a virtue that combines both patience and forbearance. The Dalai Lama writes that it "denotes a deliberate response to the strong negative thoughts and emotions that tend to arise when we encounter harm. . . . [It] provides us with the strength to resist suffering and protects us from losing compassion even for those who would harm us."[15] A virtue that provides a person with strength should not be mistaken for a character trait associated with weakness.

## Nonviolence

The virtue of patient forbearance contributes to the Dalai Lama's conviction of nonviolence, so strikingly portrayed in the film. In acquiring this virtue, we should muster tolerance and restraint when faced with provocation. In *Kundun,* the Dalai Lama is certainly provoked by Chairman Mao (Robert Lin). At first, Mao Tse-tung seems very affable as he discusses the common goals of communism and Buddhism. Acting the charming host, Mao says: "You know, I have great respect for your Lord Buddha. He was anticaste. Anticorruption. Antiexploitation. For some, politics and religion can mix." Hearing these words, the Dalai Lama is favorably impressed. He even tells his tutor, Ling Rinpoche (Tenzin Trenley): "I like what I see of Marxism. It is based on equality and justice for all. I believe Chairman Mao wishes the best for our people. Our path must be nonviolence. Cooperation." But, as the Dalai Lama leaves China, Mao tells him in a darkly menacing tone: "Religion is poison. It undermines the race, and it retards the progress of the people. Tibet has been poisoned by religion." The Dalai Lama says nothing, although he is fully aware of the implied threat behind the chairman's words. When he gets into his car, Tenzin looks straight ahead and tells a companion: "He will betray us."

The restraint the Dalai Lama exhibits in his encounter with Mao provides a model of how we can restrain ourselves from retaliating when we're threatened or attacked. If you think about it, the action of responding to an attack with violence is the reaction of a wild animal. Unlike a wild animal, a human being can choose to relinquish the negative impulses and emotions that tempt him or her to strike back at someone. Relinquishing these negative impulses and emotions removes our incentive to retaliate. But how, some may ask, can we rid ourselves of such strong emotions? Both Stoics and Tibetan Buddhists tell us that we should want to abandon negative thoughts and emotions simply because we want to be happy. If we allow ourselves to harbor these negative mental states, our actions have a destructive effect both on ourselves and on others. Causing anxiety, depression, and stress in us, they make us sick and shorten our lives. Simultaneously, they make our actions toward others violent, either verbally or physically. As a result of such considerations, Epictetus observes: "Remember that it is not he who gives abuse or blows who insults; but the view we take of these things as insulting. When therefore, anyone provokes you, be assured that it is your own opinion which provokes you."[16]

Tibetan Buddhists have a basic commitment to nonviolence, a commitment that entails refraining from verbal and physical actions that cause harm to oneself or others. No one is separate because the world is interconnected; nothing is isolated from other things. Harming one person is tantamount to harming everyone. What we do to one another we do to ourselves. Beyond not harming anyone, nonviolence requires compassion for all beings. This concept is discussed in the scene in *Kundun* when Takster Rinpoche (Jigme Tsarong), who had been living in Chinese-controlled territory, discusses the Chinese ambitions with the Dalai Lama, his younger brother. Takster warns: "The Chinese have one goal. The complete dissolution of our nation. . . . There is no room for Buddha in their world. Our only hope is to fight." Refusing to follow this advice, the Dalai Lama explains to his older brother: "Buddha teaches that we must learn from our enemy. We have compassion for all people." In his view, anger and violence are appeased and removed only by compassion.[17]

## Loving Your Enemy

Many viewers of *Kundun* may not understand how anyone can have compassion for his or her enemy. They may be familiar with the idea of nonviolence because the Gospel also tells us to love our enemies and to turn the other cheek. But they may either not accept the Gospel message or, if they do, find it too difficult to implement in their lives. It's not that people who hate their enemies lack empathy; rather, they feel that hate, anger, or bitterness is sometimes warranted. Empathizing with the Dalai Lama, these people would acknowledge that he certainly has a right to be bitter and angry about the atrocities the Chinese have inflicted on his people. Yet the scope of their empathy is limited to certain people.

In contrast to this restricted empathy, the Dalai Lama explains, our enemies can be our teachers by helping us practice patience, tolerance, and compassion. Each morning, he focuses on those Chinese leaders and officials who torture and kill Tibetans. Then he draws their ignorance, prejudice, hatred, and pride into himself. Having already acquired a virtuous character, he doesn't think that their vicious attitudes can change his behavior. But, he hopes, his practice lessens their problems. Even if it doesn't, his morning ritual has the positive effect of giving him peace of mind.[18]

While most of us don't have the virtue of the Dalai Lama, we have the potential to develop that same peace of mind and the happiness that accompanies it. We can develop this potential by recognizing that, whatever injustices others inflict on us, we don't have to bring ourselves down to their level. Epictetus tells us that we can relate to our enemies in a way that is consistent with our own character. The greatest harm to a person who is unjustly treated by another isn't the treatment he suffers but his response to the treatment. The Stoic philosopher asks us: "Is a brother unjust? Well, preserve your own just relation towards him. Consider not what he does, but what you are to do. . . . For another cannot hurt you, without your consent. You will then be hurt when you consent to be hurt. In this manner, therefore, if you acquire the habit of regarding your relations with your neighbor, citizen, commander, you will discover in this way what duties to expect from them."[19]

Likewise, the Dalai Lama counsels us to avoid those situations and people that anger us until we can develop our inner resources more. We develop our inner resources by first learning to identify negative emotions and thoughts when they first occur in us. This means that we must observe each of our actions, bodily reactions, words, thoughts, and feelings for any negativity. As we identify these feelings and thoughts, we should also reflect on just how destructive they are to the happiness we desire. When we do this successfully, we will naturally want to steer clear of the situations that stimulate these strong thoughts and emotions.[20] After all, who wants to destroy his or her own happiness?

## The Truth of Suffering

Some may still not understand how the Dalai Lama can avoid negative thoughts and feelings when he sees Tibetans suffering so greatly, especially given his compassion for his people. If we seek a greater understanding of his inner peace in the face of so much adversity, we must return to one philosophically crucial scene in *Kundun*. The youthful Tenzin is in his quarters with his tutor, Ling Rinpoche, discussing the Four Noble Truths. These truths—the truth of suffering, the sources of suffering, the cessation of suffering, and the truth of the path leading to this cessation—are the principles that Gautama Buddha taught after his enlightenment at a place called Deer Park on the outskirts of Benares. Understanding the Four Noble Truths will help us grasp the previous issues we've dealt with more deeply and appreciate the Dalai Lama's response to suffering. At the same time, we'll be able to grasp more fully why the beautiful sand mandala is swept away so casually and why the corpse of the Dalai Lama's father is cut up as food for the vultures.

The First Noble Truth begins with accepting suffering as a fact of existence. Whatever you do, wherever you go, you will confront suffering; it will inevitably show up in every situation. Certainly, the Dalai Lama has witnessed more than his fair share of suffering. *Kundun* shows us his vivid nightmare of a killing field in which hundreds of dead, maroon-robed monks surround him as he stands in the center of a courtyard. Besides the physical suffering the Tibetan people have endured, they have also experienced a tremendous amount of mental torment. In another scene, as the Dalai Lama gives audience to his people, an old woman (Gawa Youngdung), who is clearly emotionally agitated, addresses him in Tibetan. Scorsese noted that, originally, this was not part of the film; the woman actually became distressed when a real photograph of the Dalai Lama was placed before her. Since her genuine reaction was so emotionally riveting, the filmmaker decided to insert this scene into *Kundun*.[21]

The suffering we're familiar with may be less extreme than the suffering of the Tibetan people. We may suffer the physical pain of a bad back or of severe headaches. We feel mental pain when a promotion passes us by or when we fail at an important undertaking. Other mental pain occurs when we experience emotions such as hatred, anger, and jealousy. Such pain, which most of us have experienced, burns within us as we carry it around. In short, we can understand physical, mental, and emotional suffering and even empathize with others who bear such afflictions.

Yet Buddhism acknowledges another kind of suffering, one that is more difficult to understand for someone raised in a consumer culture. It maintains that suffering can come from finding pleasure in material things. Since this kind of pleasure doesn't last, we feel pain when we cease receiving pleasure from these things, as we inevitably do. We may not find what we want, or we may lose what we have. Then we want some other material thing to ease the pain—a new house, a new car, a new video game. But the problem just recycles itself since temporary things can't provide lasting pleasure. The Dalai Lama tells us that even ordinary friendship can bring us this kind of suffering: "Today your friend has a nice smiling face, but in a moment the conversation can turn sour, and you start to fight, with no trace of friendship."[22] No temporary thing or relationship can give us true happiness. In *Kundun*, we don't see the Dalai Lama receiving lasting happiness from his telescope or his car. He doesn't grow attached to these pleasures. They are merely temporary diversions, which he must leave behind when he flees Tibet.

In short, the First Noble Truth says that, if we reflect on sickness, old age, death, our coming in contact with unpleasant things, our separation from pleasant things, and our unsatisfied cravings, we will be aware of the ubiquity of suffering. Of course, many people consider it morbid to think about these things. But, eventually, these same people, like everyone else, will have to confront these problems. If we prepare ourselves mentally for sickness, death, and other kinds of suffering before they happen to us, we can cope with them better when they do occur, and we can quit being so fearful of these events. The alternative—pushing any thought of suffering out of our minds—doesn't help us cope. In fact, it will probably come as a shock to us when we inevitably experience suffering.

Buddhism maintains that our desires bring about our suffering. If we can't obtain something we desire, we feel pain and frustration. Consequently, if we don't want to suffer this frustration, Buddhism urges us to eliminate desire from our lives. In the same way, Epictetus says: "Altogether restrain desire; for if you desire any of the things not within our power, you must necessarily be disappointed."[23] By continually recycling themselves, desires eventually create an insatiable obsession. Both Buddhists and Stoics regard this as bondage; if we have such an obsession, we feel like we can't break free from it.

## What Causes Suffering?

The Second Noble Truth turns to the causes of suffering. It maintains that we suffer because our lives are guided by ignorance, attachment, and hatred. Ignorance entails delusion; we are deluded about how things actually exist. Rather, ignorance makes us perceive things as we want them to be. We live in our self-made dreams, in which we're attached to various things and we hold the erroneous belief that these things can make us happy. This causes suffering because we try to stop the change that inevitably occurs in the things we're attached to. We want to be young forever, never fall ill, and keep our relationships. But no person or thing can make us happy.

The Stoics too recognize that nothing or nobody can make you happy, angry, or sad without your allowing them to do so. When it comes to your attitudes and emotions, Stoics insist that you are in control. You may try to be young forever but suddenly be killed by lightning. You may live a healthy lifestyle so as not to fall ill but get cancer nevertheless. As horrible as such events may seem, Stoicism maintains that they shouldn't cause you to be psychologically disturbed. You permit things to affect you this way only if you let yourself grow attached to things.

It may be difficult to understand attachment as a cause of suffering because our society conditions us to believe that we can achieve success only by accumulating more possessions. We desire success so much that we give up authentic living. Our attachments control our lives. We concern ourselves with the desires of our ego, an ego that feels separate from others. The bigger our ego grows, the more we desire everything for ourselves at the expense of others. As others feel taken advantage of, they feel hatred toward us, which serves only to increase our suffering.

Often, these three causes of suffering—ignorance, attachment, and hatred—work together. Since we're ignorant of the truth, we believe that our happiness can be found in attachment to some person or thing. When we don't achieve happiness through our attachments, we're frustrated, and then hatred enters our lives. Buddhism teaches that attachment is rooted in an ignorance of the nature of persons and objects. A person who values attachments believes that persons and things are stable, unchangeable beings that can be controlled and possessed. Alternatively, a person may become so attached to something or somebody that he or she becomes completely dependent. Epictetus said that, to the extent that we "encumber ourselves with . . . body, property, brother, friend, child," we are also "weighed down" by them.[24] He saw this relation of many attachments to a poor quality of life as an impediment to living freely. If attachments increase our desire for more things, we become "unhinged." Usually, when we desire more than we have or need, we fear losing what we already possess. This fear makes us double our efforts to acquire more attachments, attachments that we also fear losing. If we reflect on this, it should be clear that the cycle is downright irrational! It would be much more rational to realize that the way to end our suffering is to give up our attachments to objects and people—to look within ourselves for happiness and to develop detachment. The Dalai Lama writes that the best way to overcome attachments "is to realize that the very nature of life is that what has gathered will eventually disperse—parents, children, brothers, sisters, and friends. No matter how much friends love each other, eventually they must part."[25]

## Diagnosing the Self

The same kind of irrationality that makes us ignorant of the nature of the things we want to possess also generates a belief that there is an unchanging self within us. If we could see through our delusions, we would know that all things are interdependent and interrelated. There is no "me" that is separate from "you." Everything is mutually dependent on everything else, and everything is always changing. Since the self is a part of everything, there is no stable self. The Dalai Lama had a perception of a self at two years old that was different from his perception of his self as a novice monk at seven. His perception of his self as a refugee was different from his other perceptions of his self. Like us, he couldn't find a self in thoughts, feelings, perceptions, and experiences because each thought, each feeling, each perception is continuously passing away. What gives us the impression that we each have a self is an appearance, a temporary unity of thoughts, feelings, perceptions, and experiences that dissipates when we breathe our last breath. And, because all things are transient, the self-gratification that anyone seeks from possessing things can't provide lasting satisfaction. If we try to get pleasure from persons and objects, ignoring their impermanence, we will find only frustration and dissatisfaction, which motivate us to seek other things of the same type to give us pleasure. Unless we appreciate the impermanence of all things and events as well as the transient nature of our own existence, "we will," the Dalai Lama teaches, "continue to perpetuate our own suffering."[26] In the same vein, Epictetus says: "With regard to whatever objects either delight the mind or . . . are tenderly beloved, remind yourself of what nature they are, beginning with the merest trifles: if you have a favorite cup, that it is but a cup of which you are fond—for thus, if it is broken, you can bear it. Eventually, a steady effort at remembering the nature of things will help to remind you that 'if you embrace your child, or your wife, that you embrace a mortal—and thus, if either of them dies, you can bear it.'"[27]

Buddhist ethics provides both a diagnosis of the human condition and a prescription for that condition. This method of healing human suffering parallels the method of a physician. A physician first notes symptoms and then looks for their causes. After finding the causes of an ailment, he prescribes a medicine. The Buddha is often referred to as a physician because he diagnoses the human condition as suffering and identifies the cause as attachment. His prescription is detachment and the Fourth Noble Truth. We see this analogy with medicine mentioned twice in *Kundun*. As a young child who represents the Buddha, Tenzin (Gyurme Tethong) is asked to recite: "May I be the doctor and the medicine, and may I be the nurse for all sick beings in the world until everyone is healed." As an adult, the Dalai Lama tells General Chian, "Buddha is our physician, General. He will heal us."

## The Mandala

The First and Second Noble Truths help us understand why the exquisite sand mandala is swept away at the end of *Kundun*. But first it may help to know more about what a mandala is as well as how it functions. The Second Noble Truth has told us that one cause of suffering is attachment. In order to stop attachment, the mind of the Tibetan Buddhist practitioner must be disciplined and trained. An external object of contemplation, such as a mandala, can be used to accomplish this task. The Dalai Lama writes that the image of the mandala "is said to be extremely profound because meditation on it serves as an antidote, quickly eradicating the obstructions to liberation and the obstructions to omniscience as well as their latent predispositions."[28] The great beauty of the mandala makes the practitioner release the negative stream of thoughts that impede him or her from reaching spiritual liberation.

Tibetan Buddhist monks have been using mandalas for twenty-five hundred years. Each mandala is a geometric diagram representing the universe in sacred terms. It contains images of a deity, usually a large buddha, surrounded by other deities as well as symbols of such virtues as compassion and wisdom. Since the symbols are created in such a way as to suit the physical and mental aptitudes of different practitioners, each mandala is unique. While some mandalas are painted, others are composed of very fine, colored sand, like the mandala we see at the beginning and end of *Kundun*. The monks create each sand mandala in a ceremony ranging over nine days of intensive concentration. Once finished, the symmetrical design of the mandala draws the eye toward the diagram's center so that one meditates deeply on the beauty of the Buddha, the Buddha's world, and its enlightened qualities. In this way, the mandala helps the practitioner actualize his own enlightenment by invoking within himself the enlightened attitudes, mental transformation, and virtues that are symbolized by the deity and the deity's realm.

Understanding the mandala's function in the light of the Second Noble Truth, we can now appreciate why at the end of the film the monks sweep the mandala away and pour the sand into water. All the mandala's elaborate symbols and images are empty of inbuilt substantive existence. That is, they are impermanent. Their only function is to facilitate the practitioner's spiritual development. The destruction of the mandala is a significant part of the ritual because it signifies the letting go of the negative thoughts and attachments that entrap people. If the practitioner treats the mandala as an object of attachment, he or she will want to make a permanent thing of something that is by nature impermanent. Realizing the mandala's true nature, it's only fitting to sweep it away. This doesn't mean that the monks who sweep it away think of it as so much garbage. Instead, the fleeting nature of this work of art can make someone appreciate it even more during the time it exists. If an object did last forever, we might be more likely to take it for granted than we would knowing that we can enjoy it for only a limited amount of time.

## Feeding the Vultures

That same line of thinking can help us understand why the Dalai Lama's dead father is cut up for the vultures to eat. But first we should know that the way in which his father's corpse is disposed of, called a *sky burial,* is the most common method of corpse disposal in Tibet. The burial occurs three days after the corpse is considered dead, allowing time for the offering of prayers and chanting. Before dawn, lamas (spiritual teachers) lead a ceremonial procession to the burial ground, chanting to guide the soul. After mandalas are marked on the chest and stomach of the corpse, the body cutters slice across the chest with large knives. Using hatchets and cleavers, they remove the internal organs and slice flesh from the bone. As the vultures gather, the bones are beaten with hammers and mixed with roasted barley flour to make them tasty. When enough flesh and bones have been prepared to feed all the vultures that have gathered, the body cutters start throwing pieces of the corpse into a flat area where the vultures devour them. As they finish eating, the skull is pulverized and the brains and skull given to the vultures.

To most Westerners, the actual ceremony is even more macabre than the one depicted in *Kundun.* Yet it illustrates the first two Noble Truths' focus on impermanence and nonattachment to the body. Agreeing to have one's body disposed of in this way is seen as a commitment to be rid of this attachment. The sky burials also remind the living witnesses that life is impermanent; death is a certainty for all beings. If we recognize the truth of impermanence, we won't be shocked by change, even the change that death brings, when it inevitably happens. Another function of the sky burials is that they represent the cyclic nature of life, the return of one's body to the environment being enacted publicly. Observing the burial, not only are Buddhists encouraged to think about impermanence, but they are also uplifted by the dead person's last token of generosity, which is seen as an act of self-sacrifice for the benefit of others. This act of giving flesh to the vultures is considered virtuous because it saves the lives of small animals that the hungry vultures might otherwise have eaten to fill their bellies.

## True Liberation

After having discussed suffering and its causes, *Kundun* shows us the young

Dalai Lama as his tutor asks him: "How does one progress from the real-ization of one Noble Truth to another?" The boy is silent for a while. After saying, "I need to squeeze this brain," he finally responds: "When one un-derstands that he causes some of his own suffering needlessly, then he looks for the causes in his own life. And when he looks for those causes, when he investigates, then he is putting confidence in his own ability to eliminate the sources and end the suffering. A wish to find a path to peace arises. For all beings desire happiness. All wish to find their purest selves."

The Dalai Lama's answer leads to the Third Noble Truth, which says we can uproot the ignorance that is the cause of suffering by understanding the true nature of persons and things. The way things appear to be and how they actually exist are two different things. If we want to uproot the ignorance that causes suffering, we should not be content with appearances. Persons and things exist contingently; their existence depends on many factors. Once we realize this, we understand the futility of wanting to possess people and things. Our separation from others disappears, and our suffering ceases. The desire to possess others and the feeling of separation are replaced by inner peace and a sense of unity.

Near the end of the film, General Chian starts conversing with the Dalai Lama in a way that clearly shows his ignorance of Buddhism. He says conde-scendingly: "We are here to heal the people of Tibet. You need reform. You have no sense of what is good for your people. We are here to liberate you!" Speaking as the secular head of Tibet, the Dalai Lama admits the need for reform, but "as Tibet needs it, not for China." He wants to makes changes in communications and in education, but he insists that these changes must be implemented in a way that serves the interests of Tibet rather than those of China. Speaking as the spiritual leader of Tibet, he says: "Buddha is our physician, General, he will heal us. Compassion and enlightenment will set us free. You cannot liberate me. I can only liberate myself."

The kind of liberation that the Dalai Lama is referring to is enlighten-ment, which can be attained only by individual effort. No one can do it for you; you have to do it yourself. Liberating yourself, by means of the Eightfold Path, brings release from the negative thoughts and emotions that produce suffering. The Fourth Noble Truth is that, to cease suffering, we must follow the Eightfold Path—right view, right intentions, right speech, right action, right livelihood, right effort, right mindfulness, and right concentration. So the liberation of which the Dalai Lama speaks is moral freedom from a bondage to undisciplined living. The moral ideal of cultivating a compas-sionate life is a way to be liberated from the bondage to attachment, hate, and ignorance. These three causes of suffering are bondage to a way of life that is unworthy of human beings, who are capable of happiness when they make an effort to liberate themselves from these negative mental states.

Contrary to General Chian's view, liberation doesn't come from reforming the external environment. It comes from knowing the nature of the mind. We can do this by learning to observe our thoughts. When thoughts arise, we can observe them. Gradually, we will develop a faculty of using our mind to watch our mind and, ultimately, transform it. By acquainting ourselves with consciousness as both knower and object known, we can perceive our mind as unaffected by desire and aversion. We can release our resentments, anger, and fear. The result is a liberation brought about by our own efforts, a liberation that can't be taken away from us. As a result, an examination of Tibetan Buddhist ethics shows us that, although the land of Tibet has been taken from the Tibetans, their spirit of liberation can never be taken away without their consent. *Kundun,* as viewed through Tibetan Buddhist ethics, is a film of liberation. Can you hear Epictetus (or his reincarnation) applauding it?

## Notes

1. The Dalai Lama writes: "In order to transform ourselves . . . it is necessary to develop . . . an *ethic of virtue.*" Like Aristotle, he tells us that, to achieve virtue, "it is essential to avoid extremes": "For example, courage taken to excess and without due regard for circumstances quickly becomes foolhardiness" (*Ethics for the New Millennium* [New York: Riverhead, 1999], 101, 112).

2. Dalai Lama, *My Land and My People* (New York: Warner, 1962), 26.

3. Francis Leach, "Martin Scorsese—*Kundun* Interview," http://www.abc.net .au/arts/headspace/triplej/creatures/scorcese. (Scorsese's name is misspelled in the URL.)

4. Dalai Lama, *Ethics for the New Millennium,* 123.

5. Dalai Lama, *My Land and My People,* 13–14.

6. Ray Greene, "Grace Period," *Boxoffice Magazine,* January 1998, cover story.

7. Dalai Lama, *Ethics for the New Millennium,* 47.

8. Ibid., 53.

9. Dalai Lama, *The Art of Happiness* (New York: Riverhead, 1998), 69.

10. Dalai Lama, *Ethics for the New Millennium,* 131.

11. Ibid., 55.

12. Greene, "Grace Period."

13. Dalai Lama, *My Land and My People,* 28.

14. The Dalai Lama mentions this set of virtues in various places (see, e.g., Dalai Lama, *Ethics for a New Millennium,* 122, and *The World of Tibetan Buddhism* [Boston: Wisdom, 1995], 64).

15. Dalai Lama, *Ethics for a New Millennium,* 102.

16. Epictetus, *Enchiridion,* segment 20, in *Discourses and Enchiridion,* trans. Thomas Higginson (New York: Walter J. Balack, 1972), 338.

17. Not only was the Dalai Lama's decision ethical, but it was practical as well. Knowing that the Chinese forces greatly outnumbered the Tibetan army, young Tenzin knew that they couldn't use violent means to eliminate the Chinese threat. Violence may have been a short-term response to the threat, but violence only triggers more violence. And the one thing that surely follows in the wake of violence is suffering. A lasting peace requires, according to the Dalai Lama, a compassionate plan of just change for all involved in a conflict. So nonviolence was the only course of action that could possibly work.

18. See Dalai Lama, *How to Practice: The Way to a Meaningful Life,* trans. and ed. Jeffrey Hopkins (New York: Pocket, 2002), 39.

19. Epictetus, *Enchiridion,* segment 30, 342.

20. See Dalai Lama, *Ethics for the New Millennium,* 91.

21. Leach, "Martin Scorsese—*Kundun* Interview."

22. Dalai Lama, *How to Practice,* 36.

23. Epictetus, *Enchiridion,* segment 2, 332.

24. Epictetus, *Discourses,* 1.1, in *Discourses and Enchiridion,* 5.

25. Dalai Lama, *How to Expand Love: Widening the Circle of Loving Relationships,* trans. and ed. Jeffrey Hopkins (New York: Atria, 2005), 99.

26. Dalai Lama, *The Art of Happiness,* 164.

27. Epictetus, *Enchiridion,* segment 3, 333.

28. Dalai Lama, *Tantra in Tibet* (London: Allen & Unwin, 1977), 77.

# Scorsese and the Transcendental

*R. Barton Palmer*

The Transcendentalist adopts the whole connection of spiritual doctrine. He believes in miracle, in the perpetual openness of the human mind to new influx of light and power; he believes in inspiration and in ecstasy.
      —Ralph Waldo Emerson, "The Transcendentalist" (1842)

Loneliness has followed me all my life. The life of loneliness pursues me wherever I go. . . . There is no escape. I am God's lonely man.
      —Travis Bickle, *Taxi Driver*

## A "Saint of Cinema"

It is hardly surprising that Martin Scorsese, an ex-seminarian turned film director, shows himself in his works to be a deeply committed moralist. Scorsese, in fact, is particularly attracted to properties that treat the vagaries of the spiritual life, in a fashion typical of the independent-minded cineaste who scorns the showbiz establishment and its entertainment product. However, it goes without saying, Scorsese is hardly an independent artiste, being rather, at least in part, the consummate Hollywood insider. For more than thirty years, he has been an enthusiastic and very public supporter of the filmmaking establishment and especially its history, which he deeply honors. Who, indeed, among his contemporaries, save Steven Spielberg, has more relentlessly and successfully pursued the media limelight in order to promote not just his own films but the American commercial product in general? Yet, with energy and commitment, Scorsese simultaneously also pursues a quite different cinematic identity, that of the European-style auteur eager to express his intellectual and formal obsessions in the practice of what he sees as an art as well as a well-paid craft. As Les Keyser so well puts it, referring to the forcefulness of the values with which Scorsese infuses his work: "The graduate of New York University does indeed struggle mightily to be 'the saint of cinema,' and more often than not he succeeds."[1]

Consider *Kundun* (1997) and *The Last Temptation of Christ* (1988), certainly two of the most unusual mainstream films of the last two decades. These very personal works demonstrate the depth and uniqueness of Scorsese's interests as well as his formal mastery of the art cinema tradition. A kind of spiritual biography that explores religious and mystical traditions barely known to most Americans, *Kundun* also engages deeply with international politics, movingly dramatizing the Dalai Lama's heroic but unsuccessful attempt to defy China's annexation of Tibet, as spiritual power finds itself unable to triumph over its material counterpart. A thematically similar project inevitably destined to create public relations problems for the director and his producers, *The Last Temptation* transfers to the screen the controversial Nikos Kazantzakis novel, which was placed on the Index of Prohibited Books by the Catholic Church because it provisionally rewrites early Christian history. Scorsese's *Last Temptation* offers an alternative version of the life of Jesus that centers on the conflict he endures between human impulse (manifested in his love for and sexual attraction to Mary Magdalene) and his divine intimations (the mission that seems to be appointed him by the Father). In this struggle, spirituality triumphs, but not before the joys of the material world, evoked hypothetically but movingly, are celebrated.

It is often not fully acknowledged that Scorsese does not explore such themes only in his art cinema work. Just as Graham Greene's Catholicism informs his "entertainments" as well as his self-consciously serious novels, Scorsese's obsession with the spiritual pervades not only his auteurist films but also his genre projects, including the neo-noirs *Taxi Driver* (1976) and *Cape Fear* (1991), as well as the Mafia trilogy of *Mean Streets* (1973), *Goodfellas* (1990), and *Casino* (1995). These last two films especially are more obviously commercial than any of his other projects, designed as they are for a national and international market in which Hollywood gangster films have for more than seventy years enjoyed substantial box office success. Yet they too are strongly marked by Scorsese's moralism as well as by his interest in probing the deeper aspects of the human condition. In particular, his protagonists often seem measured by the sense in which they, like Emerson's transcendentalist, find themselves inclined to regard "the procession of facts you call the world, as flowing perpetually outward from an invisible, unsounded centre" within. But, for Emerson, the truth that follows is that it is "simpler to be self-dependent" because "the world is the shadow of that substance which you are."[2] This existential isolationism is a view that Scorsese does not share. His films demonstrate that, for him, self-dependence is but another form of alienation, the insubstantiality of others but the barrier to the transcendence of the monistic everyday that love in its various senses can bring. Scorsese's protagonists, as Travis Bickle so accurately says of himself, are, indeed, God's lonely men, and this is a condition of internal exile that they, sometimes deliberately and sometimes fitfully, struggle to transcend.

While exploring these themes in several of Scorsese's works, this essay will focus on one of his more recent and lesser-known films, *Bringing Out the Dead* (1999).

## "Feeling the Bottom Fall Away"

Scorsese's transcendentalism, his profoundly spiritual sense of the intense subjectivity of experience, finds a perfect vehicle for cinematic expression in *Bringing Out the Dead,* a work of subtlety and heartfelt moral engagement adapted, with Paul Schrader writing the screenplay, from Joe Connelly's semi-autobiographical account of his work as an emergency medical technician in lower Manhattan.[3] In many respects, this was an ideal property for both Scorsese and Schrader, the screenwriter most famed among contemporary directors for his critical and professional interest in the transcendental, to adapt for the screen. With its moving meditations on the debts we owe to others and the mystery of salvation, the novel seemed to offer an ideal opportunity for writer and director to make an art film in the spiritual tradition of *Last Temptation* (on whose production they also collaborated). At the same time, Connelly's novel develops characters with that gritty urban realism in the tradition of noir fiction to which Scorsese and Schrader are also strongly attracted.

Though it is not a novel in which criminality and violence play a central role, *Bringing Out the Dead,* in fact, explores the same noirish cityscape that figures so prominently in their other joint projects, especially *Taxi Driver,* and also in those Schrader wrote and directed independently, including *Hardcore* (1979) and *Light Sleeper* (1992). While still in galley proofs, the book came to the notice of the agent Scott Rudin, who quickly purchased the film rights and brought the project to Scorsese.[4] The director was immediately taken with it and realized that Schrader would be the only one to do the screenplay. Scorsese saw that *Bringing Out the Dead* would both reprise and modify considerably themes that he and Schrader had earlier developed in *Taxi Driver.* He admitted in an interview: "There's a correlation to *Taxi Driver,* there's no doubt, . . . only it's twenty-five years later and we're a little mellower now. Instead of killing people, our protagonist is trying to save people. We were all about thirty, thirty-one years old—Schrader, De Niro, and myself—when we made *Taxi Driver.* But now we're fifty-six. It's a different world, and we're different too."[5] Scorsese, I believe, rightly underlines the difference between the two films. Travis Bickle (Robert De Niro), the perhaps deranged protagonist of *Taxi Driver,* is driven to violence, but his urge to purify his world of corruption is, eventually, directed toward the more manageable and particular double task of ridding the city of men running a downtown brothel while rescuing the innocent and vulnerable girl they have victimized. Like other Scorsese and Schrader protagonists, Travis Bickle and *Bringing Out the Dead*'s Frank Pierce are, in the end, both seekers after "lost sheep," whom they, if in intriguingly different ways, rescue from a degrading imprisonment within a corrupt material world. Yet Travis finds himself beyond redemption, whereas, at the end of his moral struggle, Frank experiences a profound sense of transcendence.

Like the alienated, anguished Bickle (who at one point says in voice-over: "All my life needed was a sense of direction, a sense of someplace to go"), Connelly's Frank Pierce finds his life falling apart despite his efforts to have it mean something. As he confesses: "Help others and you help yourself, that was my motto, but I hadn't saved anyone in months. It seemed all my patients were dying, everything I touched turned to shit. I waited, sure the sickness would break, tomorrow night, the next call, feeling the bottom fall away."[6] Episodic rather than tightly plotted, the novel traces Frank's Dantean journey through the grim underworld of New York's night town, a depraved public sphere populated by hordes of the disaffected, the discarded, and the dysfunctional.

Frank's intense experiences with attempting, but usually failing, to bring others back to life provide him with the opportunity to both transcend and embrace his (dis)connection to those who share the world with him. Frank yearns for, yet fears, release from his job as an emergency medical technician, which he feels inwardly compelled to do, for it holds out the promise of the ultimate high, bringing the dead back to life and, therefore, defying, if only for a time, the existential limits of the human condition. Aspiring to be God (or, rather, in some more limited and less overweening sense, to displace him), Frank is doomed to devastating failure and the resultant guilt, which he at first finds impossible to expiate.

Frank is especially haunted by the memory (or perhaps the spirit, glimpsed in moments when the mask of everydayness seems to fall away) of Rose, a young girl who died despite his desperate ministrations. The novel's decisive moment, however, comes after he has saved an older heart attack victim, only to see him enter the living purgatory of irreversible brain death and constant heart failure. Because his wife refuses to forbid resuscitation, the man's natural death is staved off each time by that dubious miracle of modern medical technology, the defibrillator. Life for the old man has, thus, become a succession of shocking, painful returns to an unconsciousness that is merely the shadow of meaningful existence. Tortured by the consequences of his successful yet also failed act to save, Frank finally allows the man to die by subverting any further heroic measures, in an act of mercy that cures his own malaise. This violation of professional ethics acknowledges the paradox of the power Frank possesses. He can give back life, but he must always and ultimately fail to reverse the course of natural deterioration that is the essential fact of the human condition.

In effect, Frank saves his patient by allowing him to die, a grace that Mary, the man's daughter, with whom Frank has become romantically involved, must hate him for offering. Frank describes her reaction to the old man's passing: "She turned to me: 'You killed him.' What was there to say? I could only marvel at the power of her hate. Enough to smash atoms if she wished, turn me to dust with the smallest snap of it, yet all she did was leave. That was the miracle."[7] Mary refuses to destroy Frank with the power he has granted her to wield over him, returning, if ironically and appropriately, the mercy he has shown her father. Mary hates Frank because her father's death deprives her of his presence, and, thus, in an ironic twist, his kindness to the old man means that Frank must forfeit the connection with Mary that has been developing because he at first brought him back to life. A giver and then a taker of life, Frank is loved but then hated for his *caritas.* Yet there is more than a bitter paradox at the heart of his experience. For it is truly a miracle that, as Mary leaves without saying more, Frank feels his spiritual crisis end. Mary delivers him from his "sickness" (the overwhelming sense of failure that steals his nightly rest) to an unguilty secret sharing with Rose, whose spirit now seems quiet and appeased. Frank is allowed the final blessing of sleep, drawing inward in an Emersonian fashion from an engagement with the outer world to his "invisible, unsounded centre." These are his final words: "I listened to her breathing and I felt myself sleeping before I was asleep. The sound of her breathing. I was going to sleep."[8]

Perhaps because of its neoexistentialist tone of cynical optimism (like Camus' "stranger," Frank finds himself delivered from anomie to the community of the self by the hatred of others), the novel turned out to be a hugely popular best seller. Connelly, apparently an avid reader of Raymond Chandler, also imbues his first-person narrator with an appealing world-weariness and an engaging eagerness for self-examination. In most ways, the adaptation remains fairly faithful to Connelly's characters and narrative. Yet, while praised by the critics, the film was generally ignored by audiences perhaps disappointed by the absence of the sensationalized violence of Scorsese's gangster pictures, which, with their highly stylized urban setting and working-class characters, this film superficially resembles. However, there is no denying Scorsese's considerable achievement. With its carefully orchestrated expressionist evocation of a heightened reality lurking behind the mundane everyday, *Bringing Out the Dead* offers the aesthetic depth and visual energy of Scorsese's best projects. In any event, the attempted marriage of intellectual engagement and eye-popping entertainment never did find its audience. *Bringing Out the Dead* provides a fitting bookend (perhaps, of course, only a temporary one) to the joint exploration of spiritual aspiration that Scorsese and Schrader began in their first collaboration on the justly renowned *Taxi Driver*, whose conclusions about redemption and deliverance it interestingly revises.

In particular, the screenplay penned by Schrader and Scorsese significantly alters the novel's ending, bringing the film more in line with the particular transcendentalism of the writer and, more prominently, of the director. For the film's Frank (Nicolas Cage), redemption is more than the bottom falling away, a temporary relief from engagement with others that is a sleep accompanied by a suddenly benevolent spirit. Scorsese's Frank is provided with a more lasting and substantial connection to life and the material world. Unlike his novelistic model, he does not simply transcend, through subjecting himself to the power of another, his own misguided assertion of self. Such revisions are in keeping with similar themes developed in earlier films and betray a deep indebtedness to the transcendental cinema of the French cineaste Robert Bresson, an admiration that Scorsese shares with Schrader, whose own projects as writer-director provide an interesting contrast to his somewhat different work with Scorsese. It is to that wider context that I first turn.

## Miracles and the "Influx of Light and Power"

How does this notion of the spiritual life (the inchoate search for meaning that is startlingly and unexpectedly followed by the decisive and transformative moment) fit into the Scorsese oeuvre more generally? It is easy enough to underestimate the pervasiveness of the transcendental—broadly conceived as the opposite of sensualism and materialism—in Scorsese's films, especially those that seem thoroughly commercial and in whose production Schrader did not participate. Consider *Casino,* in which scholars have generally displayed little interest, apparently considering it simply a competent genre exercise. Its lengthy narrative and diffuse plotting led journalistic critics to dismiss it as little more than a tiresome display of shopworn genre elements. As in *Goodfellas,* in *Casino* Scorsese seemed to be mainly interested in belaboring the contrast between the flash of mob life (all molls and money) and its ultimate banality (scary goombahs saddled with nagging wives and the deflating responsibility of kitchen patrol).

The film, so it seemed, was yet another realistic chronicle of wiseguy malfeasance in the vérité manner of *The Godfather* (Francis Ford Coppola, 1972), which, with its suite of sequels and imitations, has dominated representations of organized criminality since the early 1970s. Here is an area of cultural production that simultaneously deconstructs and furthers the romantic view of the gangster first profitably mined by Hollywood in the early 1930s. The operation of organized crime, of course, is a subject for which the American public has a demonstrably unsatisfiable hunger, as witness, among other obvious examples, the amazing popularity of Nicholas Pileggi's two exposé novels, *Wiseguy* (the source of *Goodfellas*) and *Casino.*[9] Thinking perhaps that the director was interested only in transforming a sensational pulp property into a plot-driven high-concept Hollywood film, David Denby spoke for the trade reviewers in general when he opined that *Casino* was filled with "brilliant journalism" but "left you hungry for drama."[10] But Denby and others underestimate the transformation of the eminently lowbrow material effected by Scorsese in shaping the screenplay, for which he received joint credit with Pileggi. In the film, as opposed to the novel, the "dramatic" has been emptied of suspense and, at times, consequentiality, becoming the "moral" instead.

In *Casino,* Scorsese carefully evokes a semi-Pelagian moral universe, as the expulsion from the Garden of Eden is ironically reenacted in the Las Vegas of the late 1970s and early 1980s. A gallery of criminal types, from hookers and maniac wiseguys to crime bosses and small-time hustlers, Scorsese's characters are not doomed by unelection. And they are hardly forced to play out a destiny from which the possibility of merit appears to have been excluded. Instead, flawed by greed, hubris, lust, faithlessness, and willful blindness, they struggle to succeed in what the casino manager Sam "Ace" Rothstein (Robert De Niro) declares is a "paradise on earth." This Las Vegas, part Bunyanesque allegory, part historical reconstruction, is a world unexpectedly turned upside down, where vice has become legitimate business and famed gamblers like Rothstein who have always lived outside the law find themselves leading members of the local Chamber of Commerce.

A kind of grace, perhaps satanic, is evident in this startling reversal. Yet the criminal entrepreneurs find themselves unable to prevail in their newfound legitimacy, despite an environment that, reflecting in its thoroughgoing sinfulness a human rather than a divine creative urge, has been perfectly designed to maximize the profit to be derived from the self-indulgent depravity of the marks who stream into the city like lemmings speeding toward a cliff. Reason and self-restraint fail the criminal masterminds, so the would-be exploiters become the objects of others' venality and violence, criminals higher in the hierarchy who ironically pass a harsh judgment on their brethren for their transgressions, their violations of the rule of crime.

Appropriately, the film's final distribution of fates seems determined by the iron rule of Dantean *contrapasso*. Held responsible for the nature they come to inhabit, Scorsese's characters justly suffer the consequences of their self-fashioning. The brutal thug Nicky Santoro (Joe Pesci) betrays his lifelong friend Sam and, more important, the mob bosses in Kansas City. So the man who had once without a qualm crushed a rival gangster's head in a vice in order to extract a confession is denied the mercy of the quick hit that neatly disposes of inconvenient others. Beaten horribly but not fatally with baseball bats by his erstwhile confederates, Nicky is buried alive after being forced to witness his much-beloved younger brother endure a similarly horrifying and undignified end. The two men become examples to warn off others who might similarly be tempted to disregard the will of their superiors, but they are also moral signposts of a different order—and not the only ones in the film. A former prostitute offered the opportunity for social redemption and a life of financial ease, Ace's wife, Ginger (Sharon Stone), cannot break her connection to her former pimp, Lester (James Woods), sinking back with him into a life of self-destructive drug addiction and alcoholism. Broke and abandoned, Ginger eventually dies of an overdose in a sleazy motel, demonstrating the final irrelevance of her beauty, self-possession, and considerable talent for self-advancement.

Yet *Casino* does more than dramatize the harrowing opportunity for moral choice that is the correlative of free will, two orders of existence that Scorsese shows shape human destiny. To exclude the possibility of grace and irresistible transcendence would be to deny the divine, whose presence must be noted, even if only ironically, in a world that is, morally speaking, turned upside down. The divine is, in fact, invoked at the outset, along with the possibility of salvation. The precredit sequence takes up the narrative in medias res, with the world that Rothstein has constructed already falling to pieces.

As he gets into his car, Ace says in voice-over: "When you love someone, you've got to trust them. There's no other way. Otherwise, what's the point? And for a while that's the kind of love I believed I had." With these words, the car suddenly catches fire and explodes, hurling him into the air, which gradually turns into, first, flames and, then, an abstract design through which he tumbles, quite apparently unharmed, as on the sound track the massed choral voices of Bach's St. Matthew Passion proclaim loudly, and, it turns out, without irony, the mysteries of the suffering and resurrection of God.

As the narrative proper begins, Ace appears healthy and whole, his voice once again controlling the images of a long flashback and recalling the explosion that he has somehow miraculously survived. The heavenly chorus makes way for a succession of popular songs drawn from the period, signaling a return to everydayness (and materiality), the universe in which Ace, with his amazing instincts for making profitable wagers because of a fanatic dedication to detail, also achieves success, though it is eventually destroyed by those he chooses to love and honor.

*Casino*'s precredit sequence is one of the most complex in any Scorsese film and demands a lengthier reading than can be provided here. Here, I am concerned only that it raises a question central to the understanding of the director's oeuvre more generally: What are we to make of the fact of impossible deliverance, styled as something transcending the material? Ace not only survives the explosion, which seems, in some sense, the correlative of his spiritual and romantic frustration, but is sent skyward to some abstracted existential space beyond the world of disappointed commitment, misunderstood others, and imperfect love—the fallen world below to which he is then returned untransfigured. Is it in such events—which, of course, can always be assigned a realistic explanation (here, as later revealed, the imperfect skill of the mob bombmaker)—that the unmerited favor of God, and, hence, his direction of human affairs, is revealed? For Scorsese the answer seems, if tentatively at times, to be yes. As the narrative retrospectively reveals, Ace is the only character who dares to love in the way that matters, that is, risking everything, putting his faith in someone whom reason suggests is not worthy of trust. For him, calculated self-interest, the love of others that transforms them into objects to be used, is no love at all. In contrast, an Augustinian *cupiditas* thoroughly dominates Nicky and Ginger, destructive and self-destructive creatures who are defined almost completely by greed and lust.

Ace is the only main character who survives the expulsion from the "paradise on earth" that is Las Vegas. He should have perished or been killed, like Nicky and Ginger, but is saved instead. His fate recalls that of Robert Bresson's archetypal protagonist, that of *Man Condemned to Death Who Escapes* (1956; American release title: *A Man Escaped*), a film singled out by Paul Schrader in his *Transcendental Style in Film* as a masterpiece of transcendental cinema.[11] Like Bresson's resistance fighter, who must negotiate a moral dilemma that pierces to the heart of the human condition, Ace is delivered by extraordinary luck from the sinfulness of the world that would destroy him, but only after he acts powerfully in his own interest, resisting the temptation to retreat from meaningful engagement with others.

In *Casino,* Ace is preserved for solitude and exile, but, as we shall see in *Bringing Out the Dead,* deliverance for Scorsese can also be communal and integrative, the merited end of actions that free the spiritually and physically exhausted protagonist from alienation and anomie, making possible an opening up to significant connection with others.

## God's Lonely Men

What *Casino* reveals is that Scorsese's obsession with the transcendental is not dependent on the kind of intellectual synergy he has enjoyed for more than twenty-five years with Paul Schrader, who, because of his seminal critical work on the subject and his own cinematic practice, has become famously identified with this sort of cinema. It seems that, in their work, Scorsese and Schrader are both driven to represent that transforming or decisive moment when the material loses its hold on our consciousness and experience, admitting what Emerson terms the "influx of light and power," whose effect is to show those of us trapped in the empirical realm that we are, indeed, "phantoms walking and working amid phantoms" who can easily be brought to see "the solid universe growing dim and impalpable."[12]

Interestingly, in an interview done shortly after the production of *Bringing Out the Dead,* Schrader denies that his own films and screenwriting are shaped by the transcendental: "The reason why I don't make transcendental films, the reason I don't have transcendental style, is that I believe in something that is anathema or contrary to the whole notion of transcendental cinema. I have my roots in psychological realism and audience identification with character, whereas the whole notion of transcendental style is based on repudiating psychological realism."[13] But this protest is surely disingenuous, if not deliberately misleading. There seems little doubt that, as John R. Hamilton suggests, "[Schrader's] films and screenplays belie such denial," filled as they are with "self-conscious replications of the Bressonian decisive moment."[14] And it is these decisive moments that are to be found as well, though not as consistently, in the films of Martin Scorsese, particularly (but not exclusively, as we have seen with *Casino*) in the projects scripted by Schrader.

According to Schrader, the decisive moment in Bresson's films is a "blatant anti-realistic gesture, . . . an inexplicably spiritual act." As in the case of Ace's elevation to the heavens in *Casino,* "we have not been set up for it, yet we accept it."[15] And we do so even though "the prescript rules of everyday fall away; there is a blast of music, an overt symbol, and an open call for emotion."[16] Such moments of transformation do not necessarily involve an unambiguous form of deliverance or redemption. At the end of Bresson's *Pickpocket* (1959), the thief Michel loses his freedom, and it is in jail that Jeanne, a family friend, finally offers him her love. Hitherto an unfeeling, even anomic man, Michel unexpectedly and inexplicably accepts, wondering why it has taken him so long to realize the possibility that such a gift exists. Released from the prison of his own solitude, Michel thus finds a spiritual freedom even as he is in no sense liberated from the literal incarceration he must endure as the just reward for his *moyen de vivre.* This is a scene that Schrader replicates almost exactly at the end of his *American Gigolo* (1980).

*American Gigolo* is Bressonian in a theological as well as a formal sense. In *Pickpocket,* there is no question of Michel's meriting the deliverance from solitude that he finally accepts from Jeanne. So in *Gigolo,* Julian Kaye, a prostitute who unconvincingly considers his work to lonely women a kind of ministry, does not in any sense earn the offer of love he receives from Michelle Stratton (Lauren Hutton). Like Ace Rothstein, Michelle has wagered everything on this offer of trust and connection. Asked by Julian why she has decided to love him, Michelle answers: "I had no choice. I love you." Like Michel, Julian unexpectedly accepts the grace of this offer, no longer proving able to resist this secular form of election: "Oh, Michelle, it's taken me so long to come to you."

In Bresson's decisive moments, Schrader discovers an underlying Calvinism. Bresson, a Catholic, was much influenced by Jansenism, an austere form of the faith influenced by Calvin's doctrine of predestination. And such complex meditations on the mysterious intersection of free will and determinism are reflected in Schrader's own practice. He might be speaking of his films when he observes of Bresson's: "Grace allows the protagonist to accept the paradox of predestination and free will. . . . But it is not enough for grace to be present, man must choose to receive it." It is in such an assent to the irresistibility of election that the paradox of free will and predestination is resolved: "Man must *choose* that which has been predestined."[17]

In its most extreme form, such a transformation simply repeats the fact of election, the limited atonement that means that some, not all, are to be saved. In the Calvinist view, such salvation is perdurable (this is known officially as the doctrine of the persistence of the saints, the belief that grace once bestowed never loses its salvific efficacy). God's truly lonely man is, thus, always already the one for whom salvation has not been destined. As Travis Bickle suggests, in a bit of self-analysis that pierces to the heart of his condition: "There is no escape."

This theme is clearly developed in the most autobiographical and personal of Schrader's films. *Hardcore* dramatizes not the plight of those who have been from the beginning of time excluded from eternal light but the challenge that the utter depravity of human nature poses to the self-assurance and elitism of the elect, their error in believing that, once determined, salvation might exclude suffering. Jake VanDorn (George C. Scott) is a successful furniture manufacturer in Grand Rapids, Michigan, a widower whose two comforts are his Dutch Reformed faith and his daughter, Kristen (Ilah Davis). On a church-sponsored trip to California, Kristen is convinced by a local boy to run away from the group. Disappearing into the secular wasteland that is Los Angeles, she is soon drawn into the shadowy world of pornographic moviemaking. VanDorn goes west to rescue her but, as himself, finds it impossible to carry the investigation very far, so different are his values and manner from those of sleazy producers and the "talent" they employ. He must adopt the disguise of being what they are, participate in doing what it is they do. In this way, he meets a young porn actress named Niki (Season Hubley) who agrees to help him track down Kristen, which she succeeds in doing. Reunited with his daughter, VanDorn at first must listen to her spiteful refusal to accept her rescue and return to her previous life, but suddenly, inexplicably, she agrees.

The film ends with the restoration of the VanDorns to their true (i.e., saved) natures and the consignment of Niki, to whom VanDorn had become close, to the living hell from which he had helped her temporarily emerge. Because Niki is, in the film's terms, self-evidently unjustified, she cannot be rescued, as the fashion in which limited atonement plays out in human affairs is heartbreakingly dramatized. In *Hardcore,* the decisive moment simply recapitulates a decision made before time began. This truth is more obscurely, and less certainly, developed in Bresson, where the process of discovery shapes the very act of filming. Bresson preferred models to actors in part because of his belief that human behavior is absolutely unpredictable, human motives knowable (and known) only to God. His protagonists do not so much act as find themselves acted on, demonstrating their necessary surrender to the destiny mapped out for them by Providence.

## "A Communion of Wounded Sinners"

In contrast to the bleaker spiritual landscape limned by those two other transcendental filmmakers, Bresson and Schrader, Scorsese offers in *Bringing Out the Dead* a world in which moral progress, enabled by grace, can be attained through individual effort. Writing of the film, Richard A. Blake observes that the decisive moment in this film is in no sense predetermined but results from the attempt to persevere in virtue in the company of fellow sufferers: "Redemption in Scorsese's Catholic universe arises from just such a communion of wounded sinners. . . . They inhabit a sinful world that grinds down such as they, but their recognition of a need for communion with one another . . . offers the possibility of salvation."[18]

In the film, as in the novel, Frank is brought to the recognition that he is not God—he must undo the salvation he has brought to Mary's father, returning him to the destiny marked out for him by God. If, like Jake Van-Dorn, Frank must suffer the utter depravity of his fellow men, this is a fallen condition he shares with them and they with him. Original sin, after all, is the foundational bond that unites humanity. Frank's communion with the hopeless, the self-destructive, and the dispossessed is no disguise that he can remove (as Schrader's VanDorn does) when the special fact of ineluctable grace reasserts its powers of difference, marking off God's sheep from the goats. Frank reveals this deep connection to his world in voice-over: "What haunted me now was more savage: spirits born half finished, homicides, suicides, overdoses, innocent or not, accusing me of being there, witnessing a humiliation which they could never forgive."

The novel's Frank, it is true, also experiences a profoundly transcendental sense of community, especially after he allows Mary's father to die. But the way in which he feels the burden of self being lifted seems more a Neoplatonic release from the material than an entry into fellowship: "I felt myself expanding through all the pieces of people that had passed through me, and as a medic, I was very proud of this, a billion lives to every life. There was an infinite completeness to the thing, a madness close to ecstasy."[19] In the novel, Frank's communion with others is found, first, in his acceptance of Mary's rejection and her mercy and, second, in the companionship that he achieves with Rose, a spirit brought to life by his sense of failure and now quieted by the mercy he has shown another. Ultimately, Rose, of course, is nothing more than an object present to his consciousness, not a creature of flesh and blood.

Throughout the film, a different sense of community emerges as the spirit of Mary's father (Cullen O. Johnson) continually speaks to Frank, asking to be released from the existential misery in which Frank's ministrations have confined him. From the hospital bed, he begs Frank: "Let me go." To perform this act of mercy, Frank disconnects him from his monitoring equipment, attaching it to his own body and, thus, subverting the alarm that would otherwise go off when the heart stops beating. In a larger sense, Frank takes on the burden of the other, in fact, becomes the other, transcending his sense of self through an intimate gesture of empathy. Here is no release from the materiality of existence but an embracing of it, an *imitatio Christi* or replication of the actions of the Redeemer. When the old man is finally at rest, Frank goes to Mary (Patricia Arquette) to tell her the news. In his mind, she becomes Rose (the inner vision merging with existential reality), and Frank asks for her (their?) forgiveness.

The camera shows us Rose's face, but it is Mary's voice we hear, speaking the words that release Frank from his self-inflicted pain: "It's not your fault. No one asked you to suffer. That was your idea." Because, as Rose appears to affirm, Frank's embrace of human brotherhood causes his spiritual crisis, it is fitting that this display of love finds itself acknowledged and reciprocated. As the scene ends, Mary, no longer the bearer of transindividual truth, becomes Mary again, marking the return to the communal, material world. She asks Frank: "Would you like to come in?" And, like Michel in *Pickpocket* and Julian Kaye in *American Gigolo,* Frank says yes to this simple offer of fellowship and communion. In the film's last image, he and Mary have assumed the archetypal position of Mary and Jesus in the *Pietá:* fully clothed, she sits on her bed, cradling his head on her breast. As in *The Last Temptation,* the material world of human sexual love is not rejected but subsumed in the realm of the perpetually reenacted spiritual mystery of death and deliverance.

## "An Angel out of This Open Sewer"

In *Taxi Driver,* Travis Bickle is appalled and sickened by the spectacle of utter depravity that he moves through and continually engages with. But then he is moved deeply by the image of a young girl he spies one day on a midtown sidewalk: Betsy (Cybill Shepherd). He says in voice-over that she "appeared like an angel out of this open sewer. Out of this filthy mass. She is alone: they cannot touch her." Betsy, he soon discovers, belongs to

a world that he cannot enter; he is forever divided from her by the operation of that destiny we can call *grace*. Travis's act of mercy, his rescue of the
young prostitute Iris (Jodie Foster), purchases him a miracle of sorts: that
he comes to be regarded as a hero for his violent assault on Iris's tormentors,
an act committed out of an anger that only we know could just have easily
been directed at the patrician liberal politician Senator Palantine (Leonard
Harris), whom Travis had originally thought to assassinate. At the end of
the film, Travis meets Betsy one more time, and she is as unattainably re-
mote as she was the first day he saw her. He remains just as alone as before
because their encounter proves transient and changes nothing. Obviously,
the "they" who "cannot touch her" are the unsaved goats, among which he
must number himself.

*Taxi Driver* represents the harsh fact of limited atonement without the
religious trappings; its moral vision, at least in this sense, belongs more to
Schrader than to Scorsese. Travis's tragedy is that he recognizes the fact of
depravity and is sickened by what he senses he is somehow above. "They're
all animals anyway," he observes of those he sees on the city's sidewalks, offering, like Jake VanDorn, a disgusted catalog of their fallen state: "All the
animals come out at night: whores, skunk pussies, buggers, queers, fairies,
dopers, junkies, venal." Yet Travis can find no exit from this unredeemed
community where he has been confined. His only hope is apocalyptic: that
it will all be washed away someday by a clean rain, a violent end to pervasive
iniquity that will also destroy him (as his attempted suicide after rescuing Iris
indicates). At the very end, the possibility of purity and cleanness imaged
by Betsy remains hopelessly out of reach. She has for Travis been reduced
to a vision that he can spy only fleetingly in his rearview mirror. It seems
clear that his world does not offer the prospect of salvation for those not
called to election.

*Bringing Out the Dead*'s finale, in contrast, puts forth a different view
of human existence. In this collaboration, Scorsese's belief in the power of
active, willed transcendence makes itself decisively felt. The sublunary realm
of sinfulness and death that we inhabit, a place where no elect make their
appearance to image our own depravity back to us (Mary, mired in her own
sinfulness, is no Betsy but a fellow traveler), can be transcended through the
acknowledgment of our failure to rise completely above our own inevitable
limitations. The key gesture that Frank makes is a request for forgiveness,
the acknowledgment of fault that, in the Christian tradition shaped by the
doctrine of original sin, provides the basis for human community. And,
as Rose and Mary jointly suggest, forgiveness lies in the recognition that
our sense of inadequacy, the pain we suffer, is what we inflict on ourselves.

Frank must come to understand that, while the dead can be brought out, they cannot, then, like Lazarus, be brought back to life.

The film's last images echo the Bressonian decisive moment as it takes shape particularly in his *Pickpocket* and Schrader's *Gigolo*. But, if Bresson portrays the shock of Michel's acceptance, Scorsese and Schrader here emphasize the suffering that, with its sharing, is alleviated. As Richard Blake suggests, *Bringing Out the Dead* "introduces more than ever before [in the Scorsese oeuvre] the possibility of redemption in this infernal landscape."[20]

## Notes

The first epigraph to this essay is taken from Ralph Waldo Emerson, *Essays and Lectures* (New York: Library of America, 1983), 196.

1. Les Keyser, *Martin Scorsese* (New York: Twayne, 1992), 13.

2. Ralph Waldo Emerson, "The Transcendentalist," in *Essays and Lectures,* 195, 195–96.

3. See Joe Connelly, *Bringing Out the Dead* (New York: Vintage, 1998).

4. These negotiations are discussed briefly in Jim Sangster, *Scorsese* (London: Virgin, 2002), 263.

5. Quoted in ibid., 266.

6. Connelly, *Bringing Out the Dead,* 26.

7. Ibid., 321.

8. Ibid., 322.

9. See Nicholas Pileggi, *Wiseguy: Life in a Mafia Family* (New York: Simon & Schuster, 1985), and *Casino: Love and Honor in Las Vegas* (New York: Simon & Schuster, 1995).

10. Quoted in Sangster, *Scorsese,* 251.

11. See Paul Schrader, *Transcendental Style in Film: Ozu, Bresson, Dreyer* (Berkeley: University of California Press, 1972), esp. 59–108.

12. Emerson, "The Transcendentalist," 194.

13. Michael Bliss and Paul Schrader, "Affliction and Forgiveness: An Interview with Paul Schrader," *Film Quarterly* 54, no. 1 (2000): 9.

14. John R. Hamilton, "Transcendental Style in Schrader: *Bringing Out the Dead,*" *Literature/Film Quarterly* 32, no. 1 (2004): 26.

15. Paul Schrader, "*Pickpocket* II," in *Schrader on Schrader and Other Writings,* ed. Kevin Jackson (London: Faber & Faber, 1990), 44.

16. Schrader, *Transcendental Style,* 79.

17. Ibid., 92–93.

18. Richard A. Blake, "Playing God," *America* 181, no. 21 (2000): 20.

19. Connelly, *Bringing Out the Dead,* 316.

20. Blake, "Playing God," 21.

# Contributors

JEROLD J. ABRAMS is assistant professor of philosophy at Creighton University. His research focuses on aesthetics, philosophy of film, pragmatism, and ethics. His publications include essays appearing in *Philosophy Today, Human Studies,* the *Modern Schoolman,* and *Transactions of the Charles S. Peirce Society.* His "From Sherlock Holmes to the Hard-Boiled Detective in Film Noir" appeared in *The Philosophy of Film Noir* (University Press of Kentucky, 2006).

JUDITH BARAD is professor of philosophy and women's studies at Indiana State University. After graduating magna cum laude from Loyola University of Chicago in 1980, she attended Northwestern University. She received her Ph.D. in philosophy from Northwestern in 1984. In 1985, she accepted a position in philosophy at Indiana State, where she eventually served as the chairperson for nine years. She is the author of three books and numerous articles on ethics, including such topics as feminist ethics, the role of emotion in moral judgments, the treatment of animals, the philosophy of Thomas Aquinas, and the ethics of *Star Trek.* She has given dozens of national and international scholarly presentations and has recently been an ethics consultant for Boeing.

PAUL A. CANTOR is the Clifton Waller Barrett Professor of English at the University of Virginia. He is the author of *Gilligan Unbound: Pop Culture in the Age of Globalization* (Rowman & Littlefield), which was chosen by the *Los Angeles Times* as one of the best nonfiction books of the year in 2001. Portions of the *Simpsons* chapter of that book appeared in *The Simpsons and Philosophy* (Open Court, 2001).

MARK T. CONARD is assistant professor of philosophy at Marymount

Manhattan College in New York City. He is the coeditor of *The Simpsons and Philosophy* (Open Court, 2001) and *Woody Allen and Philosophy* (Open Court, 2004) and the editor of *The Philosophy of Film Noir* (University Press of Kentucky, 2006), and *The Philosophy of Neo-Noir* (University Press of Kentucky, 2007). He is the author of "*Kill Bill: Volume 1:* Violence as Therapy," "*Kill Bill: Volume 2:* Mommy Kills Daddy," and "*Pulp Fiction:* The Sign of the Empty Symbol," all published on Metaphilm.com. He is also the author of the novel *Dark as Night* (Uglytown, 2004).

RICHARD GILMORE is associate professor of philosophy and director of the honors program at Concordia College. He is the author of *Philosophical Health: Wittgenstein's Method in "Philosophical Investigations"* and *Doing Philosophy at the Movies.*

RICHARD GREENE is associate professor of philosophy at Weber State University. He received his Ph.D. in philosophy from the University of California, Santa Barbara. He is the coeditor of *The Sopranos and Philosophy* (Open Court, 2004) and *The Undead and Philosophy* (Open Court, 2006). He is the executive director of the Society for Skeptical Studies.

KAREN D. HOFFMAN is assistant professor of philosophy at Hood College. Specializing in ethics, she has a particular interest in the topics of forgiveness and evil as well as in philosophy of and in film. Her recent publications include "Evil and the Despairing Individual: A Kierkegaardian Account," in *Minding Evil* (Rodopi, 2005), and "Where the Rainbow Ends: *Eyes Wide Shut,*" in *The Philosophy of Stanley Kubrick* (University Press of Kentucky, forthcoming).

DEBORAH KNIGHT is associate professor of philosophy at Queen's University. Her primary research lies in aesthetics and the philosophy of art, with particular interests in the philosophy of literature, the philosophy of film, the ethical criticism debate, and art and the emotions. Recently, she has published chapters in *Philosophy of Film: An Anthology, The Philosophy of Film Noir, Dark Thoughts: Philosophical Reflections on Cinematic Horror, Literary Philosophers: Borges, Calvino, Eco,* and *The Oxford Handbook of Aesthetics.*

DEAN A. KOWALSKI is assistant professor of philosophy at the University of Wisconsin Colleges, Waukesha campus. He is the author of *Classic Questions and Contemporary Film: An Introduction to Philosophy* (McGraw-Hill,

2004), the editor of *The X-Files and Philosophy* (University Press of Kentucky, forthcoming), and the coauthor of *Moral Theory and Motion Pictures: An Introduction to Ethics* (Roman & Littlefield, forthcoming). He has also authored a handful of articles on the freedom and foreknowledge problem, including "Some Friendly Molinist Amendments" (*Philosophy and Theology*, 2003) and "On Behalf of a Suarezian Middle Knowledge" (*Philosophia Christi*, 2003). His most recent research interests include exploring various metaethical relations between ethics and religion.

JENNIFER L. MCMAHON is associate professor of philosophy at Centre College. She has expertise in existentialism, philosophy and literature, aesthetics, non-Western philosophy, and biomedical ethics. She has presented papers on diverse topics at national and international conferences. She has published articles in journals including *Asian Philosophy* and the *Journal of the Association for Interdisciplinary Study of the Arts*. She has also published essays on philosophy and popular culture in *Seinfeld and Philosophy*, *The Matrix and Philosophy*, *The Simpsons and Philosophy*, and *The Lord of the Rings and Philosophy*. McMahon earned a B.A. in philosophy from Skidmore College. She holds M.A. and Ph.D. degrees in philosophy from the State University of New York at Buffalo. She has earned several teaching awards.

R. BARTON PALMER is Calhoun Lemon Professor of Literature at Clemson University, where he also directs the film and international culture Ph.D. program. He is the author, editor, or general editor of more than thirty books devoted to film and literary subjects. In addition to numerous articles and book chapters on film noir, he has published *Hollywood's Dark Cinema: The American Film Noir* (2nd rev. and expanded ed., University of Illinois Press, forthcoming) and *Joel and Ethan Coen* (University of Illinois Press, 2004). He has also edited *Perspectives on Film Noir* (G. K. Hall, 1996). His current work on noir directors includes the forthcoming book (with David Boyd) *After Hitchcock: Imitation, Influence, Intertextuality* (University of Texas Press, 2006).

STEVEN M. SANDERS is emeritus professor and former chair of the Department of Philosophy at Bridgewater State College. He has written widely on ethics, epistemology, political philosophy, and popular culture for academic journals and other publications. He is the author, most recently, of "Film Noir and the Meaning of Life," in *The Philosophy of Film Noir* (University Press of Kentucky, 2006), and "Sunshine Noir: Postmodernism and *Miami Vice*," in *The Philosophy of Neo-Noir* (University Press of Kentucky,

2007), as well as forthcoming essays on the films of Alfred Hitchcock and Stanley Kubrick. His work in progress includes volumes on television noir and science fiction feature films.

AEON J. SKOBLE is associate professor of philosophy and chair of the Philosophy Department at Bridgewater State College. He is the coeditor of *Political Philosophy: Essential Selections* (Prentice-Hall, 1999), *The Simpsons and Philosophy* (Open Court, 2001), and *Woody Allen and Philosophy* (Open Court, 2004) and the author of the forthcoming *Deleting the State: An Argument about Government* (Open Court). He writes on moral and political philosophy, as well as television and film, for both scholarly and popular journals and books. His "Moral Clarity and Practical Reason in Film Noir" appeared in *The Philosophy of Film Noir* (University Press of Kentucky, 2006), and his "Justice and Moral Corruption in *A Simple Plan*" appeared in *The Philosophy of Neo-Noir* (University Press of Kentucky, 2007), both edited by Mark T. Conard. He is currently coediting a book on noir television.

# Index